FIRST AND ALWAYS

FIRST AND ALWAYS

A New Portrait of George Washington

Peter R. Henriques

University of Virginia Press • *Charlottesville and London*

University of Virginia Press
© 2020 by the Rector and Visitors of the University of Virginia
All rights reserved
Printed in the United States of America on acid-free paper

First published 2020

9 8 7 6 5 4 3 2 1

Library of Congress Cataloging-in-Publication Data

Names: Henriques, Peter R., author.
Title: First and always : a new portrait of George Washington / Peter R. Henriques.
Other titles: New portrait of George Washington
Description: Charlottesville, VA : University of Virginia Press, [2020] | Includes
    bibliographical references and index.
Identifiers: LCCN 2020003771 (print) | LCCN 2020003772 (ebook) | ISBN 9780813944807
    (hardcover ; alk. paper) | ISBN 9780813944814 (epub)
Subjects: LCSH: Washington, George, 1732-1799. | Presidents—United States—
    Biography. | United States—Politics and government—1783-1789.
Classification: LCC E312 .H535 2020 (print) | LCC E312 (ebook) |
    DDC 973.4/1092 [B]—dc23
LC record available at https://lccn.loc.gov/2020003771
LC ebook record available at https://lccn.loc.gov/2020003772

Jacket art and frontispiece: Bust of George Washington by Jean-Antoine Houdon, 1785.
(Courtesy of the Mount Vernon Ladies' Association)

For my beloved grandchildren

Will

Jane

Sydney

Andrew

Jon

Nicholas

Lanie

Rebecca

Matthew

Nathan

Ryan

Collin

*May each of you live your life
with integrity and promote
well-being not only for
yourself but also for others.*

CONTENTS

AUTHOR'S NOTE

AFTER I published *Realistic Visionary: A Portrait of George Washington* in 2006, the likelihood of my writing another book about George Washington seemed nil. I had retired from George Mason University, and I viewed that volume as my best effort to share with a wider readership what I had learned in many years of studying this remarkable man.

Then Ron Hurst, one of my earliest and still one of my favorite students, now vice president of Collections, Conservation, and Museums and chief curator at the Colonial Williamsburg Foundation, rekindled our friendship. Thanks to Ron's hello on Facebook, I was invited to present the 2011 Distinguished Lecture Series at Colonial Williamsburg. My appearances there before wonderfully receptive audiences led to approximately thirty other talks, almost all of them on various aspects of George Washington's life and character. Additionally, for many years I regularly discussed His Excellency at George Mason University's Osher Lifelong Learning Institute and at Gadsby's Tavern in Alexandria, Virginia, among other places.

Readying these lectures enriched my understanding of the man I thought I knew, drawing me into aspects of Washington that I had not pursued before. This additional research and reflection persuaded me that I had enough fresh material and insights to fill another volume. I have attempted in *First and Always: A New Portrait of George Washington* to deepen the portrait that I sketched in my book *Realistic Visionary: A Portrait of George Washington. First and Always* is a "new" portrait, but it is of the same man and therefore makes many of the same points as *Realistic Visionary*. Indeed, I have incorporated a few brief passages from that book. As in *Realistic Visionary*, each chapter in *First and Always* is designed to stand on its own, which means revisiting George Washington's extreme sensitivity to criticism and other themes. For these repetitions I beg the reader's indulgence.

While each of this volume's chapters is also designed to stand on its own, I hope that taken together they will strengthen the case I make in chapter 8, "What Made George Washington Tick." In that closing essay I contend that Washington was deeply ambitious, massively concerned with his reputation, and in regular search of an adoring public's approbation. His drive for honor and fame was integral to his remarkable leadership (chapter 1). Lack of praise from an unrelentingly demanding mother had left him with an unquenchable thirst for praise (chapter 2). His studiously maintained mask of revolutionary virtue led to some of the myths about him, which I dissect in chapter 3. One of the most fraught aspects of the Asgill Affair, described in chapter 4, was that Washington's own actions threatened his image as a humane and admirable leader. At the root of his breaks with five famous Virginians was his desire to protect and preserve his reputation (chapter 5). His actions with regard to his enslaved workers were often influenced by how he thought those actions might be viewed by the outside world, and he freed his slaves in part to remove a potential blot from his historical reputation (chapter 6). And the extreme partisanship he displayed at his career's end arose in part out of fear that the Republicans would undo his legacy and impel America in a wrong direction (chapter 7).

It is no secret that I have great admiration and respect for George Washington. Full disclosure—I even wear a gold coin medallion of him around my neck. That admiration acknowledges that George Washington was a man of the eighteenth century, which was a very different world from ours. Sadly, Washington's paeans of praise about promoting liberty and republican values were announced with only free white people in mind. His record with persons of color is much less admirable. His thoughts on blacks, Native Americans, and women were ahead of his times but nothing like today's. We must judge him in his context, not ours.

Despite my admiration for Washington, this book, as readers will discover, is no hagiography. George Washington was a man, not a demigod. He had flaws. He made many mistakes. The amazing thing is not that he had character flaws and made mistakes, but that despite these facts, he was able to achieve such an unmatched record of success.

America has never had a leader more important than George Washington. But for him, no single nation known as the United States of America would stretch from Atlantic to Pacific. Two seminal events characterized the founding of that nation—the winning of independence from Great Britain and the establishment of nationhood—and those two are not at all the same thing. In both of those dramatic achievements, George Washington was the central and crucial figure.

Washington or no Washington, Great Britain might not have been able to thwart the American rebellion. However, had General Washington not kept the Continental Army intact as a significant force, the empire would not have signed a formal treaty ending the war and making the new country's western boundary the Mississippi River.

Of course, Washington had critics and adversaries but consider his record: unanimously elected commander in chief of the Continental Army, unanimously elected president of the Constitutional Convention, unanimously elected the first president of the United States, unanimously reelected president of the United States, and after his presidency unanimously nominated to be commander in chief of all forces to be raised in the quasi-war with France. No other American leader can claim to have enjoyed such popular enthusiasm.

George Washington was not only popular. He was also consequential, a man of vision and action. More clearly than any other Founding Father, he advanced the concept of an American nation, using his immense stature to realize that vision as he undertook to help create institutions meant to bind Americans together. His experiences during the Revolution had led him to conclude that in order to thrive, an effective and genuinely republican union needed a strong national government. Paradoxically, GW also believed that to guarantee both states' and citizens' rights and liberties, the union needed a government strong enough to discourage the erosion of those rights through parochialism and extreme individualism.

The United States Constitution, drawn up in Philadelphia during the summer of 1787, was the result of perhaps the most consequential political gathering in history. That epic undertaking sought to correct the weaknesses of the Articles of Confederation and to establish a government strong enough to preserve the union. Washington's decision to attend the Constitutional Convention, over which he inevitably presided, lent that undertaking a prominence and gravitas otherwise unattainable. Advocates and skeptics agreed that without Washington's support and a tacit collective assumption that he would be heading the resulting government, the new constitution never would have been ratified.

Mechanisms of leadership such as the framers conceived had no real precedent. Among their most creative steps was establishing the presidency. That innovation profoundly unsettled them, insofar as a vigorous executive was hard to square with their republican outlook. The office, hedged with checks and balances as everything in the Constitution was, nevertheless endowed its occupant with very significant powers, and made the president independent of the judicial and legislative branches. The president, under the original Constitution, could serve for an unlimited number of four-year terms. He would have authority to appoint and supervise the heads of executive departments and to command the army. He would have the power to veto legislation and to issue pardons, and enjoy surprising latitude in conducting foreign affairs.

In these and other regards, George Washington, simply by being, shaped the office of the president even before he occupied it, because the Convention created the office with him in mind. According to one participant, the powers granted would not "have been so great had not many of the members cast their eyes toward General Washington as president; and shaped their ideas of the powers to be given to a president, by their opinions of his virtue." Supremely confident in Washington, delegates acted not out of fear but out of hope.

The tasks the new president faced were endlessly daunting. As Joseph Ellis notes, Washington's "achievement must be recovered before it can be appreciated, which means that we must recognize that there was no such thing as a viable American nation when he took office as president." At least, beset by their particular grave crises, Abraham Lincoln and Franklin Delano Roosevelt were operating in the context of an established government. Washington, however, had to take the republic from drawing board to three-dimensional human reality, along the way helping to fashion a new nation out of a gaggle of newly independent states, each jealously guarding its own interests and fearful of anything resembling a strong central government.

To forge and temper the union, Washington effectively used Americans' love for him. It is difficult to imagine another figure being accorded the trust and public confidence required to establish a stable and effective system of government and to convince most of his country-men that a robust government could comport with republican liberty. Washington was the gravitational force that held the union together through its early challenges.

Washington also defined what it means to be a constitutional ex-ecutive. While a strong and energetic president, he remained always alert to the office's limitations, deferring when appropriate but, when necessary, aggressively defending his prerogatives. Traversing what he called "untrodden ground," he succeeded to an extraordinary degree at setting constitutional precedents that have endured in the United States.

Washington bequeathed to successors an office that was muscular, especially in regard to foreign affairs. The presidency is the powerful entity it is in large part thanks to George Washington's performance. He set benchmarks for all who have followed. And after eight long, difficult years in office, he again proved that his truest allegiance was to the re-public by voluntarily surrendering power. It was the first of many peace-ful transfers of power in the unprecedented American experiment.

I am convinced that George Washington would be pleased with my effort to outline his centrality to the American story. I am equally convinced that he would not be pleased with the book I have written. George Washington wanted very much to be famous—but he had no wish to be truly known. His words about the challenge facing an artist rendering an image of him apply equally to curious historians. "I fancy the skill of this Gentleman's Pencil will be put to it, in describing to the World what manner of man I am." He was as keen to shield his inner self as I am keen to examine that self.

For all his fame, Washington is the most enigmatic of the Founding Fathers. He has eluded all efforts to penetrate the myth and reach the man. There are things about him we can never know. Nevertheless, I believe that we can significantly deepen our understanding of the flesh-and-blood George Washington.

Scientists tell us that the human brain is a vast network of around 100 billion neurons that communicate with electrical impulses. As of this writing, researchers have managed to digitally reconstruct just over 100,000 of them! We may never be able to fully understand the brain and human consciousness, but that does not mean we cannot learn more about them. We can and we will. So it is with George Washington. As more and more of his papers make their way into digital form, coupled with ever more sophisticated search tools, the result will be more insightful writings that further enrich our understanding of this national icon. I hope *First and Always* marks a step in the right direction.

In quoting from Washington's letters, I have occasionally standardized the original spelling, capitalization, and punctuation to make the language clearer, but in no instance have I changed the meaning of what he wrote.

1

Matchless

THE LEADERSHIP OF GEORGE WASHINGTON

GRANTING THAT George Washington was the remarkable leader I sketch in the author's note compels the question of how he was able to achieve such success. In my view, he triumphed thanks to a combination of ten somewhat overlapping factors. They are:

Fortune
Physicality
Ambition
Determination
Passion
Courage
Toughness
Realism
Talent
Character

Fortune

Great good fortune was certainly essential to George Washington's extraordinary success. As Thomas Jefferson noted, "Never did nature and fortune combine more perfectly to make a man great." Although asserting that GW was the luckiest human being who ever lived might be a stretch, he surely remains at the pinnacle of good fortune. George Washington came of age during a crucial era in human history, a time, in John Adams's words, "when the greatest lawgivers of antiquity would have wished to live." Of course, like his fellow founders, Washington had the benefit of coming to maturity at a time when his latent talents were not blocked by the hidebound norms of an aristocratic society,

George Washington's fearlessness in the face of danger was one of the important reasons for his success as a leader. (Courtesy of Mount Vernon Ladies' Association)

while at the same time he did not have to deal with the liabilities of a fully egalitarian society in which an elitist sense of superiority was forbidden. Washington flourished in such an environment.

Time and time again, in an almost uncanny way, George Washington proved to be the right man in the right place at the right time. He was born in Virginia, by far Britain's wealthiest, largest, and most important colony. In the struggle to gain control of the Northwest Territory, it had to be both surveyed and fought for, and Washington was both a surveyor and a soldier. For every epic event of the second half of the eighteenth century, he was precisely the proper age to engage meaningfully with its principals and its events: the French and Indian War (in Europe, the Seven Years' War), the American Revolution, the Constitutional Convention, and the founding of the American Republic.

His older half-brother Lawrence, the master of Mount Vernon, lived near the powerful Fairfax family and their manor home, Belvoir. Lawrence married into the Fairfax dynasty, opening all manner of possibilities for his younger sibling. GW rose both as a surveyor and as a military man thanks to the patronage of the powerful William Fairfax, who became the youth's mentor and champion. In a bittersweet twist, Lawrence's early death at thirty-four eventually put Mount Vernon under Washington's control.

His good fortune continued when he successfully courted Martha Custis, the wealthiest widow in Virginia, after the sudden death of her husband, Daniel Parke Custis. That marriage made Washington master of one of Virginia's largest and most profitable estates. It consisted of nearly 8,000 acres in six counties, along with slaves valued at 9,000 pounds Virginia currency, and accounts current and other liquid assets in England of approximately 10,000 pounds sterling. George Washington's marriage ensconced him in the topmost tier of a thoroughly hierarchical culture.

Fortune also blessed Washington in that a series of impending eventualities, any one of which would have derailed his ascent, did not come to pass. Had his mother allowed him to join the Royal Navy; had his long and tireless campaign for a commission in the king's army borne fruit; had Sally Fairfax, his first love and his good friend's wife, encouraged him into a reckless affair; had one of those bullets that ripped through his uniform during the French and Indian War been aimed more keenly; had the plot hatched early in the Revolutionary War to kidnap or assassinate him succeeded; had the great British sharpshooter Patrick Ferguson, seeing in his sights near Brandywine Creek an anonymous American officer, not spared the fellow out of admiration for his carriage, George Washington's story would be very different—and so would America's.

Physicality

Physique ranked high among George Washington's assets, and he made the most of nature's gifts. Truth be told, an essential factor in Washington's success was his physicality. Throughout his life GW's grace and strength amazed onlookers. He possessed a very impressive exterior and looked the part of a leader, especially a military leader. But for terrible teeth, which he rarely showed, Washington was a superb physical specimen. He was cut, in Abigail Adams's phrase, from "majestic fabric." The brand-new uniform he wore to the second Continental

Congress highlighted this physicality. Roughly six foot two inches tall, equivalent to a man of six foot five today, he was powerfully built, combining prodigious strength with an elegant carriage and a majestic stride. He took fencing lessons, not because he expected to have to run a man through, but rather to improve his nimbleness and the grace of his movement. This graceful movement allowed him to become a marvelous dancer, a much-admired social skill, once dancing with General Nathaniel Greene's pretty and flirtatious wife for three hours straight. Nowhere were his graceful movements put to better show than in his horsemanship. He was widely recognized as the best horseback rider in Virginia, a society that greatly admired that skill.

Innumerable contemporary accounts testify to Washington's charisma, a characteristic clouded over by time's passage. James Monroe testified that Washington possessed "a deportment so firm, so dignified, but yet so modest and composed I have never seen in any other person." Of his bearing, Jedidiah Morse recollected, "There was in his whole appearance an unusual dignity and gracefulness, which at once secured him profound respect, and cordial esteem. He seemed born to command his fellow men." Mercy Warren, the sister and spouse of important political figures and therefore accustomed to the company of powerful men, declared that Washington was the most accomplished gentleman that she had ever met. His "public & private Virtues place Him in the first class of the Good & Brave & one really of so High a stamp as to do Honor to Human Nature."

While perhaps influenced by the eighteenth-century cult of sensibility, the image portrayed in countless quotes is revealing. "You may laugh, but he has a most beautiful face," a young woman from Massachusetts wrote. "Did you ever see a countenance a thousandth part so expressive of the goodness, benevolence, sensibility, and modesty which characterize him?" The French foreign minister, Count de Moustier, noted that Washington "has the soul, the look, and figure of a hero united in him." "I sat down beside him," Polish nobleman Julian Niemcewicz wrote. "I was moved, dumb, and could not look at him enough. It is a majestic face, in which dignity is united with gentleness." His nephew Howell Lewis declared, "I have sometimes thought him decidedly the handsomest man I ever saw; and when in a lively mood, so full of pleasantry, so agreeable to all with whom he associated, that I could hardly realize that he was the same Washington whose dignity awed all who approached him." To Abigail Adams he was "polite with dignity, affable without familiarity, distant without haughtiness, grave without austerity: Modest, wise, Good."

Gouverneur Morris asserted, "No man could approach him but with respect—none was great in his presence." Henry Knox noted how, upon being presented to General Washington, an aide to General William Howe appeared "awestruck," as if encountering the supernatural. A man who met Washington after having been presented to the king of England and the king of France said neither monarch had exerted the effect Washington had upon him. French officer after French officer offered similar assessments based on personal interchanges with His Excellency. Washington had so much "martial dignity" that one "could distinguish him to be a general from among 10,000 people," Benjamin Rush said, adding that, placed alongside Washington, any monarch in Europe would look like a valet. His personal magnetism and charisma were crucial to his success as a leader, but other factors were of equal importance.

Ambition

George Washington's ambition is difficult to exaggerate, although he was not ruthlessly or unethically ambitious but rather cleverly and determinedly so. What Edmund Morris wrote about Ronald Reagan, "He was ambitious enough to crack rocks," seems applicable and echoes the line William Shakespeare put in the mouth of Henry V: "If it be a sin to covet honor, [he was] the most offending soul alive." Washington hungered for honor and for history's most elusive prize—fame across the ages. Essentially, he desired secular immortality, and to achieve it he would pay a fearsome price. No doubt, he would have identified with the words of the Greek soldier who declared, "What toils do I undergo, O Athenians! that I may merit your approbation." Washington strove not only to outdo all competitors but also to conquer and surpass himself. He pursued magnificence. In Paul Longmore's telling words, "Throughout his life, the ambition for distinction spun inside George Washington like a dynamo, generating the astounding energy with which he produced his greatest historical achievement—himself."

Determination

Encountering adversity and disappointment, Washington parried them with tenacity and perseverance. One might call it "the audacity of determination." His indomitable will made him a formidable adversary. As Robert Morris, the financier of the American Revolution, expressed it, General Washington "feeds and thrives on misfortune by finding resources to get the better of them," whereas lesser leaders "sink under their weight, thinking it impossible to succeed." Morris saw in the general a "firmness of mind" and a "patience in suffering" endowing him with an "infinite advantage over other men."

In nearly nine years as commander in chief of the Continental Army, Washington needed every bit of determination and "patience in suffering" he could muster in order to surmount an avalanche of obstacles and disappointments. His letters and official correspondence convey nearly a decade of extraordinarily wearisome and nerve-wracking frustration: "I am bereft of every peaceful moment, wearied to death all day with a variety of perplexing circumstances. . . . You can form no Idea of the perplexity of my Situation. No Man, I believe, ever had a greater choice of difficulties and less means to extricate himself from them. . . . Such is my situation that if I were to wish the bitterest curse to an enemy on this side of the grave, I should put him in my stead with my feelings." Unquenchable thirst for enduring fame gave him the wherewithal to withstand such disappointments and setbacks.

Passion

Washington's ambition and determination had their match in his passion. The common image of Washington is of an aloof, passionless, and distant figure, a man rendered by reputation into a statue. In fact, Washington was a man of the most intense passions. "Those who have seen him strongly moved will bear witness that his wrath was terrible," said Gouverneur Morris, his most perceptive eulogist. "They have seen boiling in his bosom, passion almost too mighty for man."

Studying Washington's visage, the eminent portraitist Gilbert Stuart, famous for the "dollar bill" Washington, discerned in his subject's face features "totally different from what I had observed in any other human being. The sockets of the eyes, for instance, were larger than what I had ever met before, and the upper part of the nose broader. . . . All his features were indicative of the strongest passions. . . . Had Washington been born in the forests . . . he would have been the fiercest man among the savage tribes." Washington's temperament featured a volatile temper that, in Jefferson's words, "was naturally irritable and high-toned." When "it broke its bonds, he was most tremendous in his wrath." Such temperaments can unleash havoc, but Washington's did only rarely because, over time, he achieved what Eliza Powel referred to as "empire over yourself." His blend of explosive temper and imposing persona had genuine power. Visibly controlling the one while exhibiting the other helped ensure Washington's rise. He told his granddaughter passion "ought to be under the control of reason," an axiom his behavior illustrated.

For example, his thinking as a military man was instinctively aggressive, but he regularly subordinated his impulses to his broader understanding of the revolutionary struggle, his troops' limitations, and his advisers' counsel. Save for a few lapses, he was a man of granite self-control. This took enormous effort. Being an intensely passionate man with tremendous urges to satisfy, only remarkable powers of self-control could master them. "Like Socrates," Washington possessed "great self-command that always made him appear a man of a different cast in the eyes of the world," Gilbert Stuart said.

Washington's passion was not limited to his temper. He was as prone to tears as to temper. The warrior who described himself as "a votary of love" felt at a profound depth. Events often moved him to tears. His stepdaughter Patsy's death, taking leave of his officers at Fraunces Tavern, speaking of his dear friend Lafayette, responding to Bostonians' cheers—these and other moments brought out his lachrymosity, as did memories collected long ago. Thirty years after Braddock's defeat, Washington invoked shocking scenes of "the dead—the dying—the groans—lamentations—and cries along the Road of the wounded for help" that he felt would pierce a heart of stone. As he was recounting to Virginia governor Robert Dinwiddie the suffering he had seen on the frontier during the French and Indian War, GW soliloquized, "The supplicating tears of the women and the moving petitions of the men melt me into such deadly sorrow that I solemnly declare . . . I would offer myself a willing sacrifice. . . . If bleeding, dying! would glut their insatiate revenge—I would be a willing offering to Savage Fury: and die by inches, to save a people!"

Courage

Although perhaps an example of rhetorical excess, Washington's passionate statement quoted above points to another key aspect of his personality, namely his courage. Humankind esteems bravery, and George Washington was a paragon of courage. As an untested soldier eager to prove himself in battle, he wrote, "I flatter myself, [I have] resolution to Face what any Man durst, as shall be proved when it comes to the Test." It certainly was. During the French and Indian War, he risked having his brains blown out in his efforts to gather supplies crucial to the campaign. In an episode he later described as the most perilous of his career, he intervened in an incident of friendly fire by knocking soldiers' rifles up with his sword in an effort to keep them from injuring comrades. Washington "seemed incapable of fear, meeting personal dangers with the calmest unconcern," Jefferson wrote.

His displays of courage as commander in chief of the Continental Army worried aides, but inspired the ranks. In a typical comment, John Howland, a private, said, "The firm, composed and majestic countenance of the General inspired confidence and assurance." Artillery major Samuel Shaw echoed, "His personal bravery, and the desire he has of animating his troops by example, make him fearless of any danger." "His appearance alone gave confidence to the timid and imposed respect on the bold." General Washington's behavior at the Battle of Princeton, where he was hardly farther from the enemy than a baseball batter is from a pitcher, at Brandywine and at Monmouth, his almost foolhardy valor amid falling shells at Yorktown—"cool like a bishop at prayer"—showed a man transcending fear. As Nathaniel Philbrick has observed, the General had "as commanding a physical presence as ever led an army [and] exuded the dignified grace of an Indian sachem." "I heard the bullets whistle," Washington said of his baptism by fire, "and there is something charming in the sound." Not many men are wired that way.

Toughness

At the core of his being was a steely will. Following a visit with Thomas Jefferson in 1799, a British visitor by the name of Joshua Brooks summarized in his journal what he believed was Jefferson's view of George Washington. According to Jefferson, channeled through Brooks, Washington was "a hard master, very severe, a hard husband, a hard father, a hard governor. From his childhood he always ruled and ruled severely. He was first brought up to govern slaves; he then governed an army, then a nation. He thinks hard of all, is despotic in every respect, he mistrusts every man, thinks every man a rogue and nothing but severity will do." Of course, it is impossible to know how accurately Brooks recorded Jefferson's views, and certainly the assessment is biased and unfair. Washington was certainly not "despotic," and while he had a dark view of mankind, he certainly didn't mistrust everyone. But Brooks gets right a key aspect of the general—his toughness, a characteristic he carried for better and for worse.

George Washington was a hard man in different ways. First, there is simply the matter of Washington's physical toughness. As a young man, Washington wrote Virginia's governor Robert Dinwiddie, declaring, "I have a Constitution hardy enough to encounter and undergo the most severe trials." His wilderness journey over many hundreds of miles in the dead of winter to warn the French to stay out of the Ohio territory became the stuff of legend. When, traversing the Allegheny River on a raft in winter, he and rugged frontiersman Christopher Gist capsized, it was Gist, not Washington, who came away frostbitten.

In a much-polished and perhaps inflated story, a Revolutionary War veteran described a 1775 incident in which Washington came upon a brawl between Virginia riflemen and members of the Marblehead Regiment. "With the spring of a deer," the raconteur continued, Washington leapt from his saddle and plunged into the melee. He spied two major protagonists, grabbed each by the throat, and, holding the men at arm's length, alternately shook them and spoke with them, defusing the moment. As a military disciplinarian, Washington refused to flinch from ordering harsh punishment that cost miscreants the skin off their backs and even life itself.

Typically, while he hoped that no such scoundrels would be found in the Continental Army, his General Orders declared, "It is the General's express orders that if any man attempt to skulk, lay down, or retreat without Orders he is to be instantly shot down as an example." He believed the only way to stop desertions was to terrify the soldiers from such practices. At the siege of Yorktown, the general ordered that any American deserter "found within the Enemies lines" should be "instantly hanged." Washington likewise advised a New Jersey magistrate that "the most effectual way" of curtailing the traitorous practices of violent Tories was by "shooting some of the most notorious offenders wherever they can be found in flagrante delicto." Meeting with President Washington, the Seneca Indian chief Cornplanter reminded the American leader that Cornplanter's people referred to him as Town Destroyer. "To this day, when that name is heard, our women look behind them and turn pale and our children cling close to the neck of their mothers."

As master of hundreds of enslaved workers, Washington was occasionally willing to send recalcitrant slaves to certain death in the Caribbean; if necessary, he authorized the use of the whip to enforce compliance; to discourage thievery, he had slaves' dogs drowned to deprive their owners of four-footed lookouts. Isaac, an enslaved worker, described how, when his tree-felling displeased the proprietor, Washington, without a word, "gave me such a slap on the side of my head that I whirled round like a top and before I knew where I was Master was gone." (Chapter 6 examines some of GW's relations with enslaved workers in more depth.)

Washington wore the same impermeable carapace in business, relentlessly seeking his due, striving constantly to increase his wealth, ever wary of being hoodwinked. There can be little question that GW had a great fondness for money—getting it, keeping it, and making sure that no one took more of it from him than what was due. Typically, he wrote one agent, "As you are now receiving my money, your time is not your own; every hour or day misapplied is a loss to me." Or again, "If then a man receives [pay] for his labor and he withholds that labor or if he trifles away that time for which he is paid, it is a robbery—and a robbery of the worst kind because it is not only a fraud but a dishonorable, unmanly and a deceitful fraud."

Washington's hard shell enabled him to make and hold to unpopular but necessary decisions. One was refusing to authorize a plan to free captured American officers because of what it would mean for those troops left incarcerated. In another incident, he refused to exchange POWs because the swap would have benefited the British more than the Americans. Despite great pressure to the contrary, he authorized the hanging rather than the shooting of the widely admired Major John Andre, caught participating in Benedict Arnold's treasonous plot. His Excellency felt the noose was the correct penalty for treason. As president, he signed the much-scorned Jay Treaty of 1794 out of conviction that the arrangement was in the nation's long-term interest. And, as Rick Atkinson eloquently noted, Washington, who once said, "What brave fellows I must this day lose," learned and lived "the hardest of war's hard truths—that for the new nation to live, young men must die, often alone, usually in pain, and sometimes to no obvious purpose." No less tough on himself than on those he commanded, he had the ability to make tough—if unpopular—decisions to promote his ultimate goals.

Realism

George Washington's worldview informed and underpinned his leadership. He was that rare combination of visionary and realist. Seeing a coastal string of thirteen elbow-throwing colonies, he could envision a large, powerful, independent United States of America based on republican principles. Though a visionary, George Washington was not a utopian idealist ("utopia" is a combination of two Greek words meaning "no place"), but a practitioner of what statesmen today call Realpolitik, the hard-nosed, hard-knuckled school of the possible. He was a "rock-ribbed realist." Washington, a product of a pre-democratic and pre-egalitarian world, looked skeptically upon the common man. While he would have agreed with Lincoln's latter assertion that government was to be "of the people" and "for the people," he would never have agreed that it should be "by the people."

He had an unblinkingly practical view of the world's workings and a shrewd understanding of human nature, perhaps because instead of going to college he went to war and saw life's rougher side. Gouverneur

Morris said Washington's grasp of human character was "an inestimable gift to his country." And Washington would have agreed with Morris's assertion, "It happens somewhat unfortunately that the men who live in the world are very different from those that dwell in the heads of the philosophers." Viscerally understanding the world's caprice, GW viewed humanity darkly. "What, gracious God, is man!" he wrote, "that there should be such inconsistency and perfidiousness in his conduct?" Or again, "I have seen so many instances of the rascality of mankind, that I am convinced that the only way to make them honest, is to prevent them being otherwise." George Washington's starting point was clear. "We must take the passions of men as nature has given them." He held that what drives nations—and men—is interest. "A small knowledge of human nature will convince us that, with far the greatest part of mankind, interest is the governing principle and that almost every man is more or less under its influence. . . . Few men are capable of making a continual sacrifice of all views of private interest, or advantage, to the common good." "The motives which predominate most in human affairs [are] self-love and self-interest." He declared, "It is vain to exclaim against the depravity of human nature on this account; the fact is so, the experience of every age and nation has proved it and we must in a great measure, change the constitution of man, before we can make it otherwise. No institution, not built on the presumptive truth of these maxims can succeed." Without a clear understanding of the nature of mankind, GW believed it would be impossible to create an effective republican government.

He knew from experience that only "interest" could bring about any societal embrace of virtue because "interest" is "the only cement that will bind." This open-eyed annealing of idealism and aggrandizement was a theme Washington believed in utterly and often acted upon. "We must make the best of mankind as they are, since we cannot have them as we wish them to be."

Talent

George Washington was able to "make the best of mankind as they are" because he was "awash in talents." Foremost among his many talents were a keen intelligence, a phenomenal memory, very astute judgment, and, perhaps most importantly, an intuitive and profound understanding of power and how best to exercise it.

Absolutely crucial was Washington's very impressive intellect. Almost all Washington biographers recognize his good heart, but most give his head short shrift. Marcus Cunliffe writes that he "never became what might be called an intellectual." Historian Alexander DeConde declared that "lacking broad intellectual qualities" Washington was "slow of mind." More recently, first-rate scholars Andrew Burstein and Nancy Isenberg insist in their book, *Madison and Jefferson,* that Washington had "an intellect no better than average." Such assertions miss the mark. A combination of both a good heart and a good head helped Washington succeed both as a general and as a president.

William Ferraro, associate editor of the *George Washington Papers,* characterizes that intellect in glowing terms. "Washington's writings at almost any period of the Revolutionary War reveal an impressive mind that could aggregate and retain information on widely divergent topics and shift nimbly among complex subjects—strategic planning, intelligence operations, supply issues, rank disputes, recruitment, prisoner management, congressional relations, finance, diplomacy—being but a partial list." While the general had a great many different aides writing for him, the communications throughout the war were consistent because a single mind—his own—held sway over the many hands putting pen to paper.

Washington's memory was phenomenal, as seen in a vignette during which he startled a visiting Polish nobleman by apparently naming virtually every river, creek, and lake in a 2,000-mile arc from Portsmouth, Maine, to the Mississippi River. A masterly executive, Washington could ingest and distill huge reams of data and quickly act on the resulting analysis. He knew how to get things done. Washington's "executive talents are superior, I believe, of any man in the world," Jefferson asserted.

Washington's astuteness as a judge of character and of ability and of situations was crucial to his genius. He had few peers in his ability to appreciate and utilize the expertise of men who, as he himself once put it, had "much abler heads than my own." In the service of advancing his aims he opened doors for brilliant young generals like Henry Knox and Nathaniel Greene and brilliant young statesmen like James

Madison and Alexander Hamilton, among many others. Comfortable in his skin, confident in himself, clear about his beliefs and goals, and always willing to deploy his charisma, he recruited and cultivated these blossoming geniuses and inspired them to greatness without yielding control or compromising himself.

Besides a keen intelligence, a phenomenal memory, and astute judgment, Washington had a profound understanding of power and how best to exercise it, either directly or through others. Think of power as the ability to achieve intended effects. In his small but perceptive book, *The Genius of George Washington,* Edmund Morgan argues that Washington's genius lay in his grasp of both military and political power. He was a better politician than a general, and in many ways, a political genius. The British diplomat Edward Thornton praised President Washington for possessing "the two great requisites of a statesman, the faculty of concealing his own sentiments, and of discovering those of other men." John Adams noted that Washington "possessed the gift of silence," which Adams described as "one of the most precious talents."

Another aspect of Washington's genius lay in what might be called "the politics of self-presentation." Few men had a finer sense of how to conduct themselves in the public arena. Acutely sensitive to perceptions and expectations and intensely aware of the scrutiny attending any man of his station, Washington rigorously cultivated his public image.

Not a reflective writer, he nonetheless had a reflective side. British actor John Bernard, after a far-reaching talk with Washington in 1797, commented, "He spoke like a man who felt as much as he had reflected and reflected more than he had spoken." Washington never left an option unconsidered. "He was habituated to view things on every side, to consider them in all relations, and to trace the possible and probable consequences of proposed measures," David Ramsey wrote in 1789.

George Washington was never "one of the boys." As a commander and as a civilian leader, he maintained a correct distance from those he led. Elitist by temperament, upbringing, and philosophy, he believed a degree of separation was "necessary to support a proper command." Power required a remoteness that familiarity and intimacy eroded. "To grow upon familiarity" was "in proportion to sink in authority," he said. In historical hindsight, that remoteness complicates the task of understanding him but in its time it did not repel. Instead, Washington's imposing mien was softened by his air of modesty, shyness, and a tendency toward self-deprecation, all of which helped create an appealing whole that not only made men trust him but also obey him. James Madison referenced the appeal of what he called Washington's "modest dignity," and modesty was as important a part of his personality as his courage. Abigail Adams described "a dignity that forbids familiarity, mixed with an easy affability that creates love and reverence." Frenchman Claude Blanchard said Washington had mastered the "art of making himself beloved." This ability to ingratiate himself with others helps explain GW's charismatic appeal to contemporaries and his superlative management of other leaders as general and president.

Sharply self-critical, Washington knew well his strengths and his weaknesses. He worked constantly to improve the former and to minimize, if not to eradicate, the latter. He wrote to Joseph Reed, "The man who wishes to stand well in the opinion of others" must "hear of imputed or real errors." He was no orator, for instance, but he was capable of eloquence in word and gesture. A life-long lover of the theater and a devotee of classical drama, he grasped the essence of playacting, which he often employed, evincing a magnificent sense of stagecraft, sometimes inciting participants to action and sometimes bringing them to tears. As British essayist Alexander Pope wrote, "Act well your part. Therein lies the honor." Washington certainly did.

Riveting examples abound. At the Second Continental Congress in May 1775, the general made a profound impression by appearing in his new military uniform. After taking a great risk and attacking the Hessians at Trenton in December 1776, he utilized the Continental Army's victory to persuade soldiers to reenlist, preserving battlefield momentum. At Monmouth in 1778, he dramatically rallied his troops to snatch a draw from the jaws of defeat. With his officers near mutiny at Newburgh in 1783, he neutralized their ire using only reading glasses as a prop. Later that year he moved his officers to tears with his farewell encounter at Fraunces Tavern in Manhattan, effectively employing the power of silence, which was one of his trademarks. As he later expressed it, "Unutterable sensations must then be left to more expressive silence." At Annapolis at the end of the war in 1783, he returned his commission to an emotional Congress and announced his reentry into private life. He awed members of the Constitutional Convention in

1787 with his displeasure when a participant violated the stated policy of secrecy by leaving a confidential paper on his desk. And in 1797, following John Adams's inauguration, Washington insisted that the new vice president, Thomas Jefferson, precede him in procession, reinforcing his status as a private citizen.

These emotionally charged scenes did not occur by accident. Washington had a magisterial way of directing major scenes in his life. Not only did he perform well, but he apparently also examined his performances and the reactions they elicited. He was not only a consummate actor; he was also an accomplished director of the man in the mirror. Crucial to his success as the leader of the new nation, Washington learned how to render a concern for appearance and a love of theater into a convincing presentation of republican power. But do not simply take the notion of Washington as actor at face value. In Greek, "actor" means "hypocrite," one pretending to be what he is not. Washington was no hypocrite. He believed in and lived the role he played—the embodiment of revolutionary virtue, a symbolic figure around whom countrymen could rally. He applied his great skill in the "politics of self-presentation" to unite the people behind American independence and republican government. Don Higginbotham argued that he should be known as "The Unifier," a phrase that succinctly captures what Washington sought to achieve.

Committed to collaboration, Washington often put aside personal animus to further larger goals, a generosity of spirit he encouraged in others. During the Constitutional Convention, he changed one of his votes because the issue, while not crucial to him, was so to others who, if disappointed, might oppose other points of real merit. During the war, he declared, "I have undergone more than most men are aware of, to harmonize so many discordant parts." His praise for French admiral François-Joseph-Paul de Grasse gives insight into how he conducted himself. "A great Mind knows how to make personal Sacrifices to secure an important general Good." Washington had that rare capacity to rise above emotions and recognize genuine value. "Let it suffice for me to add that I am acting on the great scale, that temporary evils must be endured where there is no remedy at hand."

Washington constantly tried to create a community of open discourse and a spirit of mutual forbearance. He was a good listener. As both general and president, he sought unity above all. When a disgruntled general threatened to resign, Washington defused his ire by paraphrasing Cato: "Surely every post ought to be deemed honorable in which a man can serve his country." Again and again, he urged that people not let personal pique overpower the greater cause.

Two quotations, one from the war and one from his presidency, sum up his view. "How strange it is that Men, engaged in the same Important Service, should be eternally bickering, instead of giving mutual aid! Officers cannot act upon proper principles, who suffer trifles interposed to create distrust and jealousy." In seeking to defuse the feud between Hamilton and Jefferson, he wrote, "How unfortunate, and how much is it to be regretted then, that whilst we are encompassed on all sides with avowed enemies and insidious friends, that internal dissensions should be harrowing and tearing at our vitals. . . . In my opinion the fairest prospect of happiness and prosperity that ever was presented to man will be lost—perhaps forever!" He did not want "passion to interfere with our interest and the public good."

Character

Character is often a nebulous term and difficult to define. The ancient Greeks, for whom character was destiny, codified that aspect of humanity into four virtues—fortitude (or courage), temperance, prudence (or wisdom), and justice. Washington possessed all, and in abundance.

Fortitude is strength of mind along with the physical and moral courage to persevere in the face of adversity, and Winston Churchill opined, "Courage is rightly esteemed the first of human qualities . . . because it is the quality which guarantees all others." Washington always admired and practiced stoical courage. "I hope I shall always possess a sufficient degree of fortitude to bear without murmuring any stroke which may happen."

Temperance is the self-discipline needed to rein in appetites and passions. Washington came to embody the wisdom of the Stoic philosopher Epictetus, who said, "No man is free who is not master of himself." GW reserved some of his sharpest words for drunkards and their implicit lack of self-control.

18   FIRST AND ALWAYS

Prudence is the practical wisdom that enables a person to make the right choices in specific situations. One of Washington's most impressive traits was his judgment. He had the ability to make sober and highly realistic assessments of the various options facing the infant American republic, and time and time again he decided correctly. Temporary evils must be patiently borne if there is no immediate remedy at hand.

Justice collects beneath its rubric fairness, honesty, lawfulness, and the dutiful keeping of promises. According to Dwight Eisenhower, a great leader must possess absolute integrity, and Washington had that. In 1786, he told a friend, "I do not recollect that in the course of my life I ever forfeited my word, or broke a promise made to anyone." Impartiality was among his most admired traits. Jefferson avowed, "His justice [was] the most inflexible I have ever known, no motives of interest or consanguinity, of friendship or hatred, being able to bias his decision." To conduct oneself with integrity, especially in a time of crisis, is the fundamental test of character. As Epictetus said, "It is difficulties that show what men are."

George Washington was a great man. Fortunately for America, he was also a good man, indeed the greatest of good men and the best of great men. He sought not mere celebrity but "honest fame," the path to which, Socrates tells aspirants, requires one to "study to be what you wish to seem." Washington did become the man he wished to be—the embodiment of revolutionary virtue. It is striking how closely his behavior reflected his ideals, and how hard he worked to enter the temple of fame by way of the temple of virtue.

In George Washington, charisma and leadership melded in such a way that, in Abigail Adams's words, he could have been "a very dangerous" man—but because, as she also recognized, he was "one of the best intentioned men in the world," he put his talents to work not in self-aggrandizement but to lead his country in the "glorious cause" of establishing and expanding liberty and republican values. It was a priceless gift.

2

"Complicated, Very Complicated"

GEORGE WASHINGTON'S CONTROVERSIAL RELATIONSHIP
WITH HIS MOTHER, MARY BALL WASHINGTON

IT IS IMPOSSIBLE to write at any length about George Washington's relationship with his father, Augustine, who was often away and who died when George was only eleven years old. An examination of the massive volume of Washington's papers reveals how surprisingly infrequently he makes even fleeting mention of his father, and never does he do so in a reflective manner. His father's influence must forever remain beyond the historian's grasp. There is not even enough material for informed speculation.

This leaves as the central adult figure of George's formative years his mother, Mary Ball Washington. The variety of comment in two centuries on her presence in his life recalls the Russian saying that the past has become less predictable than the future. Mary Ball Washington's image has toggled from exaggerated saintliness ("Mary, the Mother of Washington," reminding one of "Mary, the Mother of Jesus") to unalloyed shrewishness (with the very influential Washington biographer James Flexner entitling one of his chapters "Termagant [Mother] . . ."). Ron Chernow, author of a Pulitzer Prize–winning biography of Washington, basically sides with the shrew crew. In his extremely well-written and often very insightful best seller, Chernow paints Mary Ball Washington as a "crude," "slovenly," and "illiterate" woman whose "failure" to find a second husband "imposed inordinate burdens on Washington as the eldest son." Chernow sees a quiet antagonism between the son and his "hypercritical" and "difficult" mother, who withheld "loyalty" from her son and "leveled a steady stream of criticism at him."

Perhaps the clearest example of Chernow's attitude comes when he writes, "George Washington defined himself as the *antithesis* of his mother [emphasis added]. If his mother was *crude* and *illiterate*, he would improve himself through books. If she was *self-centered,* he would be self-sacrificing. . . . If she was *slovenly,* he would be meticulous in appearance. If she *disdained fancy society,* he would crave its acceptance. . . . And if she was a veteran *complainer,* he would be known for his stiff upper lip." While not without merit, this assessment inadequately understands both Mary and her relationship with her firstborn son.

Who was Mary Ball Washington? What was her background? What kind of woman was she? We know far less about her than we would like. However, thanks to scholars Paula Felder, Martha Saxton, and others, we know a good deal more about Mary Ball Washington than we once did.

In many ways, Mary had a difficult and challenging life, one that almost inevitably created a sense of insecurity. This tough and strong-willed but self-centered woman's search for security may go far to explain her and her relationship with her famous son.

Mary Ball was born in either 1708 or 1709, the only child of Colonel Joseph Ball of Lancaster and his wife, Mary Johnson Ball. The parents' backgrounds could not have differed more. Joseph Ball was a member of the Virginia elite—an officer in the militia, a churchwarden, a vestryman, and at times a member of the House of Burgesses, high sheriff, and justice of the court. His estate's inventory makes clear the Balls were very prosperous. Even compared with their peers' furnishings, the Ball household's floor coverings, curtains, silver service, and matched chairs were unusually sumptuous for the era. Not so the background of Mary's mother. While inconclusive, the evidence indicates that she was born Mary Bennett and was brought over from England as an indentured servant. She married a man named Johnson, gave birth to two children (Elizabeth and John), and soon after her first husband's death married the much older Ball, who was fifty-nine and the father of grown children. Unfortunately, the exact dates of their marriage, sometime in 1708, and of Mary's birth, sometime in 1708 or 1709, are no longer extant. Mary's mother must have had particularly attractive attributes to win the affection of so powerful a man in so hierarchical a society.

Little Mary had not turned three when Colonel Ball died. His will indicated he was enamored of his "beloved wife" and fond of their daughter. Joseph specified that "during her natural life" his widow would be able to "peaceably enjoy the homestead." Among his generous bequests, Joseph Ball left his widow a white horse, Dragon, along with "her" bridle, sidesaddle, and other "furniture." To toddler Mary, her father left three slaves and four hundred acres north of the Rappahannock near Fredericksburg. About a year after Joseph Ball's death, Mary Bennett Johnson Ball married her third husband, Captain Richard Hughes, who may have spelled his surname "Hews," "Hewes," or "Hues." As the colonel had, the captain died only a few years into the marriage. Evidence is strong that Richard cared greatly for Mary, since he agreed to provide for her two children, John and Elizabeth, by her first husband. Anticipating future developments, it is significant to note that the Hughes farm at Cherry Point, near the Potomac River, was very close to the home of George Eskridge. Mary's mother described Eskridge, a wealthy attorney and member of the House of Burgesses, as her "trusty and well-beloved friend." Later, her will named him an executor, and she put her daughter Mary "under the Tutelage and governorship of Captain George Eskridge during her minority."

We don't know how her stepfather's death affected six-year-old Mary. Surely, however, the deaths from disease in the winter of 1720–21 of her stepbrother John and especially her mother were a great tragedy for the girl, who was only about eleven years old. The mother's will reflects the affection between the Marys and their shared love of riding. Bequests to young Mary included fine bed furnishings, two gold rings, and a "good pacing horse," with instructions to Eskridge that on the girl's eighteenth birthday he purchase for her a plush silk sidesaddle and a "likely young negro woman." Clearly Mary Bennett Johnson Ball Hughes did what she could to protect her namesake and to give her daughter at least the possibility of remaining in the world she herself had briefly enjoyed as wife to the wealthy and powerful Joseph Ball.

While speculative, it is plausible to argue that the death of her father, stepfather, stepbrother, and mother all before she became a teenager weighed heavily on young Mary. With the central supports in her short life washed away, she was now forced to look to her older married stepsister, Elizabeth, for help and a place to live. Elizabeth had married Samuel Bonam, the nephew of Eskridge's first wife, a fact that connected the families more closely. Undoubtedly, Mary endeavored to act in a way that would make her welcome in her new home, and the evidence that she was in fact welcomed is supported by Mary's decision, after her marriage to Augustine Washington, to name her first daughter after Elizabeth. When Elizabeth's husband Samuel died in 1724, he left Mary a "young dapple-gray riding horse," a sign of his affection and further evidence of Mary's love of horses.

How did Mary Ball come to wed Augustine Washington, an ambitious member of the Virginia gentry, and noticeably higher on the social hierarchy scale than she? In the strange ways of fate, George Eskridge would play a key role in linking Mary to Augustine because of his close connection to both parties. In addition to essentially being Mary's guardian, Eskridge was also Augustine's brother-in-law— Eskridge's wife was the sister of Augustine's wife, Jane Butler.

Tragedy struck in 1730, when Jane, the mother of the Washingtons' three surviving children, Lawrence, Augustine, and Jane, died suddenly while Augustine was in England on business. Returning to the shock of that news, Augustine not only had to deal with his grief but also needed a caregiver for his three motherless children. Mary, now in her early twenties, was experienced in this regard, having lived with her half-sister, Elizabeth, and having helped run the house and care for Elizabeth's two orphaned children. There was another factor that made a union with Mary Ball appealing to Augustine. With the death of her half-brother, John, Mary had acquired six hundred acres of potentially valuable land near the location on which Augustine had built his ironworks. The stars seemed to be aligned. Augustine found a helpmate and caretaker and control over valuable acreage, and Mary moved up the social ladder. The couple wed on March 6, 1731.

The Washington family Bible picks up the story. "George Washington Son to Augustine & Mary his Wife was born the 11th Day of February 1731/2 about 10 in the Morning & was baptized the 5th of April following." Interestingly, recent careful examination has shown that this entry was in fact made later by George Washington himself. As John Rhodehamel notes, "That the young man should register his birth was emblematic of his emerging character: George Washington was a record keeping animal." That calendar entry—February 11th, 1731/32—became obsolete in 1752, when the British adopted the more accurate Gregorian calendar by adding eleven days and starting the year with the month of January, thus making Washington's birth date under the new style February 22, 1732. Under the old Julian calendar, the year had begun on

March 1—hence September, October, November, and December, corresponding to the Latin for seven, eight, nine, and ten.

George, undoubtedly named for George Eskridge, was the first of a succession of six children in eight years—Betty, Samuel, John, Charles, and Mildred. All except Mildred lived to adulthood. Mildred's death at sixteen months was not the only death of one close to her that Mary had to deal with. Her stepdaughter, Jane, died in 1735 and, more significantly, her beloved half-sister, Elizabeth, died in early 1742. Elizabeth's death was a profound blow to Mary; the two had grown very close. As Martha Saxton explains, for Mary "this was an irreplaceable intimacy, a lifelong companion, now of middle age, who had sheltered her when their mother died, labored with her at domestic chores and helped her learn to manage a house." A far graver blow fell in 1743. Augustine Washington suddenly expired from "gout of the stomach," perhaps pancreatic cancer. Mary suddenly found herself a widow with five preteen children to care for and with an estate that was radically reduced by about 60 percent due to the fact that her husband had granted his most valuable properties, Mount Vernon and Wakefield, to Lawrence and Augustine, his sons by Jane Butler. Augustine's will made no sentimental bequests to Mary or any reference to her as his "beloved wife." Additionally, he stipulated that his widow would lose her control over her widow's third if she remarried.

I believe Mary's personality and perhaps her societal circumstances guided her decision not to remarry. To do so would mean once again molding herself to yet another man's expectations and domination, as she would have been legally under the direction and control of her husband, who may or may not have respected her property rights. For whatever reason or combination of reasons, she would not do it. That obdurate independence placed her in a difficult position, for she was responsible for raising five preteen children to maturity and doing so on rather limited resources because of her reduced estate. In an age that often saw single parents parcel out children, rather than bear the financial and emotional burden of going it alone, Mary kept her children under her own roof and raised them herself, an achievement of no small scale. The challenging task would not be done without problems, but it was done, and the reason it was done was due in no small measure to the type of woman she was.

Contemporary comments, positive and negative, portray Mary as very imposing, with undeniable strength and toughness. There seems little doubt that she ran her household, including her slaves, with something of an iron hand. As Henry Cabot Lodge expressed it, "She was an imperious woman, of strong will, ruling her kingdom alone." Douglas Southall Freeman observed, "In her dealings with her servants, she was strict. They must follow a definite round of work. Her bidding must be their law." Stories survive of her meting out punishment to disobedient slaves.

As a widow in an era in which a woman's declaration of any authority automatically invited challenge, Mary found the habit of command particularly useful. She instinctively knew she had to dominate her environment. One vignette describes Mary's farm manager scoffing at her instructions, saying his way was better. "And pray, who gave you any exercise of judgment in the matter?" she replied. "I command you, sir; there is nothing left for you but to obey." To relent, especially in the presence of her own slaves, would be to lose power. As great-grandson George Washington Parke Custis expressed it, "The matron held in reserve an authority, which never departed from her."

Probably the most famous observation about her powerful persona is the one by George's cousin Lawrence of Chotank, Virginia. "Of the mother I was ten times more afraid than I ever was of my own parents." Though presenting a rather frightening image, there is a second part of that quote that is usually omitted and which is important in rendering an accurate assessment. "She awed me in the midst of her kindness, for she was, indeed, truly kind. I have often been present with her sons, proper tall fellows too, and we were all mute as mice; and even now, when time has whitened my locks. . . . I could not behold that remarkable woman without feelings it is impossible to describe." Betty's children spoke similarly of their grandmother. Strictness and kindness are not necessarily incompatible.

If an imposing personality and strong will were an important part of Mary's makeup, so were her strong religious views, which were robust and informed. A close examination of George Washington's library suggests that his supposedly "illiterate" mother read more than commonly thought. Two important books on her shelf were John Scott's *The Christian Life from Its Beginning to Its Consummation* and Thomas

Comber's *A Short Discourse on the Whole Common Prayer.* While Jane Butler was still alive, Augustine had bought and inscribed this copy of Comber's book, whose author intended his words "to furnish devout sons of the church with profitable meditations." Mary, who later added her name, apparently gave George his father's copy of Comber when the boy was about thirteen. George signed it, too, adorning his autograph with ornate flourishes.

There seems little dispute that Mary's favorite book was Matthew Hale's *Contemplations Moral and Divine,* which had belonged as well to Augustine's first wife. Mary proudly signed her name under Jane's, and either she presented the Hale book to George or he added it to his library after his mother died. Hale begins his interdenominational discourse on Christianity by focusing on the "latter days," the need for all to be ready to die, and the surety that only faith in Christ guaranteed immediate passage to eternal life. It was up to people to be ready for death at all times, but also to live good, uncomplaining lives. Hale assured readers that death opened the door to either eternal happiness or eternal misery. The crucial goal—much more important than honor, fame, and wealth—was to win eternal happiness. True wisdom, he wrote, teaches us to view the honors of the earth as "rust" in comparison to the Glory offered by God. "Labor to get thy peace with God through Jesus Christ our Lord," Hale wrote. "When this is once attained, thou art set above the love of the world and the fear of afflictions because thou has the assurance of the greater treasure than this world can give or could take away."

Contemporaries viewed Mary in her later years as a devout woman. George Washington Parke Custis recalled his grandmother poring over and reading from Hale's book to her children and her grandchildren. Young Custis remembered Mary retiring daily to a secluded grove near her dwelling where she engaged in private devotions; "abstracted from the world and worldly things, she communed with her Creator in humiliation and prayer." Custis's recollection is supported by Lawrence Lewis, Mary's grandson who lived nearby at Kenmore. He remembered his grandmother having a favorite rock that offered a lovely rural view of the surrounding countryside. It "was upon this spot . . . she impressed on our infant minds the wonderful works of the Great Creator of all things, his goodness, his mercy to all who love and obey him." Another grandson, Robert, remembers her reading to him and his siblings from the family Bible. In her will, Mary, unlike both her husband and later her son, expressly recommended her soul "into the hands of my Creator, hoping for a remission of all my sins through the merits and mediation of Jesus Christ, the Savior of all mankind."

Mary Ball Washington's relationship with and influence on her son is best examined from two angles. The first perspective is on George's youth; the second focuses on his maturation into a man of increasing influence and importance. The early years best bear scrutiny in reverse. With no father to serve as a patron and with limited financial resources in Virginia's deeply hierarchical and patriarchal society, young George, in order to advance, needed to forge alliances with men of years and wealth—and he did forge those alliances. Douglas Southall Freeman explained why: "Powerful Virginia elders, who saw much loose living and indolence around them, found stimulation and reassurance in a young man of unassailed morals and of mature, sound judgment, who was full of energetic vigor." Washington could hardly have attracted favorable notice if he were clumsy or socially inept or of poor moral character. Certainly, considerable credit for George's early success must go to his mother, and Mary deserves admiration for what she accomplished. As George Washington Parke Custis said, she "taught him the duties of obedience . . . the levity and indulgence, common to youth, were tempered by a deference and . . . restraint." Young Washington respected her moral authority and adopted much of her philosophy as his own. Even as a teenager, George wrote his older sister-in-law, Ann Fairfax Washington, with mature advice. "I hope you will make use of your natural resolution and contentedness as they are the only remedies to spend time with ease and pleasure to yourself."

The George Washington Foundation is supporting interesting archeological work at Ferry Farm, George Washington's boyhood home just outside of Fredericksburg. Their findings support the thesis that Mary Ball Washington was more fashion conscious than typically portrayed. "The careful analysis of small finds, such as figurines, tea wares, and needlework tools, demonstrates that she took deliberate measures to engage in fashionable, social customs of the time and, furthermore, to train her children in the skills and behaviors associated with these customs," the archeologists report. "Such training equipped them for their adult roles in the refined society to which they aspired." Martha Saxton pointed out another example. "The long-ago inventory of textiles in her father's estate and her store accounts in Fredericksburg show Mary's lifelong connoisseurship of fabrics. She made fine distinctions among different fabrics, artfully deploying their character and strengths. George learned about textiles, their properties and care at his mother's house." This may in part account for his interest in his own meticulously chosen wardrobe. (This point will be expanded upon in chapter 8.) As only a sixteen-year-old, he made a note of what he was bringing on a visit to Belvoir: "7 Shirts 2 Do Carr[ie]d by Mr. Thornton 6 Linnen Waistcoats 1 Cloth Do 6 Bands 4 Neck Cloths 7 Caps." Another gauge of Mary's status awareness can be seen in daughter Betty's ownership of pewter teaspoons engraved with her initials, as well as Betty's mastery of needlework and penmanship, which led to marriage into the very respectable Lewis family. Mary clearly labored to provide her daughter with social and household skills that compensated for a small dowry.

I don't doubt that ultimately the Fairfax family at Belvoir, including the alluring Sally Fairfax, was George Washington's finishing school, or that his elder half-brother, Lawrence, was an important role model. My point is that all those influences built upon a foundation that George acquired from his mother at Ferry Farm. Contrary to portrayals of the Washington home at Ferry Farm as a cultural wasteland, and Mary as a pipe-smoking proto-hillbilly, such simply was not the case.

Much of George Washington's childhood relationship with his mother lies behind an impenetrable veil of blankness. The best-known and best-documented episode involving young George and his mother revolves around Mary's refusal to allow her fifteen-year-old son to enlist in the Royal Navy. Additionally, it provides a good example of Mary's strong will. The idea began with Lawrence, who had served in the Royal Navy under Vice Admiral Edward Vernon, for whom Lawrence named the estate he inherited from his father. Lawrence's plan was supported by Colonel William Fairfax, the wealthy owner of Belvoir, and family friend Robert Jackson, who was a Fredericksburg merchant and one of the executors of Augustine's will. Jackson described Mary's objections to her son going to sea as typical of "fond and unthinking mothers."

In fact, Mary did not make the decision lightly, asking the advice of her older half-brother, Joseph Ball, living in England. It is unclear whether his advice was decisive or simply confirmation of what Mary had already decided. He was certainly clear. The British Navy was a very dangerous institution in the eighteenth century. The class-ridden Royal Navy, which dated to its creation by King Henry VIII, would deny a young colonial like George, lacking effective social connections, pedigree, and income, "any considerable preferment," Joseph Ball warned. Were George to enlist, he said, superiors likely would "cut and staple him and use him like a Negro, or rather, like a dog." He opined that even a captain of a merchant vessel would not live as well as a Virginia planter with "three or four hundred acres of land and three or four slaves."

In short, Mary's decision seems logical and reasonable, especially since young George was in time to inherit a six-hundred-acre farm at Deeps Run, and it was not simply fueled by the irrational fears of an overly fond mother, worried about losing her firstborn, which is how the very influential biographer Douglas Southall Freeman portrayed the incident. "Mistress of much or of little, mistress she resolved to be, and in nothing more certainly than in deciding what should be done by her firstborn, her pride and her weakness. She would hold him fast, safe from the temptations of a sailor's life." How different American history might have been if she had not had the temerity and strength of character to resist the entreaties of such influential males! And Mary Washington's apron strings, while strong, were not permanently entangling. I think it worth noting that she gave her permission shortly afterward for the sixteen-year-old George to go on his first great adventure as a member of the Fairfax surveying party across the Blue Ridge Mountains and into the Shenandoah Valley, undoubtedly because she believed such a trip would advance his future prospects.

In short, Mary did not unthinkingly say no. And it is interesting to note that, however much Mary and Lawrence may have disagreed on the best course for George's future, they both had his best interests at heart and the two apparently maintained a good relationship. For example, in those days, death among the elite occasioned the giving of mourning rings to significant survivors to be worn in memory. When Lawrence died in 1752, his will stipulated that his stepmother—"mother-in-law" in the language of the day—was to receive a mourning ring. That her stepson would thus honor her testifies to Lawrence Washington's high regard for Mary.

Mary was no doubt a strict and demanding mother, but she clearly had a special relationship with her eldest son and favorite child, the boy who became the man of the house at age eleven. It required George to be mature beyond his years, because at that tender age George had to navigate a very complicated relationship with a mother inclined by temperament and experience to be constantly demanding. Beneath her poses of strength and independence, Mary Washington suffered from insecurity and abandonment issues. It would have been natural in widowhood for her to turn for support to her eldest child, making of George a kind of emotional crutch. The struggle of growing up with and separating from this complex woman while remaining loyal to her prepared her son for a lifetime of accommodating difficult but necessary relationships and soldiering through challenging experiences.

I do think his upbringing left George Washington with insecurities. He never was able to obtain his mother's unalloyed approval, nor could he completely satisfy her. Mary always appears to be lavish in her demands and stinting in her praise. Two of George Washington's most salient traits were extreme sensitivity to criticism and an intense desire for approval. He feared words of criticism in a way he never feared enemy bullets. It is certainly reasonable to posit that this endless quest for approval was rooted in part in his relationship with his demanding and apparently never satisfied mother.

A good snapshot of their changing relationship from George the adolescent to Washington the man is his decision to join General Edward Braddock on Braddock's ill-fated 1755 march to retake the Ohio country from the French. Washington saw great potential for advancing his military career in being a personal, if unofficial, aide to the general. On the eve of his joining that undertaking, he wrote that he would be delayed slightly in joining the expedition. He explained that his mother, "alarmed at the report of my intentions to attend your fortunes," had hurried to Mount Vernon to attempt in person to discourage him from participating in the expedition. Whatever exchange occurred—there is no record—Mary obviously failed in her mission. While committed to his mother's welfare, George Washington would not be dissuaded from seeking fame and glory, even if it meant risking his life and leaving her behind.

In studying their relationship of more than thirty years—from the French and Indian War to Mary's death in 1789—an examiner of the record must acknowledge that, especially in Mary Ball Washington's later years, George Washington had a strained and often contentious relationship with his mother. Her favorite author, Matthew Hale, instructs Christians to bear burdens cheerfully. However, Mary Washington was not one to forgo complaint, a characteristic that wore on her increasingly famous son. Their few surviving letters make abundantly clear that Mary was focused narrowly on her own needs, and she seemed unconcerned or oblivious to the problems facing her son, both in the French and Indian War and later in the American Revolution. A particularly revealing glimpse of how his mother expected her son to meet her needs is seen in a letter she wrote him during the first conflict. With Washington hard-pressed on the Virginia frontier, Mary entreated him to find her a Dutchman (German) to help her at Ferry Farm and, even more impossible, to acquire butter for her. However shocked Washington might have been by the unreasonable request, he gently replied that butter "cannot be had here."

Mary bemoaned her life during this period: "I never lived so pore in my life." She hoped for better days with the war's end. She wrote her half-brother, Joseph Ball, "There was no end to my troubles while George was in the army, but he has now given it up." Between the end of the French and Indian War and the Revolution, George Washington's account books show significant outlays on behalf of his mother. Often, perhaps to have a witness to call on later, he notes who was present when he gave her money. According to his father's will, George was to inherit Ferry Farm when he turned eighteen in 1750. However, for over an additional twenty years, Mary continually occupied, managed, and derived income from the property as if it were her own, with her son never claiming his share. Finally, in 1772, Washington convinced his mother, now past sixty, to relocate to Fredericksburg and bought a house for her (still standing today) near her daughter, Betty, and her husband, Fielding Lewis, who would be situated to help her as needed. Washington absorbed all the myriad expenses incurred in this move, including 275 pounds for the house.

No doubt, the Revolutionary War years were difficult for Mary. Her firstborn was far away, leading what to her must have seemed a forlorn and dangerous crusade. Son-in-law Fielding Lewis, who, along with daughter Betty oversaw Mary's wellbeing, was overworked and ill. Fielding died in 1781, a serious blow not only to Betty but also to Mary. The hard times she suffered were the background for her complaints that led to one of the most embarrassing moments of George Washington's career. His friend Benjamin Harrison, speaker of the Virginia assembly, wrote the general in early 1781 to alert him that there was a move in the Virginia legislature to treat Washington's mother as an indigent woman, preparatory to paying her a state pension. (It should be noted, despite James Flexner's claims to the contrary, that there is no clear evidence Mary had any direct involvement in this move.) One can only imagine how General Washington, ever extremely sensitive about anything that might damage his reputation, felt on reading this letter. Washington immediately directed Harrison to squash the petition, declaring that it was both unnecessary and embarrassing. "Confident I am that she has not a child that would not divide the last sixpence to relieve her from *real* distress. This she has been repeatedly assured of by me: and all of us, I am certain, would feel much hurt, at having our mother a pensioner, while we had the means of supporting her; but in fact, she has an ample income of her own."

Following Harrison's receipt of Washington's letter, no more was heard about the pension petition, but carping from Mary clearly kept coming, as demonstrated by Washington's letter to his favorite brother, Jack, in 1783. "I learn from very good authority that she is upon all occasions, and in all Companies complaining of the hardness of the times, of her wants and distresses; and if not in direct terms, at least by strong innuendos inviting favors which not only makes her appear in an unfavorable point of view but those also who are connected with her. That she can have no real wants that may not be supplied I am sure of; imaginary wants are indefinite and oftentimes insatiable, because they are boundless and always changing." Admitting that a mere letter from him would not suffice, Washington urged his brother to "represent to her in delicate terms, the impropriety of her complaints and acceptance of favors even when they are voluntarily offered, from any but relations."

Mary's constant complaining may have led some to think her a Tory sympathizer. A remarkable 1782 journal that French officer Count de Clermont-Crevecoeur kept as he rode with General Rochambeau and his troops north following the British surrender at Yorktown mentions the rumor. "Fredericksburg is where General Washington's mother lives. We went to call on her but were amazed to be told that this lady, who must be over seventy, is one of the most rabid Tories." The charge is most likely inaccurate. Note that Mary did not tell Crevecoeur and his party this directly, but they "heard" about it from someone else. More plausibly, Mary, who certainly had little or no affection for the military, regularly expressed unhappiness with a war that once again took her son—and his attention—away from her. One remembrance has her saying, "This fighting and killing is a sad thing! I wish George would come home and look after his plantation." If Mary had in fact been a "rabid Tory," I doubt the Virginia legislature would have considered giving her a pension, or that the citizens of Fredericksburg, in the immediate aftermath of the war when feelings against Tories still ran high, would have heaped praise upon her.

The final letter penned by Washington to his mother in 1787 was his longest and in some ways his most revealing. She had requested more money, and her failing health had led to discussions of where she might move. In sending the money, Washington made it clear that he was hard pressed himself and defensively summarized all that he had done for her in the past. Constant self-justification seems to be a key part of Washington's personality, especially the need to justify his actions to his mother. Always the dutiful son, he concluded his letter, "For whilst I have a shilling left, you shall have part, if it is wanted, whatever my own distresses may be."

The letter also touched on her failing health and the eternal topic of where an aging and ill parent might live. Earlier, unbeknownst to Mary, Washington had written Martha's mother, Frances Jones Dandridge, warmly inviting her to live at Mount Vernon. His letters to the two women differ strikingly. While saying Mary was of course welcome at Mount Vernon, Washington made clear that he did not think it was a good idea. Mary, now nearing eighty and a woman of little social polish, in Washington's view would not have fit in very well at Mount Vernon. The general brusquely wrote, "My house is at your service, and [I] would press you most sincerely and most devoutly to accept it, but I am sure, and candor requires me to say, it will never answer your purposes in any shape whatsoever. For in truth it may be compared to a well resorted tavern . . . were you to be an inhabitant of it, [it would] oblige you to do one of 3 things: 1st, to be always dressing to appear in company; 2d, to come into [the room] in a dishabille [a loose, negligent dress], or 3d, to be as it were a prisoner in your own chamber. The first you'd not like; . . . The 2d, I should not like, because those who resort here are, as I observed before . . . people of the first distinction. And the 3d, more than probably, would not be pleasing to either of us."

Interestingly, not only did Mary not come to Mount Vernon in 1787 but, as far as the record reveals, in all the years following Washington's marriage to Martha Custis in 1759, Mary never once visited Mount Vernon, although there is a reference to her planning to do so. Distance was certainly a factor, and perhaps in part she demurred because she and Martha were not at all close, but it does indicate something about the nature of their relationship.

Mary's famous son concluded the longest epistle he ever wrote her suggesting how she could raise enough money for comfortable, care-free final years. By following "the mode I have pointed out, you may reduce your income to a certainty, be eased of all trouble, and if you are so disposed, may be perfectly happy; for happiness depends more upon the internal frame of a person's own mind, than on the externals in the world. Of the last, if you will pursue the plan here recommended, I am sure you can want nothing that is essential. The other depends wholly upon yourself, for the riches of the Indies cannot purchase it." Here Washington was parroting one of the points made by religious writer Matthew Hale. Unfortunately, Mary's personality made it unlikely that she would follow this good advice, for her eye for pain was much keener than her sense for pleasure.

Always defensive about aiding his mother, Washington often explained how much he did for her. And he did a great deal. After his mother's death from breast cancer in 1789, Washington listed his filial good works for his sister Betty in a tone of exasperation, if not hostility. "She has had a great deal of money from me at times, as can be made appear by my books, and the accounts of Mr. L. Washington during my absence; and over and above this has not only had all that was ever made from the Plantation but got her provisions and everything else she thought proper from thence. In short to the best of my recollection I have never in my life received a copper from the estate, and have paid many hundred pounds (first and last) to her in cash. However I want no retribution; I conceived it to be a duty whenever she asked for money, and I had it, to furnish her notwithstanding she got all the crops or the amount of them, and took everything she wanted from the plantation for the support of her family, horses, &c. besides."

Perhaps Washington was defensive because he recognized he could never really satisfy his mother, nor gain her unalloyed approval. Mary seems to have resented rather than appreciated her son's meteoric rise, probably because she perceived that his ascendancy meant less attention for her. No evidence shows her praising her son for his achievements— and there is clear evidence of her declining to do so. Her one letter to him that survives from the period shortly after Yorktown makes no reference to that remarkable victory. A vignette survives of Mary's sharp reply to word that there was to be a ball in honor of His Excellency. "His Excellency! What nonsense!" Even the memoirs of her great-grandson, George Washington Parke Custis, eulogistic as they are, make clear that Mary was very sparing with her praise for her firstborn.

The negative picture sketched above is not the entire story. It must be tempered by more positive vignettes in order to achieve a better sense of the complicated relationship Washington had with his mother. There is no question that Mary cared deeply for her son. No doubt part of her anxiety about Washington's putting himself in harm's way came from her fear that he would not be able to look after her properly, but certainly much of it was because she cared for him. It is worth noting that the first time Mary appears in the documented record with her firstborn involves her concern for his wellbeing, and the last documented reference expresses the same concern. There is a little-noted letter from Betty Lewis to her famous brother, now the president of the United States, and recovering from an illness that nearly cost him his life. Interestingly, Betty notes that their mother, although gravely ill and on her deathbed, "wishes to hear from you; *she will not believe you are well till she has it from under your own hand*" (emphasis added). This sounds like the response of a loving mother, and perhaps it is worth noting that in the only extant letter after Yorktown, Mary describes herself as "your loving and affectionate mother." Mary died shortly after Betty's letter to Washington expressing her concern for her famous son, and her last will and testament last will and testament made him the primary benefactor and the sole executor. "I give to my son, General George Washington all my land in Accokeek Run, in the County of Stafford, and also my negro boy George, to him and his heirs forever. Also, my best bed, bedstead, and Virginia cloth curtains (the same that stand in my best bedroom), my quilted blue-and-white quilt, and my best dressing glass."

How did Washington feel about his mother? Did he reciprocate her affection? Douglas Southall Freeman—and many others—would say no. Freeman declared that "the strangest mystery of Washington's life [was] his lack of affection for his mother." I think he overstates. Several bits of primary evidence, taken together, collectively make a strong case that George Washington in fact felt a certain amount of affection for his mother. Perhaps signing most of his letters "your affectionate son" might be dismissed as simply pro forma—like "your humble and obedient servant"—but Washington's gestures on behalf of his mother went well beyond what duty would have demanded. Examples would include purchasing for her a long red hooded cloak worth ten pounds and a riding chair worth forty pounds, not to mention the large amounts of cash and the new home he built for her in 1772.

There is a little-noted letter in which Washington indicates that he plans to visit her, and he does so not only out of duty but by "*inclination*" as well (emphasis added). Washington's dear friend the Marquis de Lafayette was one of the few friends of the general who had actually met his mother. Consequently, Lafayette often sent her his regards, once referring to Mary as "[your] respected mother" and again as "[your] venerable mother." In 1786, his wife, Adrienne, Marquise de Lafayette, wrote Washington and asked him to send special best wishes to his mother. In this case, the general wrote back to Madame Lafayette, "My Mother will receive the compliments you honor her with, as a flattering mark of your attention; and *I shall have great pleasure in delivering them myself*" (emphasis added).

Washington clearly enjoyed being able to tell his mother that so prominent a figure had sent her special greetings. Would you enjoy pleasing someone for whom you felt no affection? In another letter Washington explained to a correspondent that he been called suddenly to go to Fredericksburg to bid, "as I was prepared to expect, *the last adieu to an honored parent*" (emphasis added). The major beneficiary of Mary's final will and testament, Washington had no need of the things his mother left him but declared that because they had been hers and because he knew she wanted him to have them they had special meaning: "In this point of view *I set a value on them much beyond their intrinsic worth*" (emphasis added).

A final important piece of evidence for Washington's affection for his mother is the general's response to a welcome from the citizens of Fredericksburg on his first visit to the town in 1784 after his great victory at Yorktown had led to the winning of American independence. In inviting him, townspeople wrote, "It affords us great joy, to see you Once more at the place which claims the Honor of your growing infancy, the Seat *of your Venerable and Amiable Parent* and Worthy Relations" (emphasis added).

The general's response to his welcome in Fredericksburg is highly pertinent. He wrote his comments himself and, as numerous revisions and corrections indicate, took care and thought in doing so. He declared his pleasure in his welcome was heightened by "the honorable mention which is made of my revered Mother; by whose Maternal hand (early deprived of a Father) I was led to Manhood." "Revered Mother" is what he wrote and what he said. In its coverage, the *Virginia Gazette* erroneously printed "reverend," a mistake widely replicated since. "My revered Mother" is unexpectedly strong language from a man who supposedly held the kind of negative feelings that many historians assert.

I am not trying to sugarcoat the relationship and make it into an ideal mother/child connection. My point is that while it was a conflicted relationship and, undoubtedly, Washington was often exasperated and even angered by his mother's actions. Yet there was in him a sense of a debt owed her, grudging admiration that strength pays to strength, and some affection tempering his frustration and annoyance.

There may be elements of understanding as well. One of the chapters in my book *Realistic Visionary* deals with Washington's relationship with Alexander Hamilton. A clash between the two during the

Private conversations between George Washington and his mother are lost to history and remain only among mythmakers. (Courtesy of Mount Vernon Ladies' Association)

Revolution could have led to permanent estrangement but for Washington's forbearance. I argue that Washington's empathy and tolerance for Hamilton's antics stemmed in part from the fact that Washington saw much of himself as a young man in the French and Indian War in the young Colonel Hamilton of the American Revolution. Both young men were brash, impulsive, quick-tempered, overly ambitious, and eager for fame. Perhaps, as he did with Hamilton, Washington made allowances for his mother because in many ways she and he were alike. Whether George Washington ever acknowledged it, he was in *many ways* his mother's son—not only by genetics and heredity but by upbringing and example. He even inherited his bad teeth from her. They both loved horses and excelled as riders. They both loved gardening and trees and nature.

She had great physical endurance.

So did he.

She was strong-willed, determined, and powerful.

So was he.

She was acquisitive, with a materialistic strain.

So was he.

She was demanding and hard to satisfy.

So was he.

She was controlling and defensive.

So was he.

She had an independence of spirit and a tenacity of purpose.

So did he.

She was physically impressive.

So was he.

She projected an aura of authority.

So did he.

Indeed, as a relative wrote, "Whoever has seen that awe-inspiring air and manner so characteristic in the Father of his Country will remember the matron as she appeared when the presiding genius of her well-ordered household, commanding and being obeyed." Of course, Mary Ball Washington and George Washington differed starkly in important ways. Washington developed into a remarkable leader with a very broad view of the world and the willingness to sacrifice for a cause larger than himself. One does not see that with Mary. In some ways, Mary seems stunted and short-sighted, unable or unwilling to grow. Her determination and force of personality appeared focused on herself, earning her a reputation for hardness. In Washington's case, his willpower and force of personality earned him a reputation as a model of republican virtue, putting America's welfare before his own.

No doubt, Mary Ball Washington mattered immensely in the life of America's matchless man. Though not a great figure herself, she accomplished admirable things. Her various actions and examples—both positive and negative—helped shape George Washington into the remarkable man that he became. Perhaps she deserves her own monument in Fredericksburg after all.

3

"I Cannot Tell a Lie"

MYTHS ABOUT GEORGE WASHINGTON
THAT SHOULD BE DISCARDED

JOHN RHODEHAMEL succinctly summarizes why it is important to challenge and discard the many myths that have grown up around George Washington. "The most successful statesman in American history is often best remembered as a boy with a hatchet or as a simpleminded prig kneeling in the snow to pray. A tawdry mythological excrescence oozing Victorian pieties and wooden teeth has gained a greater hold on our national imagination than the epic of Washington's indispensable leadership in the making of the great nation that probably would not have come to be without him."

Not to put too fine a point on it, but the world is awash in nonsense about George Washington. Some of that nonsense is innocuous, like the claim that Washington wore a wig or had wooden teeth. Some is absurd, such as the canard that he fathered Alexander Hamilton. Some is anachronistic, such as the notion that he was a big marijuana grower. But certain Washington myths are harmful because they obscure the singular reality of this complex, subtle, and shrewd man to whom we owe so much.

The three most famous myths are that George Washington cut down his father's cherry tree, had wooden teeth, and that he prayed on his knees at Valley Forge.

Pervasive Myths about Washington

THE CHERRY TREE

Certainly, the most iconic of all the myths is that of young George cutting down his father's cherry tree. Here is the original account: "When George was about six years old, he was made the wealthy master of a *hatchet!* of which, like most little boys, he was immoderately fond, and was constantly going about chopping everything that came in his way. One day, in the garden, where he often amused himself hacking his mother's pea-sticks, he unluckily tried the edge of his hatchet on the body of a beautiful young English cherry-tree, which he barked so terribly, that I don't believe the tree ever got the better of it. The next morning the old gentleman finding out what had befallen his tree, which, by the by, was a great favorite, came into the house, and with much warmth asked for the mischievous author, declaring at the same time, that he would not have taken five guineas for his tree. Nobody could tell him anything about it. Presently George and his hatchet made their appearance. *George,* said his father, *do you know who killed that beautiful little cherry-tree yonder in the garden?* This was a *tough question;* and George staggered under it for a moment; but quickly recovered himself: and looking at his father, with the sweet face of youth brightened with the inexpressible charm of all-conquering truth, he bravely cried out, 'I can't *tell a lie, Pa; you know I can't tell a lie. I did cut it with my hatchet.'* . . . *Run to my arms, you dearest boy, cried his father in transports, run to my arms; glad am I, George, that you killed my tree; for you have paid me for it a thousand fold. Such an act of heroism in my son, is more worth than a thousand trees, though blossomed with silver, and their fruits of purest gold."*

Obviously, despite its implausibility to modern ears, one cannot definitively prove that George didn't cut down the cherry tree because one can't definitively disprove a negative. A couple of points are worth keeping in mind. The story, which has absolutely no contemporary evidence to support it, was only first reported in the fifth edition of Mason Locke Weems's extremely influential *Life of Washington.* Best known as Parson Weems, he should be more properly viewed as a preacher rather than as a historian. His George Washington is a model for the youth of America to follow. Weems is not concerned with being historically accurate but rather with conveying what he believes are important truths. For example, he has Lawrence Washington weeping with joy at George's early triumphs in the French and Indian War, when in fact Lawrence died two years before the war began.

Or, to give another example, Weems describes the scene at George Washington's death where the dying man asks all present to leave him

"Parson" Weems is the source of the most famous myth about George Washington, namely that he cut down his father's cherry tree and boldly confessed to his action. (Courtesy of Mount Vernon Ladies' Association)

alone to commune with his God, and Weems tells his readers what Washington said in his very private final prayer! Weems then describes what happened following the great man's passing. "Swift on angels' wings the brightening saint ascended while voices more than human were heard (in Fancy's ear) warbling through the happy regions, and hymning the great procession towards the gates of heaven. His glorious coming was seen far off, and myriads of mighty angels hastened forth, with golden harps[!], to welcome the honored stranger." In short, readers must treat Weems's statements of fact with great caution. The cherry tree story is included to demonstrate both the importance of telling the truth and that George Washington was a very honest person, and perhaps to encourage parents to reward honesty instead of punishing misdeeds. It should not be accepted as a factual event, especially since there is no contemporary evidence to support the story.

One of my students challenged that assertion. On a recent visit to the Weems-Botts Museum in Dumfries, Virginia, she had learned that there was an eighteenth-century German tankard decorated with the initials "GW" and an image of young Washington cutting down a cherry tree. This position is well stated by historian Peter Lillback, in his book *George Washington's Sacred Fire:* "The story must have had some circulation. The evidence for this is a vase made in Germany around the time of the American Revolution (between the 1770s and 1790) honoring its leader, by depicting George as a young boy with a hatchet and bearing the initials, GW." The claim intrigued me. If true, scholars should be giving the story more credence than they do. The results of my research were fascinating and an excellent example of how people like Lillback, eager to have their views substantiated, are likely to seize upon a source that confirms their position without worrying about the reliability of the source.

Happily, I discovered a richly detailed color photograph of the tankard in question in R. T. Halsey's 1889 book, *Pictures of Early New York on Dark Blue Staffordshire Pottery.* Examining the photo, I found that the tree depicted is not a cherry tree, but rather a nondescript, barren tree and that the male figure is not a child but a man. Even more significant, careful examination discovered the initials on the mug were not in fact "GW" but rather "CW." In short, the mug has absolutely nothing to do with George Washington.

HIS WOODEN TEETH

The story of George Washington having wooden teeth is almost as well known as the cherry tree myth, but it is easier to debunk. That is because several sets of Washington's dentures survive, and one of them is on display at Mount Vernon's Education Center. Indeed, they are presented in a well-lighted display case much like ones used to present crown jewels. And they are not wooden. Exactly how the myth that they were wooden originated is unclear. The likeliest explanation, offered by dental scientists and historians, is that over time food and drink stained Washington's false teeth to resemble wood.

In fact, the false teeth Washington wore were fashioned from the teeth of cows and humans, as well as from elephant and hippopotamus ivory. Denture makers set these facsimiles in a lead frame fitted with hinges and springs which, while uncomfortable, allowed the general to open and close his jaws and to chew. One little known, although gruesome, fact is that Washington purchased teeth from his own slaves and most likely used some of them in his dentures. It should be noted that he purchased them and didn't simply yank them out of his slaves' mouths as has sometimes been reported. Although the story is unsubstantiated, he may have used some of them in an experiment to implant healthy teeth, as there were efforts to do that during this time period.

PRAYING AT VALLEY FORGE

Pointing out the mythical nature of the cherry tree story and the wooden teeth is unlikely to upset many Americans. Declaring that the account of George Washington praying on his knees in solitude for divine intervention at Valley Forge is a myth is something else. It is one of the most iconic images of the American story. Reproductions of Arnold Friberg's well-known *Prayer at Valley Forge* adorn the Mount Vernon gift shop in a variety of sizes and prices. In 1982, President Ronald Reagan declared that "the most sublime picture in American History is of George Washington on his knees in the snow at Valley Forge." In the vivid language of historian Joseph Ellis, the Continental Army's trial by adversity in 1777–78 enshrined Valley Forge "as a kind of American Gethsemane, where Washington, the American Christ, kneels in prayer amidst bloodstained snow beseeching the Lord for deliverance." The power of the image was brought home to me vividly when one of my students at George Mason University dropped my course after I expressed doubt about the scene's provenance. She was not about to spend time and money listening to some left-wing, liberal professor undermine American values and denigrate American heroes!

At first glance, there are many points that would make such a story plausible. Certainly, George Washington believed in a divine power, which he usually referred to as "Providence," but also by a great many other names, including "God." And while Washington's God was inscrutable, all-wise, and all-powerful, his God also directly intervened in human affairs and specifically in his own life. Furthermore, Washington believed in the efficacy of prayer. Thus, there is nothing inherently implausible about him, amid his troops' suffering at Valley Forge, praying for divine help.

Even so, an examination of the story shows it has no basis in fact and does not comport with what we know about the commander in chief and his personal religious practices. That type of flamboyant prayer is simply not in accord with Washington's character, habits, and gentlemanly reticence in such matters. For example, one of Washington's pastors wrote that while in church the president did not pray on his knees. Washington always stood at prayers in church. And one author jibed that praying on his knees in the snow "would have soiled his uniform, a result he would have abhorred." Then there is this question: If Washington left the camp to pray in solitude, why was he praying so loudly that he could be clearly heard a good distance away?

Despite the durability of the legend of Washington at prayer, no contemporary evidence validates the tale. When, in 1918, believers in the prayer story lobbied the Valley Forge Park Commission for a monument on the spot where Washington supposedly was seen kneeling in prayer, the commission scoured the Library of Congress and other places with Revolutionary War records and then issued a report stating that "in none of these were found a single paragraph that will substantiate the tradition of the 'Prayer at Valley Forge.'"

It is pertinent to note that this tale debuted with the seventeenth edition of Parson Weems's *Life of Washington*. Weems claims that Isaac Potts, the owner of Washington's temporary headquarters (still standing), watched in awe as the general, done with his devotions, returned to his command center with "a countenance of angelic serenity." Potts, identified as a Quaker Patriot, exclaimed to his wife, Sarah, that seeing Washington pray had convinced him that all would end well. "If George Washington be not a man of God, I am greatly deceived, and still more shall I be deceived, if God do not, through him, work out a great salvation for America." Versions of the story have been published since, some making Potts a Tory and changing the name of his wife.

There are two red flags about the validity of Weems's story. Weems has Potts calling out to his wife, "Sarah, my dear Sarah! All's well!" In fact, Potts did not marry Sarah until 1803. His wife in 1777 was named Martha. More significantly, Isaac Potts was not even at Valley Forge during the time in question. According to the Bryn Mawr College archivist, Lorett Treese, Potts was in Pottsgrove, Pennsylvania, between 1774 and 1782. The current tenant of his farmhouse was a relative, Mrs. Deborah Hawes. This conclusion is supported by the fact the rent for the headquarters was paid to Mrs. Hawes, not Potts, and the receipts were made out in her name.

Myths about Washington's Character and Personality

There are several myths about Washington's character and personality that have to a degree replaced reality. The more important ones are that he was a great curser, that he was cold and humorless, that he was a womanizer, and that he fathered a child by a slave mistress.

A GREAT CURSER

Several accounts have His Excellency uttering a string of profanities when his men retired without firing a shot at the Battle of Kips Bay, near the present-day location of the United Nations building, when the British made an amphibious assault on New York City in the summer of 1776. Certainly it was a low point for Washington who, in a paroxysm of rage when his troops broke and ran, threw his hat on the ground three times and cried out, "Are these the men with whom I am to defend America?" According to another report, he swore, "Good God! Have I got such troops as these?" His Excellency was certainly greatly agitated and in despair, but there is no contemporary evidence that he actually cursed.

The more famous incident revolves around Washington's clash with General Charles Lee during the Battle of Monmouth in the summer of 1778. Lee infuriated Washington by ordering his troops to withdraw in the face of what Lee considered superior British force. According to Colonel Charles Scott of Virginia, the commander in chief "swore that day till the leaves shook on the trees." "Charming! delightful!" Scott continued, "never have I enjoyed such swearing before or since. Sir, on that memorable day he swore like an angel from heaven!" No doubt, in the minds of many people both then and now, General Lee deserved every well-delivered epithet. Yet, if we wish to take a true view, we can't simply believe what is pleasant over what is less colorful in spite of the evidence. And the evidence is that nothing like this happened.

Colonel Scott was recounting many years after the fact a scene he most likely did not witness in person. We do have on the record the testimony of Alexander Hamilton, who was actually present at Monmouth that day. He testified that, in regard to Lee's misbehavior, "Washington was careful of his words. He had not time to curse. He had to retrieve the day." Later, asked about the cursing, Major Jacob Morton, also present at Monmouth, declared, "No sir! no sir! . . . I heard all that passed between General Washington and General Lee on that occasion."

No doubt, George Washington was a man of the most intense passion, capable when provoked of using strong language. One witness described him as "violently excited" at Monmouth, where he forcefully remonstrated with General Lee. Yet, His Excellency prided himself above all on maintaining the self-mastery of the complete gentleman. Not only was cursing aloud the opposite of self-mastery, but foul language was impious. In General Orders issued not long after Monmouth, Washington criticized "the wanton practice of swearing" as a vice "productive of neither advantage nor pleasure." Or again: "The foolish and wicked practice of profane cursing and swearing is a vice so mean and low that every person of sense and character detests and despises it . . . we can have little hopes of the blessing of heaven on our arms, if we insult it by our impiety."

In fact, the strongest proof against the validity of Colonel Scott's recollection is the official record of Charles Lee's court-martial. In the bitter aftermath of the battle, Lee, feeling himself the injured party, wrote letters attacking General Washington, for which a military court tried and convicted him of treating Washington disrespectfully—and furthermore of disobeying orders and conducting an unnecessary, disorderly, and at times a shameful retreat. The extensive files from Lee's court-martial make clear that Washington was not the one to curse. In his defense, Lee rationalized his actions by declaring that Washington's body language toward him in the moment was stronger "than the expressions themselves." Had Washington cursed as recollected by Colonel Scott or cursed at all, Lee certainly would have incorporated some mention of foul language on Washington's part into his court-martial defense. The fact that he did not is telling.

A COLD AND HUMORLESS MAN

Few myths are more entrenched than the one that claims that Washington was a cold and remote leader, essentially a stiff without any sense of humor. This is best illustrated by an alleged encounter between Washington and Gouverneur Morris, which is well told by historian Edmund Morgan. "During the meeting of the Constitutional Convention in Philadelphia in 1787, a group of Washington's friends were remarking on his extraordinarily reserved and remote manner, even among his most intimate acquaintances. Gouverneur Morris, who was always full of boldness and wit, had the nerve to disagree. He could be as familiar with Washington, he said, as with any of his other friends. Alexander Hamilton called Morris's bluff by offering to provide a supper and wine for a dozen of them if Morris would, at the next reception Washington gave, simply walk up to him, gently slap him on the shoulder and say, 'My dear general, how happy I am to see you look so well.' On the appointed evening a substantial number were already present when Morris arrived, walked up to Washington, bowed, shook hands, and then placed his left hand on Washington's shoulder and said, 'My dear general, how happy I am to see you look so well.' The response was immediate and icy. Washington reached up and removed his hand, stepped back, and fixed his eye in silence on Morris, until Morris retreated abashed into the crowd."

This story does convey a truth. Washington's gravitas could convey reserve, even aloofness. Raised in a prominent family in eighteenth-century Virginia's deeply hierarchical society, Washington marinated all his life in elitism, a condition reinforced by his military career. As he advised Colonel William Woodford, be "not too familiar, lest you subject yourself to a want of that respect, which is necessary to support a proper command."

That said, I strongly believe that this tale is one more myth about Washington that should be discarded. In the first case, as is the case with virtually all myths, no contemporaneous sources lend this anecdote credence, and the details of time and place defy reconstruction. Historian Garry Wills summarizes the ostensible incident and its persistence: "The first record we have of this story appeared as third-hand gossip in a book printed 80 years after the purported event—in Martin Van Buren's posthumous book on the political parties. From there it was repeated in James Parton's 1874 *Life of Jefferson*, whence Max Farrand included it in his massive records of the constitutional convention, and from that source it has been endlessly parroted. That is a flimsy foundation for a story so out of character for both men."

The last sentence makes a crucial point. A compelling reason to be very skeptical of this story is that it portrays Washington in a fundamentally flawed way. Even assuming Morris acted as claimed, a highly dubious assumption, we have very good reason to doubt that General Washington would have behaved as represented in the story. By the time he took command of the Continental Army in 1775, Washington had developed a character no less impressive and perhaps even more impressive than his military bearing. "He is a complete gentleman," delegate Thomas Cushing from Massachusetts wrote. "He is sensible, amiable, virtuous, modest, and brave." It should be noted that the word "amiable" was often used by contemporaries in describing Washington, but it is used much less in later accounts.

In his eighteenth-century amiability, Washington showed himself to be a courtly man whose social address and deferential manners made him agreeable to all. The essence of a gentleman was courtesy—a term derived from the word "court" and encompassing how one was to behave at court. Again and again, acquaintances commented on Washington's genuine politeness and ever-correct manners. To embarrass another in any way would violate the *Rules of Civility* he not only copied out of a book as a youngster but also strove to live by as an adult. Given such a philosophy and character, Washington would have been most unlikely to behave deliberately in a way that would embarrass his friend, Gouverneur Morris, in the fashion described in the story.

It is more revealing to reflect on Washington's particular fondness for Morris, well known as a rake and prankster. As James Flexner observes, "those who believed George Washington was always proper and grave could not understand why he was intimate with such a man. They did not know that Washington relished scapegraces that kept him amused." Morris understood what fans of the mythical Washington overlook—namely, that George Washington had a sense of humor. In the words of James Madison, "the story so often repeated of his never laughing . . . is wholly untrue; no man seemed to more enjoy gay conversation, though he took little part in it himself. He was particularly pleased with the jokes, good humor, and hilarity of his companions." Washington himself wrote, "it is assuredly better to go laughing than crying thro' the rough journey of life."

Washington not only had a sense of humor, but an earthy one at that. This is clear from some of Morris's comments to the president, a man for whom he had the utmost respect. For example, Morris casually mentions bedding his French mistress and celebrating "the Cyprian mystery" to her great satisfaction. Exactly what erotic experience Morris was referring to is unclear, although Cyprian refers to Aphrodite, the goddess of love. He would not have dared be so salacious in a letter unless he knew for sure that Washington would appreciate or at least take no offense at his bold jests. Morris also shared with the president jokes that had strong bawdy overtones. "I promised you some Chinese pigs—a promise which I can only perform by halves for my boar, being much addicted to gallantry hung himself in pursuit of mere common sows. And his consort, to assuage her melancholy (for what alas can helpless widows do) took up with a paramour of the vulgar race. Thus her grunting progeny have jowls and bellies less big by half than their dam. Such however as I have such I send unto you."

A wonderful example of Washington's own earthy sense of humor can be seen in a rather remarkable letter he wrote upon learning that a fellow Revolutionary War officer had wed. "I am glad to hear that my old acquaintance Colo. Ward is yet under the influence of vigorous passions—I will not ascribe the intrepidity of his late enterprise to a mere flash of desires, because, in his military career he would have learnt how to distinguish between false alarms & a serious movement. Charity therefore induces me to suppose that like a prudent general, he had reviewed his strength, his arms, and ammunition before he got involved in an action—but if these have been neglected, & he has been precipitated into the measure, let me advise him to make the first onset upon his fair [lady] . . . with vigor, that the impression may be deep, if it cannot be lasting, or frequently renewed." That may not seem like something the mythical George Washington would write, but the flesh-and-blood George Washington did so.

A WOMANIZER

Given our fascination since early times with celebrity and sex, it was perhaps inevitable that the catchphrase "George Washington Slept Here" would acquire a salacious overtone. James Flexner noted that Washington was supposedly known as "the stallion of the Potomac"; no pure woman could without danger be left alone in his presence. The famous English historian Arnold Toynbee vented his spleen concerning American disobedience during the Revolution by stating that Washington died because of a chill caught on an illicit visit to an adolescent girl in the slave quarters. The *Washington Post* once printed a story that claimed Washington used a secret code to categorize female slaves he bedded. Numerous people have told me that he died of syphilis.

At one of my teacher symposiums at Mount Vernon, a participant, clearly expecting to be let down, asked me, "Was President Washington faithful to his wife, Martha?" My answer then was the same as I would give now. "I don't know, but I have never seen any credible evidence to the contrary, so I think it behooves us to give him the benefit of the doubt." Although pragmatism may have trumped passion in GW's courtship of Martha, genuine love bloomed between them and remained until his death.

Certainly, as his friendship with Gouverneur Morris illustrates, Washington was no prude. He was able to flirt and banter with women under the right circumstances. For example, Mrs. Theodorick Bland, wife of a Virginia colonel, wrote her sister-in-law about going on riding parties with the commander in chief. "General Washington throws off the hero and takes on the chatty, agreeable companion. He can be downright impudent sometimes—such impudence, Fanny, as you and I like." Annis Boudinot Stockton of Princeton, New Jersey, an ardent admirer of Washington who composed poetry in his honor, was frequently the recipient of some well-directed barbs of wit: "You apply to me, My dear Madam, for absolution as tho' I was your father Confessor; and as tho' you had committed a crime, great in itself, yet of the venial class. You have good reason, for I find myself strangely disposed to be a very indulgent ghostly Adviser on this occasion; and, notwithstanding 'you are the most offending Soul alive' (that is, if it is a crime to write elegant Poetry) yet if you will come and dine with me on Thursday and go through the proper course of penitence, which shall be prescribed, I will strive hard to assist you in expiating these poetical trespasses on this side of purgatory." Later he warned her, "Once the Woman has tempted us and we have tasted the forbidden fruit there is no such thing as checking our appetites, whatever the consequences may be."

A similar sense of earthy humor is shown in a letter to his dear friend Lafayette, about his wife, whom Lafayette said was enamored of the general. "Tell her . . . that I have a heart susceptible of the tenderest passion, and that it is already so strongly impressed with the most favorable ideas of her, that she must be cautious of putting loves torch to it; as you must be in fanning the flame." A final example is Washington's exchange with the fascinating Eliza Powel, with whom he had a particularly close relationship. When the general had to spurn an invitation from Eliza to attend a production of Richard Sheridan's entendre-laden comedy *The School for Scandal,* he wrote to her that he could "but regret that matters have turned out so unluckily, after waiting so long to receive a lesson in the school for scandal."

Of course, sexual banter was one thing. Having sex was another, and, as indicated above, the available evidence points to Washington's fidelity to Martha. Even in the midst of growing partisanship and anger at the president during his second term and the furor over Jay's Treaty, critics leveled many very harsh charges against Washington, but none of the attacks accused him of marital infidelity. It is true that there were wartime stories involving General Washington with a washerwoman's daughter, Kate, and with a woman by the name of Mary Gibbons. All have been shown to be slanders directly linked to British propaganda operatives, who released forged letters in an effort to undermine support for America's commander in chief.

THE FATHER OF WEST FORD

In more recent years, an oft-heard claim has been that Washington fathered, with a concubine named Venus, a slave child, West Ford, a view initially based on the Ford family's oral history. Frankly, this rumor has received vastly more attention than it deserves. There is an entire book on the subject, *I Cannot Tell a Lie,* by Linda Allen Bryant, which is basically historical fiction. Here is an excerpt from the book after the reader is informed that Venus, a slave belonging to GW's brother John, was a virgin on the night she was sent to "comfort" the old general. "After that fateful night, whenever the massa's brother visited Bushfield or when Venus accompanied her mistress to Mount Vernon Venus was made available for his *comfort.* She became his personal property and only he could touch her sexually. Massa

Washington never knew that Venus didn't come to him of her own free will. And she never told him. He treated her very gently during his visits and she came to care for him. And only when it was obvious that she was with child was she finally left alone." In a recent book, *Ties That Bound: Founding First Ladies and Slaves,* the author, Marie Jenkins Schwartz, states it is "possible—if not probable—that George [Washington] was West's father."

More significantly, the historian Henry Wiencek spends consider-able time examining the claim in the much more scholarly work *An Imperfect God.* While Wiencek, in appearances after the book's publi-cation, declared he personally did not believe the story, he never ex-plicitly denies it in his book, whose publicity highlights the new evi-dence about the possible truth of the claim. Instead, Wiencek writes, "The possibility remains that George Washington could have been West Ford's father," and "We will probably never be certain one way or the other." In my judgment this is not good historical scholarship.

Some see the claim that Washington fathered a slave child by Venus as comparable to that of Thomas Jefferson fathering slave children by Sally Hemings. And Wiencek himself asserts that generations of ear-lier scholars argued that it was not possible that Jefferson, given his character and beliefs, would have done such a thing, only to change their minds. In fact, there is no comparison between the two claims. Whether one accepts as fact the relationship between Thomas Jeffer-son and Sally Hemings, one must admit that there is a very significant corpus of evidence, much of it from contemporary sources and mod-ern DNA results, that makes such a relationship at least plausible. In contrast, the Washington/Venus/Ford story is a gossamer of fabrica-tion. Of course, the descendants of West Ford and anyone else have the right to believe whatever they wish, but the facts do not support the claim. Let me explain why.

First, absolutely no primary documents link Washington to either Venus or to West Ford. Despite the fact that Washington was a pro-digious recordkeeper, neither name appears in his extensive personal records. There was a Venus, but she was not a Mount Vernon slave but rather the property of his brother John, who lived at Bushfield Planta-tion, roughly fifty miles from Mount Vernon. Venus would have been at Washington's home on few, if any, occasions, and she was merely a child when General Washington went off to war in 1775. West Ford did not come to Mount Vernon until after the general's death.

Additionally, whatever the Ford family oral tradition may have been, there appears to be nothing extant in the written record for approximately two hundred years after Washington's death that in any way hints that any of this might be true. The first certain reference is not until 1940. Believers make a huge leap of faith merely placing Washington in the same vicinity as Venus nine months before West Ford's birth.

The child probably was born in the second half of 1784, although Mary Thompson, Mount Vernon's very knowledgeable historian, believes it was more likely in 1783 or the first part of 1784. Regardless of the exact date, if West was born before 1785, Washington was off at war and could not possibly have been his father. If West were born in 1785, which is unlikely but possible, George Washington could have been his father—provided one places Venus and Washington together, a daunting task. It is daunting because Washington did not visit Bushfield in the immediate aftermath of the war and before John died in 1787. John's wife and a "maid" briefly visited Mount Vernon in 1784. If that visiting maid was Venus—and there is no way to know for sure—she and Washington could have been together, theoretically positioning Washington to father a child by Venus. While it might seem difficult to credit, in fact that is the extent of the case, other than oral history of the Ford family, that anyone can make: namely, that Washington and Venus could have been together nine months prior to the birth of West Ford—if that birth occurred in 1785.

Of course, this theory does not explain why George Washington—happily married, America's most famous man, a man fanatically dedicated to guarding his reputation—would dally with his visiting sister-in-law's servant under his own roof. It is not explained, because no reasonable explanation can be given. And it might not be amiss to note that while it cannot be proven, a strong possibility exists that Washington was sterile and never fathered any child, black or white.

How then did the current situation come about? West Ford was clearly a special individual who merits more attention than space allows in this chapter. In her will, Hannah Washington, the widow of Washington's brother John, declared that the "lad West" was to be immediately inoculated against the smallpox, bound to a "good tradesman" until age twenty-one, "after which he is to be free for the rest of his life." In the same document, Hannah kept Venus and West's younger sister, Bettey, in perpetual slavery.

Why did Hannah favor West? While admittedly in the realm of speculation, the most likely explanation is because the father of West was one of her three sons, Bushrod, Corbin, or William Augustine. (Hannah would have been much more likely to be concerned for the fate of the child if it were fathered by one of her sons than if fathered by her husband.) The best case can be made that the father was her youngest son, William Augustine, called Augustine by the family. Augustine was killed in a tragic incident at the age of seventeen, when a schoolmate accidentally discharged a shotgun, its full force smashing into the young man's chest, killing him almost instantly. Hannah was devastated at the loss. As her husband wrote Washington, "the shock was too great for her infirm frame to bear with any tolerable fortitude. Upon the first communication she fell into a strong convulsion, which continued for some time, and when that went off, she lay for near four hours in a state of insensibility. When her reason returned, her grief did also and she had a return of the fit. She is now in a very low state both of body and mind."

As indicated in the wonderful journal of Philip Vickers Fithian and other sources, often the young white men of the plantation, as their hormones raged and they reached young manhood, would take advantage of the easy access to black female slaves. Augustine was about the same age as Venus and had grown up with her. If he were the father, it would explain Hannah's particular interest in West. However "tainted" his birth by a slave woman might be, West was still her grandson and the offspring of her lost son. Consequently, Hannah took action to see that West was not just another slave for life. Her other sons, without a great stake in the matter, appeared happy to grant their mother's wish in this matter. (If either Bushrod or Corbin had a long relationship with Venus, it seems less likely that Venus, after West's birth, would have given birth to a child with a slave father.) One final point: West Ford's first son was named William, which might be another bit of evidence that William Augustine was the father of West Ford. (The *George Washington Papers* incorrectly identified William Augustine as George Augustine, a mistake the editors acknowledge.)

West Ford was directly related to George Washington, but he was not directly descended from him. (Courtesy of Mount Vernon Ladies' Association)

The available evidence thus strongly supports the contention that West Ford is directly *related* to George Washington even though he is not directly *descended* from him. There is an extant sketch of West Ford from 1858 that shows features prominent in the Washington family as well as a photograph of him as an older man. Isn't it plausible that somewhere along the line of transmitting the story to various descendants, the claim of a relationship to George Washington was replaced with the claim of being descended from him? Given the available information, it makes the most sense that the oral history of the Ford family that they had Washington blood in their family tree over time became they had George Washington's blood in their family tree.

Washington, Power, and Presidential Precedents

There are also several myths involving George Washington in regard to power and the presidency that should be discarded. They are: George Washington's supposed internal struggle over whether to be a king; his purported addition of the phrase "So help me God" to the presidential oath; that he was a "figurehead" president controlled by Alexander Hamilton; and that he established the tradition that a president should serve no more than two terms.

WASHINGTON AS KING

It is widely believed that Washington could have been a king if he had decided to go down that path. An exhibit at the Education Center at Mount Vernon encourages this misapprehension by having a display case with revolving images—one of Washington in civilian clothes, the other of him wearing a crown and other kingly trappings. Of course, the conclusion in the exhibit is "He would not be King."

The idea of George Washington selflessly refusing the offer of a crown at the close of the Revolutionary War has so much appeal to both readers and writers of history that leaving it out of the historical record would seem almost criminal. Mount Vernon's curators could not resist the appeal, but the exhibit is misleading on two points. Never for a moment did Washington consider being a monarch, a role fundamentally at odds with his self-image as the embodiment of revolutionary virtue and republican belief. An avid reader of Joseph Addison's *Cato*, an immensely popular and influential rendition of the last days of the Roman Republic, General Washington was always exquisitely self-conscious about his performances on the public stage and of the need to adhere to the loftiest standard of republican virtue and self-sacrifice. As Alexander Hamilton expressed it, Washington would "never yield to any dishonorable or disloyal plans into which he might be called; that he would sooner suffer himself to be cut into pieces."

Washington had a chance to make his views crystal clear when he received a letter from Lewis Nicola, a former British army officer who served as colonel of the Continental Army Invalid Regiment, in 1782, seeming to imply that the answer to the current crisis would be for Washington to become king in all but name. Washington replied to Nicola in a blistering letter, "You could not have found a person to whom your schemes are more disagreeable. . . . No occurrence in the course of the War, has given me more painful sensations than your information of there being such ideas existing in the Army as you have expressed and as I must view with abhorrence and reprehend with severity." He considered his response important enough to insist for the only time during the war that his aides provide proof that the letter was properly sealed and sent. He wanted no possible misunderstanding on this point. (Nicola was so shocked by the general's upbraiding that he wrote three separate letters of apology.)

Washington made a similar point to his officers during the Newburgh Conspiracy against the Continental Congress in 1783: "As you value your sacred honor . . . express your utmost horror and detestation of the man who wishes, under any specious pretenses, to overturn the liberties of our Country." As Joseph Ellis perceptively noted, Washington "saw himself as a mere steward for a historical experiment in representative government larger than any single person, larger than himself; an experiment in which all leaders, no matter how indispensable, were disposable, which was what a government of laws and not men ultimately meant."

The second misleading aspect of the Mount Vernon exhibit is that it presupposes that Washington could have in fact become king if he had chosen to do so. James Madison is on target. "I am not less sure that General Washington would have spurned a scepter if within his grasp, than I am *that it was out of his reach, if he had secretly sighed for it*" (emphasis added). Americans loved and admired Washington because of his unshakeable commitment to republicanism. Had he tried to rule as a monarch, the people would have experienced tremendous shock. How could the man they so trusted violate that trust! A Washington who sought to be king would have been viewed as a worse traitor than Benedict Arnold.

THE PRESIDENTIAL OATH

Rather than seeking to become a king, Washington only reluctantly agreed to be president under the newly ratified United States Constitution, and he was inaugurated on April 30, 1789. Until early in this century, it was simply accepted that President Washington added the words "So help me God" to the oath prescribed in the Constitution. Exemplary of this view is Peter Lillback in his massive tome, *George Washington's Sacred Fire.* "Probably the most startling example of a living oral tradition that is accepted by everyone in regard to Washington is the continuing use of his own words at his inauguration as the first president under the Constitution. The famous phrase, 'So help me God,' is not found in Washington's vast writings, because it was not written down by Washington. Nor is it in the Constitution, yet, every president following Washington has said these same words when he has taken the oath of office. The reason those words are still used today is due to the fact that this oral tradition was later recorded by others, who claimed to be eyewitnesses of Washington having said those words. Each president following Washington has kept this oral tradition of Washington's words alive." (Despite Lillback's assertion, the first president to definitely add the phrase "So help me God" to his constitutional oath was Chester A. Arthur in 1881.)

In fact, the evidence is overwhelming that Washington did not do so. No contemporaneous evidence avers that President Washington altered the oath stipulated in Article 2, Section 1 of the Constitution: "I do solemnly swear (or affirm) that I will faithfully execute the office of president of the United States, and will to the best of my ability, preserve, protect and defend the Constitution of the United States." The French foreign minister, Comte de Moustier, who attended the 1789 ceremony, described that event in considerable detail in a letter to his home government. Moustier transcribed the oath as in the Constitution, and made no mention of "So help me God" being added by the president. Another eyewitness, Eliza (Susan) Morton Quincy, later wrote, "Chancellor Livingston read the oath according to the form prescribed by the Constitution; and Washington repeated it, resting his hand upon the Bible."

Apparently, sixty-five years later the story of Washington adding this phrase appeared in *The Republican Court,* an 1854 book by Rufus Griswold, who based his account on a childhood memory attributed to the novelist Washington Irving. Researcher David Parker recently scanned multiple online databases for the phrase "So help me God" used in connection with Washington's inauguration. In searching millions of entries, Parker found that before 1854 no accounts exist of Washington appending "So help me God" to the oath. From 1854 on, however, the "So help me God" assertion took flight, becoming so pervasive through most of the twentieth century that virtually no one, including reputable historians, questioned it.

There are additional reasons for doubting the assertion beyond the complete lack of any contemporary evidence. By his very nature,

George Washington would not have tampered so blatantly with the constitutional text. He had presided over the 1787 Constitutional Convention and revered the resulting Constitution. In many ways, Washington was a constitutional literalist. Would such a man, in the very act of becoming the nation's first president, glibly alter an oath written into the nation's fundamental charter? On that august occasion, George Washington would have acted out of political philosophy, not religious belief.

Proponents of the myth accurately contend that Washington never expressed a personal objection to saying "So help me God" and had routinely taken such oaths during the colonial era. Perhaps, they contend, he simply added it as an afterthought or because he was caught up in the solemnity and reverence of the moment. While at first glance this is plausible, any modification of the oath would have certainly created contemporary comment that would have survived in the historical record.

Here's why: In April 1789, the month Washington was being inaugurated, the First United States Congress was debating what oath to require of new members of the federal government under Article 6 of the new constitution. Article 6 does call for an oath but also states, "No religious test shall ever be required as a qualification to any office or public trust under the United States." Early arrivals to the House of Representatives, however, did take an oath that included "So help me God."

Following the lead of a committee chaired by Alexander White and James Madison, the House on April 27, 1789—three days before Washington's swearing-in—passed a new oath act pointedly excluding the phrase "So help me God." The Senate, after adding unrelated amendments, passed the House bill on May 5, 1789, less than a week after the inauguration. Would the Senate have passed an oath bill without the words "So help me God" only five days after the great hero of the American people conspicuously added those words to his own oath? To do so would clearly be a rebuke to the newly elected president. And to do so without anyone anywhere commenting about it? It is simply not plausible.

In summary, the combination of lack of contemporaneous evidence or any other evidence over the next fifty years, Washington's philosophy of strictly adhering to the Constitution, and the parallel congressional debate over the wording of oaths under the new Constitution makes it virtually certain that George Washington did not add the phrase "So help me God" to his inaugural oath.

Does it make any difference whether he added the words or not? Beyond the desire to reconstruct the past as accurately as possible, the story has pertinence to our current debate over the proper relationship between the national government and religion. The founders were clear on that point and were fully aware of the danger of government involvement in matters of religion. As Madison asserted in the Virginia Ratifying Convention, "There is not a shadow of right in the general government to intermeddle with religion. Its least interference with it, would be a most flagrant usurpation." It would be in this spirit that George Washington would not consider altering the constitutional oath by introducing a religious reference.

A FIGUREHEAD PRESIDENT

There has been considerable historical debate over what type of president George Washington was. Entirely too many people think that, although he made a great figurehead, President Washington was not really the leader of his administration. Rather, in the words of Ron Chernow, critics viewed Washington as "a dim-witted tool in the nimble hands of Alexander Hamilton." This reading of Washington as president can be traced primarily to Thomas Jefferson, and it is worth remembering that most historians are Jeffersonian. Jefferson's archnemesis was Alexander Hamilton. He believed Hamilton was a monarchist, a champion of the rich, and an enemy of ordinary people. Jefferson's dilemma stemmed from the fact that President Washington, a man he genuinely admired, often seemed to agree with Hamilton's views. How could this be the case? Did Hamilton's views represent a legitimate alternative? Jefferson could not accept that possibility. Or, conversely, was the president also among the politically damned? That conclusion was equally unacceptable to Jefferson. The way Jefferson resolved his dilemma was by portraying the aging and increasingly failing president as a good man hoodwinked by a cleverer, sinister man. This enabled Jefferson to admire Washington the man and oppose his administration, but it has left posterity with a distorted view of Washington.

Happily, in recent decades, a spate of first-rate scholarship, including works by Joseph Ellis, Ron Chernow, Robert O'Connell, and John Rhodehamel, has been published demonstrating the genuine force and strength of Washington's personality. Washington might have been courteous, deferential, soft-spoken, and amiable, but at his core lived a steely will. He would not be any man's marionette. Nevertheless, the myth of Washington as merely a figurehead still holds sway with many today and hinders people from recognizing his greatness.

THE TRADITION OF THE TWO-TERM PRESIDENCY

A final myth is that George Washington started the tradition that no person should serve more than two terms as president. The issue was debated at the Constitutional Convention, and the decision was reached not to specify any number of terms an incumbent could serve. Of course, Washington in fact only served two terms, and no other president served more than two terms until Franklin Delano Roosevelt successfully ran for a third term in 1940. Reacting to this, Congress passed the Twenty-second Amendment in 1947, making it impossible for a president to be elected to more than two terms. The required number of states ratified the amendment in 1951.

The important point to remember is that while George Washington did not want to serve more than two terms, it was not based on a philosophical or constitutional position. Rather, it was a result of fatigue and, even more importantly, a desire to nurture the principle of peaceful transfer of power. Americans take the peaceful transfer of power for granted, but it was a radical idea at the time. Strongly desiring to do this, Washington did not want to die in office, which of course was more likely with each passing year.

The record is clear that he personally did not support mandated term limits. In 1788, when Thomas Jefferson and the Marquis de Lafayette were arguing for term limits, Washington wrote to Lafayette saying that he disagreed with the Frenchman and with Jefferson on the need to arbitrarily set limits as to how long a person could serve as president. "I can see no propriety in precluding ourselves from the services of any man, who on some great emergency, shall be deemed universally, most capable of serving the people." (It might also be noted that he did not favor term limits at the Constitutional Convention.)

Washington made a good point. Limiting the time that a president can serve may be wise, but it is undemocratic because it potentially thwarts the will of the people. Finally, Washington refused requests to run for election in 1800 for what would have been a third term, but he did not reject doing so on philosophical terms but rather for different reasons, namely that in the current situation voters would vote for a party, not for an individual (see chapter 7). The two-term tradition may be more accurately stated to have started with Thomas Jefferson, when he refused to stand for reelection in 1808 for reasons of philosophical principle.

While myths about Washington will undoubtedly persist into the foreseeable future, we have no need of a mythical George Washington. The man himself, considered strictly on his own terms, more than suffices. He requires neither inflation nor canonization. Abigail Adams was right on target when she said of Washington, "Simple truth is his best eulogy."

4

"Unfortunate"

THE ASGILL AFFAIR AND GEORGE WASHINGTON'S
SELF-CREATED DILEMMA

IN THE SPRING of 1782 George Washington decided to execute a young British captain, Charles Asgill, who had been captured when Lord Cornwallis surrendered at Yorktown in October of the previous year. The facts surrounding this little-discussed incident known as the Asgill Affair provide new insight into the political and military pressures facing Washington as the War of Independence drew to a close.

The story reminds us that the American Civil War from 1861 to 1865 was not our only civil war. In many ways, the American Revolution was America's first civil war, pitting neighbor against neighbor and sometimes family against family in conflicts that often were cruel and bloody. Parts of the country became what Robert O'Connell perceptively calls "Dangerland" in his new book, *Revolutionary*. That term can properly be applied to northern New Jersey.

In the aftermath of Washington's victories at Trenton and Princeton, the New Jersey Patriot militia had forced Loyalists by the hundreds to flee for safety into British-held New York. The Refugees—as the Loyalists called themselves—did not leave willingly, and they returned at irregular intervals in small guerrilla bands to burn, pillage, and kill. Then, in 1780, George III created a Refugee army under the direction of the Board of Associated Loyalists, headed by William Franklin, Benjamin Franklin's Tory son. Although technically under the command of Sir Henry Clinton, the Refugees were given wide leeway to act as an independent force. Thereafter, they mounted more regular attacks on New Jersey's Patriot towns. Both camps repeated horror stories of rape, mutilation, and murder that, true or not, inflamed already embittered feelings.

No doubt, reprisal and retaliation were a steady diet between Loyalists and Patriots. For example, in 1780 a band of Associated Loyalists including a determined Tory, Philip White, who had served in the British army, raided the Monmouth County, New Jersey, home of John Russell, a Patriot. Raiders burned the house, wounded Russell, killed his father, and slipped back to haven in New York. Two years later, White was again in Monmouth—for what purpose is a point of controversy but most likely to meet with his wife. In any event, Patriot militiamen caught him. Within hours, White was dead. According to Loyalist accounts, his arms had been cut off and his legs broken and his corpse mutilated almost beyond recognition and shoveled into a makeshift grave. It is worth noting that John Russell, whose house White had attacked, was among those present for these events, but militia commander Captain Joshua Huddy was not.

Destined to play a key role in the unfolding drama of the Asgill Affair, Joshua "Jack" Huddy was a controversial figure. Fearless and aggressive, he was highly regarded by the Patriots of Monmouth County as a leader who was rumored to be responsible for hanging numerous Loyalists. Huddy's footprint in the legal records, both before and during the war, does not reflect a man of sterling moral character. Born to a wealthy Quaker family in Salem County, New Jersey, on November 8, 1735, Huddy was expelled from the Society of Friends on charges that he "Suffered himself to Lead . . . into Evil and Loose Company and the Corruption of the world." Repeated legal trouble and debt forced Huddy to sell his 300-acre farm in Salem. He spent time in debtors' prison. In 1779 the Monmouth County sheriff accused him of casting his wife's three children from a previous marriage out of their home "by means of threats or blows" and of selling his wife's possessions without her consent. The final result of the case is not known, but Huddy's credentials as a strong Patriot leader may have played a factor in his not being convicted.

On August 5, 1780, the Continental Congress issued Huddy letters of marque authorizing him and his men to attack British and Loyalist ships, settlements, and outposts. He and his followers became the scourge of coast-dwelling New Jersey Loyalists, who cried out for vengeance, which occurred to a limited degree in March 1782. Troops captured Huddy at Dover, today known as Toms River, and imprisoned him in New York. The night his men captured and killed Philip White, Huddy was behind bars, but that did not prevent rumors of his complicity from spreading among Loyalists, who badly wanted to revenge White's killing. The Board of Associated Loyalists decided that Huddy would pay for White's death with his life.

To get their hands on the scoundrel, they won permission from the British commanding general, Sir Henry Clinton, to remove Huddy from prison under the false pretense that he was part of a prisoner exchange. The board had been granted the authority to exchange their prisoners for Associated Loyalists held prisoner in American hands, so the request was not likely to arouse suspicion. Led by Captain Richard Lippencott, the late Philip White's brother-in-law, a troop of Loyalists took Huddy from prison at Sandy Hook and promptly hanged him, apparently one of only two American prisoners of war executed during the war. Huddy's killers decorated his corpse with messages warning of further reprisals. A placard read "Up went Huddy for Philip White."

Huddy's compatriots retrieved his remains, lay them in state at Monmouth Courthouse, and swore vengeance. News of the outrage quickly spread. In the heat of the moment, the men of Monmouth delivered an ultimatum known as the Monmouth Manifesto. If George Washington did not offer suitable reprisal for Huddy's death, they themselves would; in so doing, they would "open to view a scene at which humanity itself may shudder."

The Monmouth Manifesto presented Washington, stationed at Newburgh, New York, with a dilemma that would in time cause the general to endure much pain and criticism—a good deal of it self-inflicted. One source of George Washington's greatness was his remarkably astute judgment, but in this incident, I believe he made two key decisions. One of them was defensible but the other less so. Indeed, the general's major error in judgment triggered the ensuing crisis. How so?

Washington's instincts led him to be skeptical of retaliation. As he explained to General Adam Stephen in April of 1777, "Tho' my Indignation at such ungenerous Conduct of the Enemy might at first prompt me to Retaliation, yet Humanity & Policy forbid the measure— Experience proves that their wanton Cruelty injures rather than benefits their Cause; That, with our Forbearance, justly secures to Us the

Attachment of all good Men." Yet, he also recognized, as he wrote John Hancock in July of 1776, "Justice and policy will require recourse to be had to the Law of retaliation, however abhorrent and disagreeable to our natures, in cases of Torture and Capital punishments." In short, under certain circumstances, the general supported retaliation, and he would in this case.

Alexander Hamilton made a point that is helpful in understanding what General Washington did and why. With his almost preternatural wisdom, Hamilton noted, "I know how apt men are to be actuated by the circumstances which immediately surround them and to be led into an approbation of measures which in another situation they would disapprove." (A good example would be the internment of Japanese Americans during World War II, an act almost universally criticized today but widely approved of at the time.) The Asgill Affair demonstrates that "in the morally ambiguous territory of irregular warfare even an operator as shrewd as Washington could stumble badly."

No doubt His Excellency was outraged by the murder of Huddy. In his perhaps over-the-top words, it was "the most wanton, unprecedented and inhuman Murder that ever disgraced the Arms of a civilized people." The men of Monmouth were clamoring for action, and the general decided to give it to them.

On weighty matters, Washington habitually consulted his officers. This time, to discourage them from discussing the matter at hand among themselves, he requested individual written opinions of twenty-four officers, including Generals Baron Friedrich Wilhelm von Steuben and Robert Howe—responses to be rendered without any type of consultation. Washington asked whether he should retaliate for Huddy and, if so, when and how. The response was overwhelming. All favored retaliation, to be taken against a British officer of the same rank—captain—as Huddy. Preferably the sacrificial captain would have surrendered without conditions such as those that applied at Yorktown protecting POWs against reprisal, but as many as eight officers said if need be, Washington should pick a man taken prisoner conditionally. A few urged immediate action without even waiting for a British response. Retaliation, a staff officer wrote, was "justifiable and expedient," both to discourage Loyalist atrocities and to keep New Jersey Patriots from seeking vengeance on their own.

Thus bolstered, on April 21 Washington sent a brief, almost blunt, note to his counterpart, General Clinton, demanding that Captain Lippencott, the leader of the hanging party, be delivered up to American hands. "In Failure of it," he added ominously, "I shall hold myself justifiable in the Eyes of God and Man, for the measure to which I shall resort." Washington's sharp words stung. "I cannot conceal my surprise and displeasure at the very improper language you have made use of," Clinton replied, describing himself as "greatly surprised and shocked" to learn of Huddy's death. An inquiry was under way, he said; based on the results, the perpetrators would be found and tried. However, Clinton declared, no matter what his staff learned about the case, he had no intention of giving Lippencott or anyone else into Washington's charge. "Violators of the Laws of War" are best "punished by the Generals under whose Powers they act," Clinton said. Discouraged by Clinton's letter, Washington wrote to Congress of his plans for retaliation; early in May he learned that members unanimously approved his proposal. "Deeply impressed with the necessity of convincing the enemies of the United States . . . that the repetition of their unprecedented and inhuman cruelties . . . will no longer be suffered with impunity," the members of Congress offered "their firmest support." Washington, "under the disagreeable necessity of retaliating, as the only means left to put a stop to such inhuman proceedings," demanded that "to save the innocent," Clinton must hand over "the guilty."

If "the guilty" party was Captain Lippencott, who was "the innocent" scapegoat? And how would he be chosen? Washington's officers had agreed punishment should be inflicted on a captain, but preferably a captain not under Convention or capitulation and rather one who had surrendered at discretion. The said captain was to be chosen by lot.

Washington tasked General Moses Hazen, the commander of the prisoner camp at Lancaster, Pennsylvania, with the unpleasant job of finding the appropriate sacrifice, but it soon became clear that such a captain was not easily found. General Washington then on his own made the crucial decision to pick the unfortunate victim from a group of thirteen British captains who had surrendered with Cornwallis in October of 1781. Washington wrote Hazen that, since no unconditional prisoner was available, "I am therefore under the disagreeable necessity to Direct, that you immediately select, in the Manner before presented, from among all the British Captains who are prisoners either under Capitulation or Convention One, who is to be sent on as soon as possible, under the Regulations & Restrictions contained in my former Instructions to you."

I find it hard to defend this decision. Indeed, personally, I can't think of a more serious misjudgment by George Washington than this one. At the time he sent his directive to Hazen, His Excellency almost certainly knew the specific terms of the surrender agreement he had signed with Cornwallis. If not, he would soon learn that he violated explicit protections. Article 14 of the capitulation ensured all those surrendering against any form of reprisal. A fair question might be asked: Was Washington justified in hanging any man whom he had pledged his own and his country's honor to protect?

The mechanism for choosing the sacrificial victim was a macabre lottery. On Monday, May 27, 1782, with the thirteen captains and other British POWs present at Black Bear Inn in Lancaster, Pennsylvania, two sets of paper slips were put into separate baskets. The slips in the first basket bore the names of the thirteen captains. The second basket also held thirteen slips—twelve blank, one bearing the chilling message "unfortunate." Since the British officers refused to take direct part in a scheme that explicitly violated the terms of their surrender, a drummer boy drew a slip from the first basket, called the name, and then took a slip from the second basket. Ten times he called names and ten times he drew blanks. The eleventh name called was that of Captain Charles Asgill. The drummer boy then reached into the second basket. The slip he pulled read "unfortunate." The sight of his fate nearly unmanned Asgill. His commanding officer, Major James Gordon, steadied him, saying, "For God's sake, don't disgrace your colors."

In the strange ways of fate, the choice of Asgill as the sacrificial offering ensured that the proceeding would draw a tremendous amount of attention. Only nineteen years old and the youngest of the thirteen captains, Asgill was a soldier with the First British Regiment of Foot (now known as the Grenadier Guards). His parents' only son, Asgill enlisted in the British army at age sixteen but went to America against his father's wishes. His pro-American father, also Charles, had been Lord Mayor of London. His mother, Sarah Theresa, Lady Asgill, was of a wealthy French Huguenot émigré family. Young Asgill, much like

Charles Asgill came perilously close to being the unfortunate scapegoat in retaliation for the unlawful hanging of Captain Joshua Huddy. (Courtesy of Historic Images / Alamy Stock Photo)

Major John Andre, the co-conspirator in Benedict Arnold's treason, had the type of charm and character that would win sympathy both from his captors and from the world at large.

Since this action was initiated to mollify the fury of Monmouth Patriots, it seemed proper that the victim be held within the lines of the New Jersey state troops, close under the eyes of those who demanded his blood. Thus, Asgill was transported to await his execution, accompanied by Major Gordon, who befriended him throughout the ordeal and did all he could to reverse the decision with appeals to both Washington and the French as well as efforts to find a captain who had surrendered unconditionally.

Washington's action outraged the British leadership in New York, who to a man had condemned Huddy's murder. As Major Gordon expressed it, "Washington had determined to revenge upon some innocent man the guilt of a set of lawless banditti." Some Americans agreed. Alexander Hamilton was the most forceful and clear in critiquing the situation. Rather than writing directly to Washington, with whom he was a bit estranged, he wrote to General Henry Knox, who better had the ear of the general. Hamilton had forcefully opposed the manner of executing Major John Andre in the Benedict Arnold treason plot. In that case, Hamilton knew Andre's life could not be spared, although Hamilton declared the manner of taking it—by hanging—was an act of "rigid justice." The Asgill Affair was of a different nature. "A sacrifice of this sort is entirely repugnant to the genius of the age we live in and is without example in modern history nor can it fail to be considered in Europe as wanton and unnecessary. . . . If we wreak our resentment on an innocent person, it will be suspected that we are too fond of executions. I am persuaded it will have an influence peculiarly un-favorable to the General's character. . . . Let not the Commander in Chief—considered as the first and most respectable character among us—come forward in person and be the avowed author of an act at which every humane feeling revolts."

Feeling empathy for Asgill, Washington confessed to his friend and secretary of war General Benjamin Lincoln that the incident "has distressed me exceedingly." General Washington viewed himself as a humane man and fervently desired to be viewed this way by the world at large, and this event threatened to portray him in a very different light. Nevertheless, he felt increasingly compelled to justify his original decision as the proper one. "Having formed my opinion upon the most mature reflection and deliberation, I can never recede from it. . . . The Enemy ought to have learnt before this that my Resolutions are not to be trifled with. . . . My resolutions having been taken up on the most mature deliberation, supported by the approbation of Congress, & grounded on the general concurrence of all the principal officers of the Army who were particularly consulted on the subject, cannot be receded from; Justice to the Army & the Public, my own honor, & I think I may venture to say, *universal benevolence,* require them to be carried into full execution" (emphasis in original). That Washington would invoke "universal benevolence" to justify ritually executing an officer protected under terms of surrender he had accepted demonstrates how hard he strove to sell himself on his own contorted logic.

He was trapped by his inability to acknowledge that he had made a mistake. He didn't know how to walk back his threat or to embrace

Hamilton's argument that in this case inconsistency trumped consistency. He had convinced himself that he could not retreat publicly without weakening his ability to lead, fearing that the people would feel they could not trust that he would do what he said.

Any chance of the British punishing Lippencott evaporated in August, when a court-martial acquitted him on grounds that in killing Huddy he had been following orders given verbally by Governor William Franklin to hang Huddy without trial. His action, the tribunal said, "was not the effect of malice or ill will, but proceeded from a conviction that it was his duty to obey the orders of the Board of Directors of Associated Loyalists." Britain later rewarded Lippencott for his wartime service with a 300-acre land grant in what is now Toronto, Canada, where he died in 1826 at the age of eighty-one.

In view of the decision, but also because the British condemned the action, did away with the Board of Directors for the Loyalists, and, most significantly, promised further investigation, General Washington wisely decided to bump the question of what to do now up to the Continental Congress for the final decision. As an excuse for further delay, Washington seized upon the statement of Sir Guy Carleton—Clinton's replacement—that he would conduct further inquiries. It seems that Washington's strategy was to avoid action, letting the affair drag on in the hope that a satisfactory solution could be found without his having to change his oft-stated position. Washington reported to Congress, "I fear an act of retaliation upon an innocent person before the result of his inquisition is known, would be considered by the impartial and unprejudiced world in an unfavorable and perhaps unjustifiable point of view." The Asgill case, the general went on to declare, had become "a great national concern, upon which an individual ought not to decide." He desired that Congress "chalk a line for me to walk." If Asgill were eventually to be sacrificed, Congress would make the final decision, not Washington.

The matter was "a great national concern" and expanded into an international cause célèbre thanks in part to Lady Asgill, who had enough influence to arouse an international outcry. "The public prints all over Europe resounded with the unhappy catastrophe," writer and diplomat Friedrich Melchior, Baron von Grimm, recorded in his memoirs. It "interested every feeling mind . . . and the first question asked of all vessels that arrived from any port in North America, was always an inquiry into the fate of that young man." "Does Asgill still live?"

Lady Asgill successfully won the intercession of Sir James Jay, the Loyalist brother of John Jay, after he visited her home. Jay wrote General Washington describing in some detail the strains that Asgill's situation was putting on that admirable family. Young Asgill was a thoroughly sympathetic personality. General Moses Hazen, in charge of his captivity and transfer to New Jersey, had been "sensibly affected" by Asgill's "most amiable character" and had hoped a more appropriate sacrifice could be found to atone for Huddy's death. The melodrama of a fatal lottery and Asgill's qualities and charms were designed perfectly to appeal to the French public at this time, and it was reported that portraits of him were selling all over Paris. As events developed, Asgill's salvation (and in a sense Washington's) would come from France. Despite the fact that Great Britain and France were at war, Lady Asgill, a French émigré, wrote a moving and what proved to be an effective letter to Charles Gravier, Count of Vergennes, France's foreign minister, who had the ear of the king.

In prose perhaps too flowery for modern ears, she pleaded for her son's release. "My son, my only son, dear to me as he is brave, amiable as he is beloved, only nineteen years of age, a prisoner of war, in consequence of the capitulation of Yorktown, is at present confined in America as an object of reprisal.—Shall the innocent share the fate of the guilty? Figure to yourself, sir, the situation of a family in these circumstances. Surrounded as I am with objects of distress, bowed down by fear and grief, words are wanting to express what I feel, and to paint such a scene of misery: my husband, given over by his physicians some hours before the arrival of this news, not in a condition to be informed of it; my daughter attacked by a fever, accompanied with delirium; speaking of her brother in tones of wildness, and without an interval of reason, unless it be to listen to some circumstances which may console her heart. Let your sensibility, sir, paint to you my profound, my inexpressible misery, and plead in my favor; a word, a word from you, like a voice from Heaven, would liberate us from desolation, from the last degree of misfortune. I know how far General Washington reveres your character. Tell him only that you wish my son restored to liberty, and he will restore him to his desponding family; he will restore him to happiness. The virtue and courage of my son will justify this act of clemency." (In fact, young Asgill was by then actually twenty years old, but his mother accurately surmised that Asgill's plight would be even more poignant and compelling if he were still a teenager.)

France had reasons besides a mother's grief to tilt Asgill's way. As a signatory to the surrender Washington had accepted at Yorktown, young Captain Asgill was France's prisoner as well as America's. French general Jean Baptiste Donatien de Viemur, Count of Rochambeau, unburdened himself to Chevalier de la Lazerne, the French minister to the United States, in a letter the minister was to share with but not give to Washington, lest it land in the official record. Rochambeau explained that he was sure Washington would not want to soil Cornwallis's honorable capitulation by a deed of reprisal that they had absolutely no right to commit, and which Europeans would regard as a barbarous injustice. Rochambeau later said that Washington, while unwilling to recant publicly, assured him in private that Asgill would not perish by his order.

Washington's preference now was to free Asgill. On October 7, he wrote Benjamin Lincoln, "Was I to give my private opinion respecting Asgill I should pronounce in favor of his being released from his Duress—and that he should be permitted to go to his Friends in Europe." Washington took pains to explain to Rochambeau that he had given Asgill parole to travel widely, indeed to the boundary between American and British turf. One wonders if Washington had hoped that Asgill would seize the moment and escape to New York City, saving Washington's honor by violating his own. Asgill did not.

Lady Asgill's letter turned the key. Touched by her eloquence, Vergennes sent her letter along with one of his own telling Washington that King Louis XVI and Queen Marie Antoinette would be very grateful if the general could see his way to mercy. "The goodness of their majesties' hearts induces them to desire that the inquietudes of an unfortunate mother may be calmed and her tenderness reassured." (There is a possibility that the actual letter was drafted by Benjamin Franklin.) Washington needed no persuading. Seeing a possible solution to the crisis, which was weighing heavily on him, Washington sent the letter to Congress by courier. It arrived in literally the nick of time.

Indeed, the crisis ended with a moment of high drama more fitting for a novel or play than for real life. While slow to operate, Congress was finally on the verge of directing Washington to execute Asgill and decided to call the question the morning of October 30, 1782. This was done despite the powerful arguments of a few members that to do so would be a serious mistake and a blot on the country's honor. Happily, almost miraculously, before the vote could be taken, Washington's letter conveying the desire of the French sovereigns arrived. Suddenly, here was a solution. Rather than seeming to give in to the hated British, America could free Asgill as a gift to France, for whom gratitude was running high. Congress voted unanimously that Asgill be freed "as a compliment to the King of France." He was ordered to be sent home.

Thus, the crisis ended. As Elias Boudinot, representative from New Jersey and later president of the Continental Congress, noted in his journal, "We got clear of shedding innocent blood by a wonderful interposition of Providence." In more mundane terms, Robert Livingston, secretary of foreign affairs, wrote to American ministers abroad, "Captain Asgill would certainly have paid the forfeit for the injustice of his countrymen, had not the interposition of their Majesties prevented." Future president John Adams, completing the preliminary peace treaty in Paris, rejoiced at the news. "It would have been a horrid damp to the joys of peace, if we had received a disagreeable account of him."

Washington was able to write Asgill with the good news—as good for Washington and his reputation as it was good for Asgill's wellbeing. However, a footnote to the affair discomfited Washington when Asgill complained that as Washington's prisoner he had been treated poorly. One of Washington's greatest admirers, Tench Tilghman Sr., the father of Colonel Tench Tilghman, Washington's aide-de-camp from the beginning to the conclusion of the Revolutionary War, informed the general of how his name was being traduced abroad. Tilghman reported that among other insults, Asgill alleged that gallows had been erected before his prison window as a taunt regarding his upcoming fate. (Asgill later wrote that no gallows was ever placed outside his prison, but reported that he was told that there was one at Monmouth with a sign on it reading "Up Goes Asgill for Huddy.") Asgill believed Washington countenanced his mistreatment and, but for Rochambeau's intervention, would have executed him.

As he demonstrated time and time again, George Washington was notoriously thin-skinned on matters that cast aspersions on his honor. Always striving to be the epitome of knightly virtue and magnanimity, the general angrily responded that he was convinced that history would vindicate him. Of Asgill's ostensible allegations, the general said such calumnies had no validity, and if Asgill had uttered them, then Washington's earlier positive view of the young officer was "forfeited." How did Asgill, Washington asked rhetorically, explain "the continual indulgencies & procrastinations he had experienced" during his confinement? How did Asgill think he came to be allowed "for the benefit of his health & the recreation of his mind, to ride . . . into the surrounding country for many miles, with his friend & companion Major Gordon constantly attending him?" Such benefits only came to him with Washington's permission.

In fact, now that he thought more about it, Charles Asgill might not have been the gentleman Washington initially thought he was. There was an indication earlier in the saga, Washington now recollected. Upon receiving Washington's letter freeing him, Asgill did not do the polite and proper thing and write the general with his thanks for the kind treatment he had received. "I was not without suspicions after the final liberation and return of Captain Asgill to New York, that his mind had been improperly impressed," Washington wrote, "or that he was defective in politeness."

In characterizing his treatment of Asgill as lenient, Washington was forgetting that in the middle of the crisis he had been anything but lenient. Learning that Asgill was being given relatively free rein, Washington had written sternly to subordinates, "I am informed that Capt. Asgill is at Chatham, without Guard, & under no constraint—This if true is certainly wrong—I wish to have the young Gentleman treated with all the Tenderness possible, consistent with his present Situation— But until his Fate is determined, *he must be considered as a close prisoner & be kept in the greatest Security*" (emphasis added). (To Washington's credit, he later qualified his claim of complete leniency when he published his official papers on the affair in the *New Haven Gazette* and the *Columbian Magazine* in January 1787.)

It is also surprising that Washington seriously expected a thank-you note from Asgill. Washington had plucked the young captain from obscure captivity and set him up to be executed as an official act of reprisal. Knowing each day might be his last, Asgill had had to write to his parents with news of his impending fate, understanding that his ill father, to whom he was apologizing in the same letter for fighting against America despite his father's wishes, would outlive him. As for not thanking Washington for not hanging him, Asgill later wrote, "My judgement told me I could not with sincerity return thanks [which] my feelings would not allow me to give vent to."

Following the war, Captain Asgill rose in the ranks to become General Asgill. Serving in Ireland during the Rebellion of 1798, he was to oversee the execution of a dashing Irish rebel named William Farrell. However, his wife, Lady Sophia Asgill, argued that since Queen Marie Antoinette's petition to General George Washington had saved Asgill's life, he was duty-bound to do the same at her request. He did as she asked. Asgill was sixty when he died in 1823, forty years after his near-execution.

The Asgill Affair could have left an ugly blot on George Washington's reputation. Asgill's execution would have been a permanent stain that would not have easily been washed away. Joshua Huddy's extrajudicial execution had presented a fiendish dilemma. Public opinion overwhelmingly favored a tough response. Had Washington not threatened retaliation, he might have lost some Patriot support, but in so doing he committed himself to a dangerous course, which he found impossible to reverse for fear of losing control. He convinced himself of the righteousness of executing a Convention prisoner even as he anguished over it. Looking for a way out, Washington bought time, pushed the issue to Congress, and gratefully took the way out offered by the Vergennes letter.

Overshadowed by Washington's many achievements, the Asgill Affair is a blip that reminds us even the greatest of men make mistakes. Thanks to a mother's love and her ability to write moving letters, the potentially tragic aspects of the mistake were mitigated, and Americans were spared the challenge of explaining why General George Washington executed a man whom he had promised to protect from any such retaliation.

5

Fractured Friendships

GEORGE WASHINGTON BREAKS
WITH FIVE FAMOUS VIRGINIANS

MANY PEOPLE view the Founding Fathers through a haze of patriotism, nostalgia, and thin to nonexistent historical knowledge. From that blurred perspective, these men appear to be a monolithic ensemble, acting as if with one mind in their struggle to make a country and to make that country great. Of course, then, as now, sharp differences set America's leaders apart and sometimes at loggerheads with one another.

One illustration of friction among the Founding Fathers is the fact, often overlooked, that George Washington severed friendships with five fellow Virginia-born revolutionaries, each in his own right famous and historically influential. One man authored the Virginia Declaration of Rights and much of the Virginia Constitution. Another served as that state's governor as well as the nation's first attorney general and its second secretary of state. The other three became presidents of the United States.

In particular, two issues embroiling the United States led to the breaks. One flash point was the debate over the Constitution and the power that document proposed to assign to the central government. The other fractious topic involved foreign affairs in the wake of the French Revolution and the ensuing war between Great Britain and France.

In the years following victory over Great Britain in the War of Independence (1783–1787), it became increasingly clear that a national government could not effectively operate under the Articles of Confederation, which had been ratified in 1781. How to correct the problem was intensely debated. George Washington was strongly in the nationalist camp and favored significantly strengthening the powers of the central government. As the late Don Higginbotham expressed it, "George Washington, more than any member of the Revolutionary generation, both by word and deed, advanced the concept of an American nation, and pressed for the creation of an institutional umbrella to bind Americans together." Washington himself summed up the woeful situation under the Articles: "The disinclination of the individual states to yield competent powers to Congress for the Federal Government—their unreasonable jealousy of that body and of one another, and the disposition which seems to pervade each, of being all-wise and all-powerful within itself, will, if there is not a change in the system, be our downfall as a nation." While admitting the Constitution's imperfections, Washington staunchly defended the instrument, which he had come to see as the only alternative to dissolving the union, a step that was, for him, anathema. "Thus believing," he wrote, "I had not, nor have I now any hesitation in deciding on which [way] to lean."

Not everyone agreed. Many Virginians felt protective of Virginia's interests—it was after all the oldest, largest, most populous, and most powerful of the states. This Virginia-first attitude remained strong even after the state narrowly ratified the Constitution in the summer of 1788. That 89–79 vote resulted from the strength of James Madison's brilliant campaign on behalf of ratification combined with General Washington's unique popularity, underpinned by a universal belief that Washington would be heading the new government.

Throughout Washington's presidency, states' rights would remain a hot-button issue, personified by the split between Thomas Jefferson and Alexander Hamilton. During Washington's second term, the main divisive factor was the aftershocks following the 1789 French Revolution. By 1793, France and England had entered into a global war. That conflict dramatically affected the young United States, a rising but as yet weak presence in international commerce, whose shipping was at the mercy of the British Royal Navy.

Differences of opinion were fundamental. From the viewpoint of Jefferson and the Republicans, France was the "true mother country" of America, while the British were "our natural enemies and the only nation on earth who wished us ill from the bottom of their souls." "The cause of France is the cause of man," declared a Republican leader, "and neutrality is desertion." They believed that those facts should shape our foreign policy. Hamilton and the Federalists believed the excesses of the French Revolution were harbingers of what might come to America, with the principles of the French Revolution and its attack on religion ultimately inflicting irreparable harm on American society.

The president, in Joseph Ellis's descriptive phrase a "rock-ribbed realist," greatly feared that excessive enthusiasm among Americans for France's cause could put America on a collision course with Great Britain. As if to bear out this analysis, Congress, led by the Jeffersonian Republicans, began moving to impose economic sanctions on Britain. The motive was to force the empire to respect American neutrality, now being violated with impunity by British warships.

Fearful that war with Great Britain and the ensuing economic disaster would be the undoing of the young republic, President Washington sought to take the crisis out of the hands of Congress by appointing John Jay as his special envoy to the Court of St. James. Jay's challenging mission was to settle conflicts with Britain and avoid war. He did manage to obtain a treaty, but it was disappointing to Washington as it won few concessions. While avoiding a clash with Great Britain, the treaty basically accepted the British interpretation of neutral rights and granted the country it favored nation status, eliminating future commercial discrimination against it for at least ten years while the treaty was in effect. The disputatious debate over ratifying the Jay Treaty rocked Washington's friendships with a number of his fellow Virginians.

And then there was the matter of Washington's personality. No man was more sensitive to the reality or appearance of criticism impugning his character. George Washington feared damage to his character and reputation more than he feared enemy bullets. Likewise, while always welcoming advice, Washington bristled at the idea that he was under the undue influence of any man or was incapable of deciding independently on the best course of action. From his perspective, "If people are convinced of my integrity, they will make proper allowances for my inexperience and frailties." As he guarded his reputation, so he guarded his purity of intent. Awareness of these sensitivities can help us understand why he came to end valued friendships and alliances with five famous Virginians, each at one time a friend or ally, most of whom continued to hold him in high regard.

While recognizing his sensitivity to criticism, it is important to emphasize that George Washington was not one to sever a close relationship over a mere disagreement, even on important matters. He understood that men of integrity often see issues differently. As he eloquently stated, "Shall I set up my judgment as the standard of perfection? Shall I arrogantly pronounce that whoever differs from me, must discern the subject through a distorting medium, or be influenced by some nefarious design? The mind is so formed in different persons as to contemplate the same object in different points of view. Hence originates the difference on questions of the greatest import, human and divine."

When Benjamin Harrison opposed the Constitution, for example, Washington wrote to his fellow Virginian using the salutation "my dear sir," which he used only with close friends. "My friendship is not in the least lessened by the difference which has taken place in our political sentiments; nor is my regard for you diminished by the part you have acted. Men's minds are as variant as their faces, and, *where the motives to their actions are pure,* the operation of the former is no more to be imputed to them as a crime, than the appearance of the latter: for both being the work of nature, are equally unavoidable" (emphasis added).

Washington viewed criticism, given honestly and unalloyed by ulterior motive, to be the mark of a genuine friend. He told his former aide and later critic, Joseph Reed, "The hints you have communicated from time to time not only deserve, but do most sincerely, and cordially meet with my thanks—you cannot render a more acceptable service, nor in my estimation give me a more convincing proof of your Friendship, than by a free, open, & undisguised account of every matter relative to myself, or conduct. I can bear to hear of imputed, or real errors; the Man who wishes to stand well in the opinion of others must do this, because he is thereby enabled to correct his faults." Later, learning that Reed had been criticizing him to others for being ineffective, the general told Reed that the specifics of his backbiting in what became known as the Conway Cabal had hurt less than Reed's failure to voice his discontent directly to Washington. The "favorable manner in which your opinion, upon all occasions, had been received—the Impression they made—and the unreserved manner in which I wished, & required them to be given, entitled me, I thought, to your advice upon any point in which I appeared to be wanting . . . censuring my Conduct to another was such an argument of disingenuity that I was not a little mortified at it."

Willing to offer what he regarded as worthwhile criticism, Washington as president sent a remarkably candid letter to Gouverneur Morris on the occasion of the latter's becoming ambassador to France in 1792. Morris had a well-earned reputation as a devastating wit. Out of friendship, the president warned the ambassador-to-be that his slashing jibes against political opponents conveyed a "hauteur" whose persistent sting was hard for its recipients to forgive. Explaining his forthrightness in reporting this, Washington wrote, "I do it on the presumption that a mind conscious of its own rectitude fears not what is said of it, but will bid defiance to and despise shafts that are not barbed with accusations against honor or integrity." In this letter, Washington endorses criticism and disagreement but only if not "barbed with accusations against honor or integrity" or tainted by impure motive. If they are, that is a different story.

The story behind each of Washington's breaks with these five men is as unique as Washington's relationship with each man, yet all five cases share significant characteristics. All involved disputes on issues of great importance. Nearly all of the breaks were total and irreversible, at least from George Washington's perspective. And, most significantly, in all five cases Washington came to believe, whether fairly or not, that his former friend had leveled criticisms "barbed with accusations against honor or integrity" that he found impossible to forgive.

George Mason

George Mason—brilliant, reclusive, and cantankerous, author of the Virginia Constitution and that state's Declaration of Rights, which preceded and influenced both the Declaration of Independence and the Bill of Rights—merits a special place in America's pantheon. He also is an outlier in the discussion at hand. Born in 1725, Mason alone among our five subjects was older than Washington and the only one with whom Washington broke before assuming the presidency. Undoubtedly, long association imbued Washington with a deep and abiding respect for Mason and his intellect. Viewing Mason as a mentor, Washington certainly had him in mind when he wrote, "Much abler heads than my own hath fully convinced me, that [British actions] are not only repugnant to natural right, but subversive of the laws and constitution of Great Britain itself." In April of 1769, Washington sought Mason's advice on how to proceed with the nonimportation proposal designed to protest the Townshend Acts and its unjustified tariffs. Washington also turned to Mason for aid in untangling the estate of Patsy Custis, Washington's stepdaughter, who died in 1773. "I could think of no person in whose friendship, care and Abilities I could so much confide." Describing Mason to Lafayette, Washington praised his neighbor as "a zealous and able supporter of the liberties of this country and a particular friend of mine."

Although the extant record demonstrates the two men were friends, it also indicates it was an uneven friendship. Mason's affection for Washington and pleasure in his company were never fully reciprocated. Differences in personality, temperament, and philosophy kept the friendship from being an intimate and affectionate one, at least on Washington's part. Mason, who lived about ten miles down the Virginia shore of the Potomac River at Gunston Hall, visited Mount Vernon far more often than Washington visited Mason at his home; he wrote

George Mason. (Courtesy of Gunston Hall)

Washington approximately three letters for each one he received; and he was constantly sending a plethora of seeds, plants, and other gifts to Mount Vernon.

By nature not an effusive man, Mason nonetheless often waxed eloquent in describing Washington, viewing him without peer among his fellow mortals. There is no reliable evidence that Mason ever changed his opinion of or affection for Washington. Even during his intense struggle against ratification of the Constitution and the new government, Mason's surviving correspondence includes not a single negative comment about Washington and many complimentary ones.

Well before the Philadelphia convention, however, the friendship was showing strains, mainly involving money. In collecting "voluntary taxes" to fund the Fairfax militia, Washington felt that Mason had his son collect from those most able and willing to pay, leaving Washington to collect from the rest as best he could. Mason would not loan Washington's neighbor, John Posey, money unless Washington cosigned and then pressured Washington to make good on the loan when Posey did not.

Nevertheless, it was Mason's conduct at the end of the Philadelphia convention in 1787 and his fight to defeat ratification of the Constitution by Virginia that destroyed Washington's friendship for him. Historians have underestimated the intensity of the animosity Washington came to harbor toward Mason for what Washington perceived as betrayal. Most academics accept that Washington entertained Mason at Mount Vernon for dinner on November 2, 1788. If Washington did so after the ratification fight, then other events must have caused the rupture that is manifested in some of Washington's later correspondence. In fact, there is no evidence that Mason was ever welcomed at Mount Vernon after he opposed the Constitution. The reference to the dinner guest on that date is not to *Colonel* George Mason but to Mr. George Mason, Colonel Mason's eldest son. Washington in his diary uniformly referred to the father as Colonel Mason and to the son, who is mentioned much less frequently, as Mr. George Mason. The error, while understandable, is regrettable. It has led to a failure to appreciate the depth of Washington's disappointment in and anger at Mason's fight to stop ratification of the Constitution, and, more importantly, the manner in which he chose to oppose it.

While admitting its imperfections, Washington was a staunch defender of the United States Constitution. Now his neighbor, a man of great ability and reputation, had decided to oppose the final product of the convention. Not only would he oppose it, but he would also actively and vigorously seek to defeat it, authoring an influential pamphlet, *Objections to the Constitution*. Washington came to view Mason as the *bête noir* of the federalist cause and interpreted Mason's opposition to the Constitution in a negative and unfavorable light. Evidence for this conclusion is strengthened by numerous letters from Tobias Lear, who became Washington's personal secretary in 1786.

Lear—competent, dedicated, utterly loyal to George Washington—does not of course explicitly speak for Washington. However, Lear's statements certainly reflect and echo the sentiments of the master of Mount Vernon. His position as personal secretary and tutor to Martha Washington's grandchildren gave him unique access to the more private life of General Washington. Lear's views on the Constitution and George Mason were filtered through his conversations with Washington. "I have no other light or information to direct me but what he possessed," Lear wrote. The words of Lear's private letters sometimes are identical to those of the general, and the secretary noted, "I have considered the General's interest in every point of view as my own." Lear's criticisms of *Objections to the Constitution,* George Mason's influential pamphlet, closely parallel comments on that broadside by Washington and by James Madison. One can hear Washington's voice in Lear's letter to Governor John Langdon of New Hampshire. "Colo. Mason is certainly a man of superior abilities—he is sensible of it, & having generally felt his weight & influence in those public bodies where he has acted heretofore, he has contracted the idea of '*aut Caesar, aut nullus,*' but finding a strong opposition to his opinion upon some points in the Convention, don't you think he felt himself piqued?" "*Aut Caesar, aut nullus.*" Either Caesar's way or no way. Lear clearly implies Mason insisted on having the Constitution his way or not at all. When his ideas were defeated, personal pique led him to bitter opposition.

Lear was not finished indicating what he learned at Mount Vernon: "Mr. Mason & Mr. [Patrick] Henry still continue their opposition with unabated violence. The opponents here . . . are now endeavoring to deprecate the characters which composed the general convention. . . .

Even Colo. Mason has descended to this low method & has declared that the Convention, generally speaking, was made up of block-heads from the northern, coxcombs from the southern, & office-seekers from the middle states." Lear's paraphrased allegations of what Mason had to say about those participating in the Philadelphia convention suggest strongly that he had heard Washington discuss *Objections* and voice criticisms of Mason.

In time, Washington did commit to paper explicit and negative comments about the man he eventually referred to as a "quandom friend." (In Latin, *quondam* means "former.") The general was unburdening himself to his good friend and physician, Dr. James Craik. Craik had written to Washington in 1789 that Mason, still dissatisfied with the government, had resigned from his position as a justice of the peace. "I always expected," the president wrote, "that the Gentleman, whose name you have mentioned would mark his opposition to the new government with consistency. Pride on the one hand, and want of manly candor on the other, will not, I am certain, let him acknowledge an error in his opinions respecting it, though conviction should flash on his mind as strongly as a ray of light." Washington's perception of how Mason conducted his opposition to the Constitution and the implications it had for Washington's self-image led the general to put an end to their friendship.

There is no compelling evidence that the breach was ever healed. Mason was no longer welcome at Mount Vernon, and the scant correspondence between the two men following the Constitutional Convention was strictly business. There is only a single reference in Washington's correspondence to Mason's death, which occurred in October 1792. Responding to a letter (now missing) from Mason's kinsman James Mercer, Washington perfunctorily wrote, "I will also unite my regret to yours for the death of our old friend, and acquaintance Colo. Mason."

George Mason never wavered in his conviction that only the highest of ideals had powered his opposition to the Constitution. "In this important trust, I am truly conscious of having acted from the purest motives of honesty, and love to my country, according to that measure of judgment which God has bestowed on me." In contrast, George Washington would agree with those viewing Mason's actions as springing more from wounded vanity than from patriotism.

Edmund Randolph

If George Mason was George Washington's mentor, George Washington was Edmund Randolph's mentor. Born into perhaps Virginia's most prestigious family in 1753, young Randolph cast his lot with the Patriot cause then led by his uncle, Peyton Randolph, president of the First Continental Congress, rather than with his father, John, a staunch Loyalist who returned to England. The younger Randolph became a Washington protégé, during the war serving for a time as one of the general's aides and during Washington's presidency as his secretary of state after Thomas Jefferson resigned. Randolph said that as a young man he was taught to "esteem" Washington and that in maturity he came to "revere" him.

Yet, in 1795, he became so upset at Washington's behavior toward him that he wrote his friend James Madison, "I feel happy at my emancipation from an attachment to a man, who has practiced upon me the profound hypocrisy of Tiberius, and the injustice of an assassin." Randolph was invoking the Roman emperor Tiberius, who poisoned

Edmund Randolph.
(Courtesy of Virginia
Museum of History &
Culture [1858.5])

his loyal nephew, Germanicus. (A year earlier Randolph, writing under the pseudonym of "Germanicus," had defended Washington's handling of the Whiskey Rebellion.) The break with Edmund Randolph, among the saddest chapters in George Washington's life, does not reflect very well on either man.

Randolph and Washington clashed amid the fight over the Jay Treaty, the most controversial episode in Washington's tenure as president. Though unhappy with the treaty, especially a passage sharply limiting the tonnage of ships allowed to trade with British colonies in the West Indies, Washington signed the document. Evidence indicates that the crisis involving his secretary of state, Edmund Randolph, spurred Washington to sign the treaty before the offending naval provision was formally changed. What was that crisis?

Edmund Randolph was the sole Jeffersonian Republican in Washington's cabinet, although many Republicans questioned the depth of his commitment. As attorney general, he had tried to minimize dissent in the cabinet and wanted to be seen as above party, a stance increasingly difficult as the French Revolution spawned a burgeoning crisis. Ever-increasing partisanship complicated Randolph's efforts, as a critic of the Jay Treaty, to stay right with both President Washington and with Randolph's Republican friends in Virginia and to do so without seeming to be wishy-washy.

Thomas Jefferson was contemptuous, describing Randolph as "the poorest chameleon I ever saw, having no color of his own and reflecting that nearest him. When he is with me, he is a Whig. When with Hamilton he is a Tory. When with the president, he is that [which] he thinks will please him." Now Randolph, who had replaced Jefferson at State, was in a position to thwart British efforts to persuade Washington to accept the treaty. The British wanted Randolph out, or at least neutralized. So did the Federalists. One weapon to aim at him was an episode in 1794. In response to the Whiskey Rebellion, an uprising in western Pennsylvania over a federal tax on distillers' output, Randolph had opposed crushing the rebels with blunt military force.

The rebellion resurfaced as a political card to play in 1795 when a Royal Navy vessel captured a French ship carrying diplomatic documents. The sheaf of papers included secret dispatches from the new French foreign minister, Jean-Antoine Fauchet, intended for his superiors in Paris. In the classified papers, Fauchet discussed exchanges with Secretary of State Randolph in which Randolph appeared to overstep. Portions of Fauchet's notes, written in his native French, could be read to indicate that Randolph was soliciting a bribe from the French. At a minimum, these passages portrayed Randolph as critical of Washington's earlier actions in the Whiskey Rebellion and additionally grossly exaggerated Randolph's influence over the president.

The British government gave the Fauchet papers to the crown's ambassador in America, George Hammond. On July 28, 1795, Hammond presented the bundle to U.S. Secretary of the Treasury Oliver Wolcott. Wolcott passed the papers to Secretary of War Timothy Pickering, who less than ably translated the documents into English and saw in the dispatches the opportunity so long sought by the Federalists to get rid of Randolph. Pickering then wrote an urgent but cryptic note to the president that he should return to Philadelphia from Mount Vernon as soon as possible.

When Washington arrived in Philadelphia, Pickering shocked the president by declaring that Randolph was a "traitor" and then shared his own version of Fauchet's damning dispatch, which implied that Randolph wanted money from the French. Was this a second Benedict Arnold affair? Washington had very unwisely trusted Arnold and been betrayed, a betrayal that had deeply impacted him at a core level. Thus, he was primed to not be deceived that way again. Perhaps Washington feared that Randolph, as Arnold had, might be angling to sell out his country for money. If so, Randolph's advice opposing the treaty could not be followed, and Washington decided to sign Jay's Treaty the next morning.

GW stewed for a week, however, before confronting Randolph about the contents of the translated Fauchet dispatch, and he did so with Wolcott and Pickering present. The president peremptorily handed Randolph the dispatch, asked him to read it and make whatever reply he chose to make as his accusers watched his reaction. One can imagine how shocked and stunned Randolph must have been to be confronted so unexpectedly, and to realize that he was under grave suspicion, and that Washington might actually imagine him disloyal or dishonest. While remaining calm and asking for time to peruse the letter more carefully, Randolph quickly concluded he could not remain in his current position. He gave instructions that his office be locked so that no one could charge that he had tampered with evidence and wrote out his letter of resignation. "Your confidence in me, Sir, has been unlimited and, I can truly affirm, unabused. My sensations then cannot be concealed, when I find that confidence so immediately withdrawn without a word or distant hint being previously dropped to me!"

The entire episode was fraught with missteps. One can properly criticize the manner in which the president handled this affair—it seems very unfair to a formerly trusted aide—but several points should be kept in mind. Washington, ignorant of French, had no idea that Pickering's ham-handed translation of Fauchet's nuanced prose gave a distorted view of the document. Additionally, Randolph's charges struck a nerve in the always sensitive George Washington. The implicit criticisms of the way Washington handled the Whiskey Rebellion and Randolph's implication that he could keep the president on the right course and away from the influence of northern bankers and closet monarchists like Alexander Hamilton inevitably engendered a strong defensive reaction. From Washington's perspective, Randolph had attacked both his competency and his control of his own administration. Washington appeared unable to forgive attitudes that implied he acted irresponsibly, especially if they stemmed from a belief that he was wrong about something because he was not bright enough to understand it. One can understand why the president felt betrayed by his protégé.

After resigning, Randolph acted like a jilted lover. He simply could not conceive that Washington, a man he had revered and struggled to please, could treat him so coldly—thus his letter to Madison characterizing the president as an "assassin." Going all in, Randolph composed and published a 100-page apologia that he entitled *Vindication,* a document which almost all scholars agree establishes that he was innocent of treason and of soliciting bribes. That said, it was done in a way certain to anger George Washington, the one person who could restore his reputation. Randolph published their correspondence, including some letters to Washington that Randolph had not yet sent to the president. To the president's credit, he said he had nothing to hide from the public and gave Randolph "full liberty to publish, without reserve, any and every private and confidential letter I ever wrote you; nay more, every word I ever uttered in your presence."

Much of *Vindication* speaks directly to Washington. Indeed, as the historian Mary Tachua notes, "Randolph sets his defense within the context of a diatribe against Washington, and the pamphlet almost explodes with Randolph's anger and hurt." Randolph declared to GW, "I hesitate not to pronounce that you prejudged the question" and then proceeded to justify what he did rather than try to discover the truth. Randolph claimed he was a "meditated victim of party spirit." "Under the influence of Wolcott and Pickering you had been in an instant transformed into my enemy." Washington took furious exception to being upbraided publicly for being in league with the Federalists. While temperament, outlook, and experience placed him in the Federalist ambit, Washington consciously prided himself on belonging to no political party.

Publicly chastising the president might have felt satisfying, but Randolph was waging a losing war. The more he attacked Washington, the weaker he became. There was no future in attacking George Washington, and the president's defenders rushed to attack Randolph. For public consumption, the president maintained an icy silence, while privately expressing scorn for Randolph. Washington was said to have flung down a copy of *Vindication* in disgust, denouncing the author in the presence of others as a liar, scoundrel, and villain. Tachua writes, "The silence that the president had maintained publicly . . . continued for the rest of his life. Washington was a proud and austere man, and it would have been difficult for him to have said that he was sorry or had been mistaken under any circumstances. It was impossible for him to reestablish contact with Randolph under these circumstances. . . . It was intolerable to him that Randolph had attacked him so bitterly and had described their working relationship so indiscreetly."

James Madison nicely summarized the pamphlet's impact. Randolph's "greatest enemies will not easily persuade themselves that he was under a corrupt influence of France, and his best friends can't save him from the self-condemnation of his political career." Unfortunately, neither man could forgive the other. Each took his hostility toward the other to the grave.

James Monroe

James Monroe differs from the other individuals discussed in this chapter in two significant ways. He had the least intimate connection with George Washington, and he lacked the intellectual clout of the other four men. No one ever accused Monroe of intellectual brilliance. Indeed, Aaron Burr's screed against Monroe on this score—"dull and stupid"—is perhaps the harshest I have read by one member of the founding generation against another.

While never close, Washington and Monroe early on had a very positive relationship. As a young captain in the War of Independence—he shed his blood and nearly lost his life during the December 1776 Trenton campaign—Monroe had deep respect and affection for the general, the epitome of a heroic commander. Monroe had lost his father at a young age, and Washington, twenty-six years Monroe's senior, undoubtedly became something of a father figure. Years later, Monroe recollected, "I saw him in my earliest youth, in the retreat through Jersey, at the head of a small band, or rather in its rear, for he was always next to the enemy, and his countenance and manner

James Monroe. (Courtesy of Library of Congress, Prints & Photographs Division)

made an impression on me which time can never efface." Washington possessed "a deportment so firm, so dignified, but yet so modest and composed I have never seen in any other person."

The general held his junior subordinate in similar regard. "He has, in every instance, maintained the reputation of a brave, active, and sensible officer." Washington, never one to offer casual praise or recommendations, wrote in a letter endorsing an officer's rank for Monroe, "The esteem I have for him, and a regard for his merit, conspire to make me earnestly wish to see him provided for in some handsome way."

What happened to dramatically change the views of both men—to cause Monroe to believe that Washington might actually seek to "enslave" the very country whose liberty he had secured, and to have Washington vent against Monroe with a sarcasm and bitterness found nowhere else in his writings?

Monroe became a strong critic of the proposed United States Constitution, but that antipathy did not dim his enthusiasm for Washington. "I have a boundless confidence in him," he told Jefferson, "nor have I any reason to believe he will ever furnish occasion for withdrawing it." When Monroe issued a pamphlet listing his objections to the new Constitution, Washington responded graciously, acknowledging their differences but also praising Monroe for his "candor and liberality," a response which encouraged Monroe to continue his political career.

The Washington/Monroe split originated in the emerging development of political parties. Monroe, who became a senator from Virginia in 1790, was an anti-Federalist. He believed it was crucial that the United States define and limit the extent of the powers granted the national government under the Constitution and firmly believed that Alexander Hamilton's vision for America, which Washington apparently embraced, would take America in exactly the wrong direction.

The real rupture, however, occurred over the French Revolution. All along, Monroe, much like his mentor, Thomas Jefferson, cheered that uprising as an extension of America's. From this perspective, the French insurrection was a seminal event in which one of the greatest nations on earth had overthrown hereditary rule and begun a republican experiment. Monroe inextricably linked the two rebellions, believing that failure of the revolution in France would endanger liberty in

America. Thus, for America to slip back into the orbit of France's mortal enemy, Britain, the apex of evil in his vision of the world, would be disastrously counterproductive and might lead to monarchy or, even worse, virtual reenslavement. Of course, the Federalists (and President Washington) saw things quite differently. They looked with disgust on the Reign of Terror, punctuated by such horrors as the September 1792 massacre of more than fourteen hundred "enemies of the revolution," and the January 1793 execution of King Louis XVI. France was moving not toward liberty but rather toward licentiousness. Many felt the excesses of the French Revolution, its radical principles, and its attacks on religion, which would destroy society, were harbingers of what might come to America.

Monroe profoundly doubted the wisdom of President Washington's response to the triangular crisis engulfing America, France, and Britain. When Washington decided to send a special envoy to Britain to resolve conflicts with that nation, Monroe requested to meet privately with the president. Monroe particularly wanted to speak against naming as Washington's special envoy his nemesis, Alexander Hamilton. Monroe was rebuffed with a sharply worded letter from the president: "I alone am responsible for a proper nomination. . . . It certainly behooves me to name such a one as in my judgment combines the requisites for a mission so peculiarly interesting to the peace & happiness of this country." If Monroe had concerns, he could put them in writing and the president would consider them! Monroe did so, blasting the possible appointment of Hamilton, although he was not much happier to learn that Washington's ultimate choice was John Jay, another object of Monroe's distrust.

Despite their testy exchange, President Washington decided to nominate Monroe to be his new minister to France—replacing Gouverneur Morris, whose recall had been demanded by the French government because they felt he was not sufficiently sympathetic to their revolution. Although the president would come to regret the decision, several factors combined to cause him to make it. Since the French were very concerned by Jay's appointment as special envoy to Britain, they might be somewhat mollified by the appointment of Monroe, whose strong pro-French views were well known. Monroe was a partisan Republican, but in 1794 the spirit of party did not appear quite so baneful to the president as it soon would become. Additionally, he had trouble finding a figure of national stature to accept the post—being rejected by his first two choices, Edward Livingston and James Madison. Finally, his secretary of state, Edmund Randolph, recommended Monroe for the post.

Washington's decision to offer and Monroe's decision to accept the post as ambassador to France led to ill feeling on both sides and the severing of their relationship. Wearing two hats—speaking on behalf of his government, yet a leader in the opposition party—Monroe found himself yanked in conflicting directions. And Monroe's unabashedly pro-French sympathies, an asset in Paris, came quickly to alarm the Washington administration. Monroe seemed willing to overcommit the United States to an alliance with France, rashly promising that America would be happy to loan France money and implying that, if need be, America would go to war on France's behalf.

Both subtly and overtly, Monroe's representations to French officials presented the Washington administration positions as contrary to American public opinion, suggesting that the French exercise patience until a Republican administration, offering a friendlier posture, was in control of American foreign policy. Monroe was treading a perilous path, serving as a spokesman for his government and at the same time acting as a political leader to promote his own party.

Events reached a climax—and the unceremonious recall of Monroe—as a result of Jay's Treaty. The more Monroe learned of the treaty's terms, the more they outraged him. As he saw it, it was a deal between Great Britain and the Anglophiles in America against the people of America. It would virtually make the United States a colony of Great Britain, her natural enemy, and ally her against France, her natural friend and key supporter. "If it is ratified, it may be deemed one of the most afflicting events that ever befell our country."

Agree or disagree with Monroe's assessment, one should not be surprised that the Washington administration recalled him. Diplomats who baldly oppose their own government's policies do not long hold their posts. James Monroe did not see it that way. "If you supposed that I would submit in silence to the injurious imputations that were raised against me by the administration you were mistaken." Administration criticism of him was "upon pretexts equally unjust, frivolous & absurd" and, in his view, rendered by knaves. "Such a collection of vain, superficial, blunderers, to say no worse of them, were never I think before placed at the head of any respectable State," he wrote to Madison.

Monroe took his case to the American people. His publication, with the almost impossibly long title *A View of the Conduct of the Executive, in the Foreign Affairs of the United States, Connected with the Mission to the French Republic, During the Years 1794, 5, & 6,* was a blistering critique of the administration's foreign affairs policy, which he viewed as catastrophic. "Our navigation is destroyed, commerce laid waste and a general bankruptcy threatening those engaged in it; the friendship of a nation lost." Monroe did not stop there. "Our national honor is in the dust, we have been kicked, cuffed, and plundered all over the ocean, our reputation for faith scouted, our government and people branded as cowards, incapable of being provoked to resist, and ready to receive again those chains we had taught others to burst."

Whatever tenderness Monroe once retained for the president vanished, at least for a time, after his recall. His enduring anger simmers in a letter to Washington, undated and unsent, in which he decried "the unceasing effort of your administration to wrest the government from the people and place it in the hands of an oligarchic faction." Monroe expressed certainty that in response Americans would rise up. "Too long have they been the dupes of a confidence which has served only to betray them." He closed by damning his one-time hero: "the labors of your more early life contributed to promote the liberties of your country; but those of your latter days to enthrall & enslave it[!]"

Although the president could not know exactly what Monroe thought about him in the aftermath of his recall, there is little doubt about what Washington thought of Monroe in the aftermath of the publication in 1798 of his book *A View of the Executive.* GW's personal reaction was made perfectly clear when, in a rare display of anger, he took up his pen to jot down in the margins of the book his fierce rejoinders. "Insanity in the extreme!" he wrote opposite one passage; "self-importance here" at another. Elsewhere in his annotations, Washington derided Monroe as "a mere tool in the hands of the French government. . . . A party man, lost to all sense of propriety." At times, the president waxed droll: "Even the acuteness and wisdom of Monroe might have erred." The editors of the *George Washington Papers* conclude that George Washington's "remarks on Monroe and his book, taken together, comprise the most extended, unremitting, and pointed use of taunts and jibes, sarcasm, and scathing criticism in all of his writing."

Washington's extensive and vituperative marginalia, locked away during his brief remaining lifetime, seemed to quench a cathartic need. Apparently, Monroe had accomplished what no enemy sharpshooter ever could—wound Washington by striking him at his tenderest spot: his reputation as the "singular figure" embodying the Revolution in its most elevated, transcendent form.

In time Monroe's fury abated, and he had many kind words for George Washington. Not so Washington for Monroe. Indeed, Washington's final recorded political sentiments referred to Monroe's election in November 1799 to Virginia's governorship. On the evening of December 13, 1799, struggling against the ailment that was about to kill him, the president was reading Virginia newspapers with his secretary, Tobias Lear. When he mentioned a speech James Madison had given nominating James Monroe for that office, Washington, Lear wrote later, appeared "much affected," and "spoke with some degree of asperity on the subject." Lear gave no more detail but did say that he tried "to moderate" Washington's anger. A day later, Washington was dead, his fury at Monroe unabated.

Thomas Jefferson

Certainly, the most notorious of Washington's five breaks was with Thomas Jefferson. As one who pursued and received a Ph.D. in American history from the University of Virginia in the late 1960s, when all things Jeffersonian were yet sacred, I found it shocking, upon embarking as a student of George Washington, to learn that Washington came to view Jefferson as a deceitful man, unworthy of trust.

Such was not always the case. For much of their relationship Washington admired few men more than he did Thomas Jefferson. It is easy to see why. Jefferson was an amiable, brilliant, multifaceted genius whose myriad accomplishments still amaze. Jefferson was eleven years Washington's junior, but that demi-generational gap did

Thomas Jefferson. (Courtesy of
Library of Congress, Prints &
Photographs Division)

not keep Washington from regarding the younger man as one of his
most important mentors. Washington often sought Jefferson's counsel on complicated matters, once requesting by letter that the other
man comment with the "fullest latitude of a friend." Responding to
Lafayette's praise of Jefferson, Washington observed that he found
Jefferson to be "a man of whom I early imbibed the highest opinion—I am much pleased, therefore, to meet confirmations of my discernment in these matters."

Once elected president, Washington eagerly sought to enlist his
brilliant young friend as Secretary of State. Jefferson not only had
cosmopolitan connections and diplomatic experience (he was at the
time America's minister to France), but the president admired his
character and their common stance on public morality and dignified
behavior. Only reluctantly accepting the top diplomatic post—and not
arriving in New York City until more than a year after Washington's
inauguration—Jefferson assured the president, "you are to marshal us
as may be best for the public good." He further pledged that he would
loyally execute "whatever you may be pleased to decide."

What happened? Why did Jefferson renege on his pledge and why did Washington in the end sever his relationship with him? This unexpected sundering arose partly out of the extent to which—to a degree neither of them recognized nor acknowledged—George Washington and Thomas Jefferson differed significantly in their political philosophies and visions for America. Washington was emblematic of the Friends of Order, who wished to harness energies released by the Revolution to build a nation, and Jefferson was emblematic of the Friends of Liberty, who feared any such effort to bring that type of order as a betrayal of the Revolution. Both men, of course, desired both order and freedom, but their points of view contrasted starkly on how to achieve them. Washington viewed a strong government as necessary for strengthening the union and thereby protecting liberty both for individuals and states. Jefferson viewed a strong government as a threat to liberty, convinced that a strong government would be ever hungrier for more and more power, always at the expense of liberty.

Alexander Hamilton's ascendancy, bringing to the fore his bold and aggressive program to enlarge government power, convinced Jefferson that the administration was moving America in the wrong direction. This awareness put Jefferson in a dilemma. As secretary of state, he was integral to an administration pursuing policies he feared as being detrimental to the republic. His dissent led Jefferson to act in ways that many scholars have found reprehensible, such as secretly undermining the Washington administration and some of its policies. A prime example was Jefferson's sub rosa support of Philip Freneau and his anti-administration newspaper, the *National Gazette,* which Washington believed regularly stirred up discontent and opposition to the administration. Freneau, a poet and Princeton classmate of Jefferson's closest ally, James Madison, held deep antipathy for Great Britain and for Alexander Hamilton's programs. He was hired by the State Department as a translator despite his lack of fluency in any language other than English. Sympathetic Jefferson biographer Noble Cunningham concludes that "attracting Freneau to Philadelphia, putting him on the payroll of the State Department, and giving him privileges denied to other editors, left Jefferson vulnerable to charges difficult to refute."

After Jefferson resigned his post as secretary of state at the end of 1793, his posture toward Washington shifted perceptibly during the president's second administration. Jefferson's worries were raised to a fever pitch by three events. The first was the president's manner of putting down the Whiskey Rebellion, which Jefferson saw as a dangerous overreach of government power. The second was the president's attack on the liberal, pro-French Democratic Societies, which Jefferson viewed as an assault on the right of dissent. Third, and most important, was Washington's decision to sign the Jay Treaty, which Jefferson believed belonged more properly in the annals of treason than in the annals of diplomacy.

As it had with James Monroe, Washington's embrace of the Jay Treaty and its aftermath brought Jefferson to the nadir of his relationship with Washington. In private correspondence, Jefferson, temporarily tormented and disillusioned with Washington's actions on the treaty, wrote a letter, a paragraph of which was to plague him for the rest of his life, going so far as to call the Father of the Country an "apostate" (one who rejects previous beliefs) to republican values. In what became a famous—or infamous—letter to his Italian friend Philip Mazzei, who had spent time with him at Monticello, Jefferson wrote in April of 1796, "My Dear Friend: The aspect of our politics has wonderfully changed since you left us. In place of that noble love of liberty and republican government which carried us triumphantly through the war, a monarchical . . . party has sprung up whose avowed object is to draw over us the substance, as they have already done the forms, of the British government. . . . It would give you a fever were I to name to you *the apostates* who have gone over to these heresies, men who *were Samsons in the field and Solomons in the council, but who have had their head shaved by the harlot England*" (emphasis added). With epic poor judgment, Mazzei gave Jefferson's letter to a Florentine newspaper editor, who published the text. Drawing interest because of the author and subject matter, in time it was reprinted in an English journal and in due course appeared in Noah Webster's *Minerva* in May of 1797. By that time Washington had left the presidency, and he never deigned to comment on it publicly. Nevertheless, there is no doubt in my mind that it was the main catalyst in Washington's decision to sever all ties with Jefferson. Given Washington's sensitivity on matters of reputation, to be called an "apostate" to republicanism was unforgivable. It is worth noting that as far as the record shows, and Jefferson later confirmed, they had no contact, written or in person, after the letter became public knowledge.

Jefferson denied that in venting to Mazzei he was attacking Washington, a protestation of innocence belied by his private correspondence with Madison, Monroe, Archibald Stuart, and others. While not as florid as his comments to Mazzei with their reference to the story of Samson and Delilah, these communiqués nonetheless are every bit as direct. In them, Jefferson makes clear that President Washington had been turned. He had become a Federalist. And, regardless of the purity of Washington's intentions, he was in fact undermining republicanism in America, which would best be served with his removal to Mount Vernon.

Although unaware of Jefferson's other remonstrations, the president knew enough from the Mazzei letter, augmented by stories of Jefferson's hostility from friends like Henry Lee, to sever his relationship with Mr. Jefferson. The depth of Washington's disillusionment with his erstwhile friend is made clear by his readiness to believe that Jefferson was involved in an underhanded effort known as the Langhorne Affair. Washington received a letter from a John Langhorne, actually written by Jefferson's nephew, Peter Carr, in an effort (how is not completely clear) to manipulate Washington into writing things that could be used to political advantage by his opponents. The important point is not whether Jefferson was engaged in the Langhorne Affair, and there is no evidence that he was. The important point is that George Washington believed him to be capable of such a dirty and shabby trick and hoped to publicly expose him.

A posthumous marker of the depth of Washington's animosity to Jefferson can be seen in Martha Washington's response to Jefferson's election as president in 1800, the year after her husband's death. She believed it was the greatest misfortune the country had ever experienced, and she explained why. Jefferson was "one of the most detestable of mankind." One hears in these bitter words an echo of George Washington's own views as he candidly shared them with his beloved wife.

James Madison

George Washington's break with James Madison lacked the fireworks or sharp words that accompanied his break with the other four famous

James Madison. (Courtesy of Library of Congress, Prints & Photographs Division)

Virginians. One cannot cite a pithy quote or anecdote of Washington directly criticizing James Madison. Personally, I view Washington's break with Madison to be the saddest of the five. In character and talent, James Madison is the most attractive of the friends Washington cast out. Madison "is uncorrupted and incorruptible I have not a doubt," Alexander Hamilton wrote. For Abigail Adams, Madison embodied Alexander Pope's axiom about "the noblest work of God: an honest man." A contemporary, Edward Coles, ranked Madison as "the most virtuous, calm, and amiable of men; possessed of one of the purest hearts, and best tempers with which man was ever blessed." Stuart Leibiger convincingly argues that during the period of 1785–1790, which saw the fight for the new constitution and the beginning of Washington's presidency, James Madison was absolutely indispensable to his chief. Exerting unparalleled influence, Madison won not only the general's confidence and respect but also his friendship. Washington was deeply and genuinely fond of his diminutive young friend. On Madison's multiple visits to Mount Vernon, the two must have presented a striking contrast, with Washington being almost a foot taller, a hundred pounds heavier, and nearly twenty years older.

By 1785, after Madison's various visits to Mount Vernon, Washington opened his letters with the infrequently used intimate salutation "My dear sir," and closed them with the infrequently used word "affectionately." Despite Washington's guarded nature, in letters to Madison he sometimes adopted a surprisingly relaxed tone. In a message about a knotty problem previously mentioned, Washington apologized to Madison for pestering him about the matter. "I am very troublesome, I know, but you must excuse me," the general wrote. "Ascribe it to friendship and confidence, and you will do justice to my motives." No record exists of what occurred on Madison's ten visits to Mount Vernon during that period involving the fight for a new constitution except evocative entries in Washington's diary noting, "Home all day with Mr. Madison." As Leibiger notes, these brief phrases reveal a great deal. It was truly remarkable for Washington, a man of strict habit, to forgo riding his lands and stay home to commune with a guest. Perhaps part of the reason for their compatibility was that Madison was always comfortable in seeing Washington as the senior partner. His ego would not get in the way of utilizing Washington's leadership and stature to achieve their common goals.

Washington and Madison's partnership ripened into as close a connection as the general ever permitted, prompting the perceptive Gouverneur Morris to observe that Washington was "immeasurably attached" to Madison. Besides helping to birth the Constitution, Madison struggled to persuade Virginia to ratify it to the point of debilitating himself. In a touching and illustrative letter, Washington, never known for urging relaxation when the nation's fate was at stake, uncharacteristically but enthusiastically pleaded with Madison to take a few days' vacation at Mount Vernon to rest and regain his strength. "Moderate exercise, and books occasionally, with the mind unbent, will be your best restoratives." The letter ends, "I can assure you that no one will be happier in your company than your sincere affectionate servant, George Washington." This may be the only occasion on record where Washington urged a colleague to take time off.

At the close of Washington's first term, Madison was among those begging him to sign on for another four years. However, when in late 1793 Jefferson resigned as secretary of state and Washington asked Madison to step in, he refused, no more eager than Jefferson to implement policies he did not support. This rejection marked a turning point not only in Washington's presidency but in the friendship. Madison's demurral left Washington complaining that those on whose aid he had counted were leaving him in the lurch. For the moment, the friendship held, however. George and Martha Washington were instrumental in the events leading up to Madison's marriage to the vivacious Dolley Payne Todd.

The break, like the others, came in the aftermath of the signing of the Jay Treaty, as much anathema to Madison as to Jefferson and Monroe, and for basically the same reasons. The Senate narrowly ratified the treaty by a 20–10 vote, but the terms of the treaty called for actions that required money, which could only come with approval of the House of Representatives. In the House, Madison led the Republican opposition, which included angry assertions that chicanery was afoot and demands to see the correspondence regarding the treaty. In a major speech, Madison argued that the commerce clause of the Constitution empowered the House to investigate and approve or disapprove portions of treaties addressing commerce, and thus it had the right to scrutinize materials connected to the treaty. In a stinging rejoinder, Washington, citing executive privilege, refused to hand over any documents at all. Meeting the Father of the Constitution head on, the Father of the Country pointed out that the Constitution assigned treaty-making power to the president and Senate alone, and not to the House of Representatives.

When the lower chamber tried to block the appropriations necessary to implement the treaty, a major showdown between Washington and Madison ensued. Ultimately, after much debate and maneuvering, the House of Representatives, by a vote of 51–48, passed the necessary appropriations, and the Jay Treaty was finally safe. Not only did Madison end up losing this fight over the Jay Treaty, which weakened his influence in the House of Representatives, but he also lost his friendship with Washington.

Certainly, political disagreements had damaged their friendship, as partisanship was increasing at a dangerous rate and affecting all participants, including Washington and Madison. Nevertheless, I believe the root cause of the permanent break was that Washington, already angry, believed that Madison accused him of usurping powers not granted to him in the Constitution. Somewhat along the lines of being called an "apostate," this was something that the supersensitive president could neither accept nor forgive. Thus, while the president did invite Madison to dinner twice in 1796 as part of a larger congressional group and did ask him to help Lafayette's son, who had fled to America after his father was arrested, the relationship was essentially severed. Never again did he ask Madison's advice or invite him to family dinners. Never again would Madison visit Mount Vernon. Indeed, in his post-presidential correspondence, Washington never even once specifically mentioned Madison in his letters or writings—apparently simply lumping him together with the radical Republicans. (In contrast, Madison continued to admire Washington throughout the remainder of Madison's long life, which did not end until 1836.) To my knowledge, the only extant specific reference to Madison from Washington in the aftermath of his presidency came the day before his death when, as mentioned previously, he criticized Madison for backing James Monroe for governor of Virginia. It was a sad ending for such an important and intimate relationship.

In this litany of friendships forged and undone, two themes emerge. One is George Washington's extreme sensitivity to criticism and to any perceived attack on his character or the purity of his motives. The other is the extent to which his philosophy of governance and his vision of America stood starkly apart from those of the fellow Virginians with whom he severed his relationships. George Washington was a supreme nationalist who envisioned a great future for a powerful "United States"—with the emphasis on the word "united." It is noteworthy that in 1792, Edward Thornton, the perceptive British ambassador to the United States, observed that President Washington was less popular in Virginia than in any of the other states in the union. Edmund Randolph shared with Jefferson that Washington confided in him that if there were ever to be a division between the North and South, Washington would align himself with the North. William Abbot called George Washington the least Virginian of all the great Virginia leaders. In truth, George Washington was an American first, a Virginian second.

6

Lives of Their Own

A CLOSER LOOK AT SOME OF GEORGE WASHINGTON'S ENSLAVED WORKERS

As GEORGE WASHINGTON's life was ebbing away on December 14, 1799, there were times when there were more black people than white people in the room with him. This fact indicates how deeply Washington's life was intertwined with slavery. He became a slaveholder at age eleven when his father, Augustine, died and left him ten enslaved Africans. Over the next fifty-six years, Washington owned or managed about 670 slaves. He spent more time managing bondsmen and bondswomen than he did supervising soldiers or government officials. At the time of his death, Mount Vernon was home to 317 enslaved workers—roughly 90 percent of the estate's residents.

In the present day, people seem particularly prone to the joys of what Philip Roth called the "ecstasy of sanctimony." We feel good and morally superior by condemning the moral failings of others, past and present. Thus, George Washington's connection to slavery blemishes his historical reputation. How, we are asked, can one admire any man willing to claim ownership of other persons? That alone should disqualify even a Founding Father from respect and admiration.

Yet a fair reading of history requires that along with damning facts we consider intangibles. We must be on guard against the fallacy of "presentism." When one takes into account that George Washington's parents, Bible, church, government, and societal leaders all gave sanction to the system of human slavery, it should not be surprising that George Washington would initially accept it uncritically as simply a fact of life. How could he do otherwise? The greater surprise is that, given this background, George Washington in the course of his life dramatically changed his view of slavery. For pragmatic, political, and philosophical reasons, he became increasingly critical of the "peculiar institution" and in his final will and testament acted to set free all of his own enslaved workers. He was the only Founding Father to do so. (It should be noted that Washington by law was not able to free those owned by the Custis estate.)

What of those enslaved hundreds who made Mount Vernon hum with industry? Can we summon these people in terms more complex than a list of names? For a few bondsmen and bondswomen the answer is yes. Among his many habits, Washington was a compulsive record-keeper. That fact, augmented by other related material, allows us to do more than simply imagine the lives and views of some of Washington's enslaved workers.

Of course, the information I present is fragmentary and incomplete and open to interpretation. With few exceptions, the material comes only from slave owners, not the enslaved individuals. A skeptic might shrug and assign the task of rendering this information three-dimensionally to a novelist rather than a historian—and there is much material worthy of historical novels. Yet, there is nothing wrong with historians speculating, as long as they make clear that such is the case. In my own narrative portraits, I often engage in informed speculation. However, I make no claim that these representations are complete or, for that matter, totally accurate. The evidence is simply too fragmentary to guarantee certitude.

That said, a treasure trove of information exists to pursue insights into the lives of some of the men and women who lived and worked in bondage at Mount Vernon. Examining these lives makes clear slavery's cruelty and, I hope, confers some understanding of their lives and the loss of identity and burden of bias they endured. No doubt, some of the vignettes reflect poorly on George Washington. Others surprised me because they did not fit preconceived notions regarding slavery. Most people don't envision that enslaved workers might own guns, be overseers, negotiate deals with their master, loan their owner their boat, return money to them, or directly threaten to physically abuse a white person who challenged them. The true story of slavery at Mount Vernon, while tragic in the extreme, is more complex and convoluted than we realize. Let's take a look.

Christopher Sheels

George Washington made his last known request on this earth to his personal body servant, Christopher Sheels, who had been standing alongside his master's bed the whole day. Washington bade Christopher sit, no doubt a welcome respite. That December night, Christopher, born about 1775, was still a young man. His grandmother Doll was the main cook and the matriarch of one of the largest families within Mount Vernon's enslaved community. His mother was Alce (not Alice), and her sister, Lucy, married Frank Lee, Mount Vernon's butler and the younger brother of William "Billy" Lee, whom Christopher had replaced as Washington's personal body servant. His father most likely was Christopher Sheldes, a white wagon-driver working around Mount Vernon at the time of Christopher's birth.

Two strikingly different vignettes trace the complicated relationship between Washington and Christopher and hint at each man's character. The first was an episode in 1797 in which a supposedly rabid dog attacked Christopher. The black youth's injuries concerned Washington enough that he may have fallen for a quack treatment. As Dr. James Craik was treating Christopher's injuries with mercury and various salves, Washington heard of a Dr. Stoy in Lebanon, Pennsylvania, who was "celebrated for curing persons bitten by mad animals." Washington not only allowed Christopher to travel roughly 300 miles to see Dr. Stoy, but also, to cover the young man's expenses, Washington entrusted him with twenty-five dollars, which, in the eighteenth century, was a very significant sum. In a letter to Dr. Stoy that he sent with Christopher, Washington wrote, "For besides the call of Humanity, I am particularly anxious for His cure, He being my own Body servant." Although Christopher could possibly have made a run for it in Pennsylvania, where antislavery feeling was strong, he came home to Mount Vernon. Cured, he declared he no longer feared a rabid dog's bite. Interestingly, Washington noted in his ledger that Christopher gave him back twelve dollars from the twenty-five dollars he had advanced him.

Yet, two years later, Christopher did plot to run away. There is an incident recounted by GW's nephew, Lawrence Lewis, which might have played some part in his decision. Lewis recounts that at dawn GW would ring a bell and summon a servant to bring his boots. (The servant is not identified, but it was most likely his valet, and based on the time Lewis was at Mount Vernon, it would have been Christopher.) Washington would silently inspect the boots. If they were not sufficiently cleaned, Lewis recounted, "the servant got them about his head but without the General betraying any excitement beyond the effort of the moment—in a minute afterwards he was no less calm & collected than usual." How demeaning it must have been to be on the receiving end of those blows.

Christopher and his new wife, a mulatto woman from Roger West's neighboring plantation, apparently schemed to slip upriver to Alexandria and catch an outbound ship. Alas, Christopher apparently dropped a note from his wife discussing the getaway plan. Washington found the message and through his close friend Dr. James Craik alerted Roger West, foiling the escape. The extant record offers no hint of Washington's reaction to learning that his personal body servant, on whom he had spent considerable money and to whom he had extended favors (including at one point while president giving him a "salary" of four dollars a month), wanted to run away. Most likely, he was disappointed but not surprised. Whatever his thoughts were, I believe it is significant that George Washington kept Christopher as his closest personal servant, and Christopher was at his post that fatal December 14. I wonder what Christopher was thinking as he removed the keys and personal effects from his dead master's pockets and gave them to Washington's secretary, Tobias Lear. Sadly, although we know Christopher was inherited by George Washington Parke Custis, at this point he drops out of the historical record.

William "Billy" Lee

And what of the man Christopher replaced, William "Billy" Lee? In his final will and testament, Washington gave ultimate freedom to all the enslaved workers he personally owned, but he conferred immediate freedom upon only one person—William Lee. In his will, Washington referred to him as "my mulatto man William" but noted that he went by the name William Lee. He was better known as "Billy," and one can understand his desire to have a full name and not simply a nickname. After the war he was called Will, which is how I will refer to him.

There is no authenticated image of William Lee, George Washington's personal body servant for over twenty years and the most famous enslaved man of the eighteenth century. (Courtesy of Mount Vernon Ladies' Association)

Will became Washington's property in 1768 when he paid a premium price to purchase him and his younger brother, Frank, from Mary Smith Ball Lee, widow of Colonel John Lee of Westmoreland County. Describing the brothers as being "mulatto" indicates that their father was white, although his identity is unknown. (In *George Washington's Mulatto Man—Who Was Billy Lee?*, James Thompson claims Will and Frank were sons of George William Fairfax and Sally Cary Fairfax, a preposterously speculative and groundless thesis.)

Will soon became Washington's personal body servant and continued so for approximately the next twenty years. One contemporary describes him as being "always at his [GW's] side." Probably Will, who ultimately became the most famous slave of the eighteenth century, spent more time with the great man than anyone else with the exception of Washington's wife, Martha. Will's story is both tragic and inspiring, and one can only imagine what tales he could have told.

Will managed to win his master's affection and admiration. Washington undoubtedly admired Will's horsemanship, which seems comparable to his own, and George Washington was known as the best horseman in Virginia. As Washington's huntsman, Will was intimately involved in the general's favorite sport, fox hunting, and Will kept up, gallop for gallop and jump for jump. George Washington Parke Custis, Martha's grandson raised at Mount Vernon by George and Martha, vividly described the hunts. "Will, the huntsman[,] . . . rode a horse called Chinkling, a surprising leaper, and made very much like its rider, low, but sturdy, and of great bone and muscle. Will had but one order, which was to keep with the hounds; and, mounted on Chinkling, a French horn at his back, throwing himself almost at length on the animal, with his spur in flank, this fearless horseman would rush, at full speed, through brake or tangled wood, in a style at which modern huntsmen would stand aghast."

Will is best known as Washington's constant companion throughout the eight-year struggle for American independence. We admire the fact and the idea of Washington bidding farewell to Martha as he left Mount Vernon to fight for American rights; few think of William Lee bidding his wife and child farewell in the same cause—in Will's case, never to see his family again, because during the war the two either died or ran away. The historical record is blank.

Numerous accounts from the war place Will often at the general's side, whether holding the reins of Washington's horse as he broke up a fight near Boston or replacing a horse that had fallen under the general during the Battle of Monmouth. The fact that Will was entrusted with the general's spyglass suggests that he was readily available to Washington during battle. At a review of troops for Indian allies, James Thacher wrote, "His Excellency, with his usual dignity, was followed by his mulatto servant, Bill, riding a magnificent gray steed." If Will had been a white man, he would have had an honored place in American history because of his close proximity to George Washington during the most exciting periods of his career.

A careful reading of Loyalist Joshua Hett Smith's account of his incarceration in the aftermath of Benedict Arnold's treason sheds a ray of light on Will's role during the war. Smith, a lawyer, had made Lafayette look bad during a court-martial proceeding, resulting in ribbing from his fellow officers that annoyed Lafayette. The interesting point is that

Smith, kept in solitary confinement, only learned about Lafayette's discomfort "from one of General Washington's domestics, who daily brought me provisions, and who was a confidential servant of the General." The confidential servant was almost certainly Will. A few points can be drawn from this small vignette. Will was not excluded from the banter of Washington's top military subordinates. He was trusted enough to be sent alone to an important prisoner, and, finally, Will felt comfortable enough to discuss a sensitive subject with a man of Smith's caliber and position.

Will passed through the war relatively unscathed, but he was not so lucky in the postwar years. During a surveying trip after the war, he slipped on some stones and fell, breaking or dislocating his patella, or knee pan as it was described at the time. Washington had to borrow a sled to get him home, "as he could neither Walk, stand, or ride." Three years later, while on an errand to the post office in Alexandria, Will fell a second time, this time landing on the other knee pan and breaking it, rendering him virtually a cripple.

The evidence is clear, at least by the prevailing standards of master-slave relationship, that Washington was uncommonly attentive toward Will and what he wanted. Two examples illustrate this point. Will had married a free black woman, Margaret Thomas (also referred to as Peggy Lee), who had been part of Washington's military household as a seamstress and washerwoman, and he asked permission to bring her to Mount Vernon. Washington's response is illustrative. Declaring that he "never wished to see her more," he confessed he could not refuse Will's request "(if it can be complied with on reasonable terms) as he has lived with me so long and followed my fortunes through the War with fidelity." Sadly, like Will's first wife, Margaret disappears from the historical record, and there is no evidence that she ever arrived at Mount Vernon.

Even with bad knees, Will wanted very much to attend the general as he traveled to New York to begin his first term as president of the new nation. A skeptical Washington reluctantly acceded. "If he is still anxious to come on here the President would gratify him altho' he will be troublesome," Tobias Lear wrote to the agent caring for Will, who had managed to get only as far as Philadelphia before his knees gave way. Lear continued, "He has been an old & faithful Servant. This is enough for the President to gratify him in every reasonable wish." After being fitted with steel braces, Will managed to make it to New

York but was unable to perform even minimal duties. Within the year he was back at Mount Vernon, where William Lee's story ends, and badly. He lost his position as body servant, his legs gave out, he took to drink, and he finished life as a shoemaker living in an outbuilding on the Washington plantation.

The exact when and why of his alcoholism is uncertain—chronic pain, perhaps, or disappointment at being sidelined except to make appearances for visitors to Mount Vernon wanting to see the servant who had been the general's body man during the war. George Washington Parke Custis provides a picture of Will meeting the old veterans who would usually leave a token of remembrance with him. "Ah, colonel, I am a poor cripple; can't ride now, so I make shoes and think of the old times; the general often stops by here, to inquire if I want anything. I want for nothing, thank God, but the use of my limbs." Sadly, in time, Will's alcoholism led to delirium tremens—"the shakes"—and ultimately efforts to relieve them by means such as bleeding failed. While many accounts, following the lead of Benson Lossing's 1850s version, put his death around 1828, the evidence is clear that in fact he died in 1810 at around the age of fifty. The general had provided a small annuity for Will, and the executor's account lists regular payments until the January 31, 1810, entry: "Paid Dr. Dangerfield for attending Old Billy Lee $5.00," followed soon after by "a charge for a coffin." His passing went unremarked upon in the press.

Ona Judge

George Washington granted William Lee his freedom, but two of the general's other most personal enslaved workers, Ona Judge (actually owned by the Custis estate) and Hercules, seized freedom for themselves. In recent years, Ona Judge, partly because of the extant material surrounding her life, has received more attention than any of Washington's other enslaved workers. Ona was called Oney when she belonged to the Washingtons, but she later called herself Ona, perhaps symbolizing her escape from Mount Vernon and a life in bondage. She was only about twenty-two in May 1796 when she suddenly and unexpectedly absconded from the president's house in Philadelphia.

Ona's mother, Betty, was a seamstress at the plantation, and her father was Andrew Judge, a white indentured tailor from England, who made the uniform that Washington wore to the Second Continental Congress. Ona was so light of skin that acquaintances described her as "nearly white." Ona, who began attending Martha Washington at ten, took up her mother's craft, in time "being Perfect a Mistress of her needle." She served Mrs. Washington in much the same manner as William Lee served the general.

Ona's escape shocked both of the Washingtons and led to unfortunate reactions. They simply could not fathom why she would run off. In Washington's words, she left "without the least provocation." From his perspective it appeared to be ungrateful behavior on the part of a young woman whom he and his wife had treated more "like a child than a servant." In Philadelphia, the Washingtons had on multiple occasions given Ona money for theater or circus tickets or to buy shoes and a bonnet. Surprisingly, Washington's account book shows that Ona, like Christopher, for a time apparently received a monthly "salary" of four dollars.

It may well grate on contemporary ears to hear that the president expected Ona to be grateful for her situation but, from Washington's patriarchal, class-tinged perspective, his vexation was justified. In this case his upbringing and caste simply blinded him to larger realities. "Oney" fled and became Ona, trading the certainty of a comparatively comfortable bondage for all the risks and rewards that autonomy conferred. As she later expressed it, "Although well enough used as to work and living, [I] did not want to be a slave always." The recent deaths of her mother and half-brother, Austin, weakened Ona's ties to Mount Vernon, but her decision to run away was apparently prompted by learning that she would be given to one of Martha's granddaughters, the mercurial Eliza Custis, who had recently entered into what turned out to be an unhappy marriage with Thomas Law.

Ona's escape doubtless was made easier by the liberty she enjoyed to walk about the city. She later said she had made friends with "the colored population of the city," and in the Philadelphia of the 1790s most African American residents were free. She somehow managed to travel to New York City, where a sympathetic ship captain, John Bowles, gave her passage on his ship, the *Nancy,* to New Hampshire, a state with a small black population and virtually no slaves. There Ona would begin her precarious new life.

In a classic display of the reasoning of an aggrieved master, the president explained Ona's flight by insisting that a Frenchman had seduced her into running away. No evidence supports this supposition, but a Philadelphia newspaper does refer to one "Wm Boussaret," a Frenchman who worked in a tobacco shop in that city and who ran away at about the same time, likely the basis for Washington's view, which he never changed.

Frankly, the president's protracted negotiations to retrieve Ona, extending even to the year of his death, do not reflect well on him, although Martha's intense desire to reclaim Ona certainly influenced his continued efforts to recapture her. GW had Frederick Kitt, his hired steward, immediately post a runaway notice and offer a ten-dollar reward for her return. In the runaway notice, Ona was described as "a light Mulatto girl, much freckled, with very black eyes, and bushy black hair," who was of medium height, "slender, and delicately made." It also noted that "she has many changes of very good clothes" but added, in an interesting and possibly revealing afterthought, "they are not sufficiently recollected to describe."

Unable to capture her in Philadelphia, by coincidental circumstances the president had the opportunity to bring her back to Mount Vernon from Portsmouth, New Hampshire, where Ona lived with a free black family and sought to support herself with her skills as a seamstress. By chance, Ona soon encountered Elizabeth Langdon, the nineteen-year-old daughter of one of Washington's close friends, Senator John Langdon, who recognized Ona from her various visits with the president and his family in Philadelphia. Having learned where she was, the president used his influence, improperly if the truth be told, writing privately to his secretary of the treasury, Oliver Wolcott, asking him to enlist the aid of the customs collector, Joseph Whipple, at Portsmouth "to seize, and put her on board a vessel" bound either for Philadelphia or Alexandria, for which Washington would pay all costs.

Whipple soon found himself in a tricky position. After meeting with Ona, he learned, as he wrote his superior, that Ona had not been enticed away by a Frenchman or anyone else, but rather "a thirst for

Ten Dollars Reward.

ABSCONDED from the household of the President of the United States, on Saturday afternoon, ONEY JUDGE, a light Mulatto girl, much freckled, with very black eyes, and bushy black hair.—She is of middle stature, but slender and delicately made, about 20 years of age. She has many changes of very good clothes of all sorts, but they are not sufficiently recollected to describe.

As there was no suspicion of her going off, and it happened without the least provocation, it is not easy to conjecture whither she is gone—or fully, what her design is, but she may attempt to escape by water, all masters of vessels and others are cautioned against receiving her on board, altho' she only, and probably will endeavour to pass for a free woman, and it is said has, wherewithal to pay her passage.

Ten dollars will be paid to any person, (white or black) who will bring her home; if taken in the city, or on board any vessel in the harbour; and a further reasonable sum if apprehended and brought home, from a greater distance, and in proportion to the distance.

FRED KITT, Steward.

complete freedom" had been her motive for absconding. Whipple did write that Ona expressed "great affection and reverence" for the Washingtons and would return if she could be assured of her freedom upon their deaths, but she would rather suffer death than return to permanent slavery.

The president would not negotiate with runaways or give any special privileges. Think of the bad example it would set! Granting her freedom, he declared, would only "discontent her fellow servants," reward bad behavior, and set a "dangerous precedent." Washington wanted her returned, forcibly if necessary. Historian Henry Wiencek notes that the president's actions violated the Fugitive Slave Act that he had signed into law. That law required the slave owner or the owner's representative to appear before a federal or state magistrate and provide evidence of ownership before attempting to transport a fugitive slave to another state. Washington wanted the transfer to be done surreptitiously, so as not to incite mob action. Ever attentive to his reputation, the president wished above all to avoid public embarrassment. If that meant he could not retrieve Ona, then so be it.

Thus, Ona became free. Early in 1797 she married a mulatto sailor, Jack Staines, and later that year or in 1798 she bore the first of the couple's three children. Interestingly, as late as 1799, Washington, on learning that his nephew, Burwell Bassett, was going to Portsmouth, made a final attempt to reclaim Ona, explaining to Bassett that such an action would please his aunt. (The evidence indicates that Ona's escape grated more on Martha than it did on her husband.) Apparently, Bassett's host, the strongly antislavery senator and now governor, John Langdon, warned Ona of the danger, and she once again avoided capture. There seemed to be a certain amount of poetic justice in this development as it was because of his daughter that Ona's presence in New Hampshire was discovered in the first place. No efforts were made to reclaim her after Washington's death.

In the mid-1840s, two abolitionist newspapers carried reminiscences by Ona Judge, the only eighteenth-century Virginia slave to leave her own very brief quasi-memoir. By then literate and a Baptist, Ona had harsh words for the life imposed on her at Mount Vernon, where she felt stunted both intellectually and spiritually. "She never received the least mental or moral instruction of any kind while she remained in Washington's family. . . . The stories of Washington's piety and prayers, so far as she ever saw or heard while she was his slave, have no foundation. Card-playing and wine-drinking were the business at his parties, and he had more of such company Sundays than on any other day." Now old and having outlived her husband and all three of their children, Ona was alone and registered officially as a pauper, but she nevertheless told her interviewers that she had no regrets. "No, I am free, and have, I trust, been made a child of God by [that] means." Ona Judge died on February 25, 1848, in Greenland, New Hampshire, almost fifty years after her former master.

Hercules Posey

In a letter, the president described Ona as "simple and inoffensive." It is hard to imagine Washington saying the same of his slave Hercules, Mount Vernon's flamboyant and admired chef. Recently discovered evidence about Hercules's escape intensifies his compelling and poignant story. Purchased in 1767 from John Posey, whose last name he apparently kept, Hercules fathered at least four children, one of whom was a dwarf. Upon his spouse's death in 1787, Martha Washington, recognizing Hercules's special role at Mount Vernon, directed that he be given three bottles of rum, presumably to share with mourners.

Hercules was about forty years of age when the president picked him to work in the kitchen in Philadelphia. Washington had objected to the white kitchen personnel at the presidential residence in New York as "dirty figures," who would "not be a pleasant sight in view (as the kitchen always will be)." While Hercules was not officially in charge of the kitchen (a white man was), he nevertheless played an important role.

There is little question that Hercules was a clever man, an excellent chef, and something of a character. He was known for his attention to sartorial detail in cloaking a physique that apparently matched his name. According to George Washington Parke Custis, "his linen was of exceptionable whiteness and quality, then black silk shorts, ditto waistcoat, ditto stockings, shoes highly polished, with large buckles covering a considerable part of the foot, blue cloth coat with velvet collar and bright metal buttons, a long watch-chain dangling from his fob, a cocked-hat, and gold-headed cane completed the grand costume of the celebrated dandy." Hercules's dress emphasized his individuality, advertising that in at least one aspect of life he was in control.

A talented manipulator, Hercules was one of the few slaves to wheedle privileges from Washington. One concession was permission to collect, sell, and keep the proceeds from bones, feathers, fat, and other kitchen "leftovers." Recycling might net Hercules as much as 200 dollars a year. And he managed to convince a reluctant president to allow him to bring his troublesome teenage son, Richmond, to Philadelphia as a scullion and chimney sweep. Additionally, Hercules was given leave to wander the city and was occasionally given tickets to the theater or circus.

When the nation's capital moved to Philadelphia, the president had to cope with Pennsylvania's Gradual Abolition Act, which allowed slaves brought to live in Pennsylvania for more than six months to claim their freedom. Washington dodged this stricture, secretly and perhaps illegally, by shifting his slaves into and out of Pennsylvania, confounding that six-month limit. "I wish to have it accomplished under the pretext that may deceive both them and the public," he wrote to his secretary, Tobias Lear. "This advice may be known to none but yourself and Mrs. Washington."

Apparently, Hercules learned that he was to be sent back to Mount Vernon and, according to Lear, took offense at the notion that Washington thought he might abandon his position as the president's chef. Lear told Washington that Hercules was "mortified to the last degree to think that a suspicion could be entertained of his fidelity or attachment to you." Lear emphasized his personal credence in Hercules's assertion. Was Hercules sincere or just playing along until the time was ripe for his flight? While we can't know for sure, Hercules may well in fact have been sincere, especially due to recently discovered information, namely that Hercules did not run away in Philadelphia, which was comparatively easy to do, but rather from Mount Vernon, a much more difficult proposition. Hercules was at the plantation because Washington, having moved his household back home from Philadelphia for a few months, did not bring the chef or his son, Richmond, back to Philadelphia for the final months of his second term as president. Richmond had been caught stealing money—perhaps, Washington may have thought, to fund a getaway for himself and his father.

At any rate, Hercules, according to farm reports and a November 1796 memo from Washington to his farm manager, was relegated to hard labor at Mount Vernon—digging clay for brickmaking, spreading dung, grubbing bushes, and smashing and grinding cobbles into sand to be mixed with paint to coat Mount Vernon's wooden exteriors to imitate stone. The reason for this apparent demotion is unclear. We know Washington expected that upon retiring from office Hercules would be his cook at Mount Vernon. In the interim, Washington likely felt it logical for his chef and other house servants, rather than idling, to be usefully employed. If so, the president badly misread Hercules, who had pledged and demonstrated his loyalty. How galling it must have been. Hercules was a proud man. After pledging his loyalty and making no effort to escape, he now found himself in an intolerable situation. Probably, he wished that he had taken flight while he was in Philadelphia, where there was a large network of free blacks and much abolitionist sentiment.

With his decision to abscond on February 22, Washington's final birthday as president, Hercules vanishes from the historical record. Or does he? He certainly vanished from his pursuers and was clever enough to avoid detection. The president unwittingly gave grudging recognition to his cleverness by warning those seeking to apprehend him that they must do it by stealth, "for if Hercules was to get the least hint of the design he would elude all your vigilance."

There has been considerable speculation that Hercules might have made it to Europe. There is a portrait, which came from an English estate, housed in a Spanish museum and attributed to Gilbert Stuart that claims to be of the cook of George Washington. That would be a wonderfully fitting end to the story of Hercules, but alas, while fine in a work of fiction, there is simply no validity to the widely repeated claim. At a 2017 day-long study of the painting by experts at Mount Vernon, the conclusion was unanimous. The painting was not the work of Gilbert Stuart. More surprising, the subject was not even a chef—and obviously not Hercules. The hat, perceived to be a chef's toque for as long as the painting has been known to modern viewers, was in fact not a cook's hat at all, but a Caribbean headdress. According to art historian Dorinda Evans, a Gilbert Stuart scholar and professor emerita at Emory University, no American cook in the colonies dressed like that, noting that the now familiar chef's toque did not appear until the 1820s. "It's a fantasized image of what people want, because people want to have an image of Hercules. And people see the things they want to see."

Although modern scholarship has discovered who Hercules wasn't, it may have also discovered what in fact happened to him. Apparently, he lived the rest of his life hiding in plain sight. Researchers have recently discovered a New York City death record for a "Hercules Posey," a black laborer from Virginia, born in 1748, who died of consumption in New York City on May 15, 1812. With that many facts connected together, it is hard not to believe that this is in fact George Washington's famous chef.

Shortly after Hercules made his escape, a French visitor to Mount Vernon asked his six-year-old daughter if she was sad that her father had gone away. Her response was that she was "very glad, because he is free now."

Sambo Anderson

Another of Washington's enslaved workers, perhaps as colorful as Hercules, was Sambo Anderson, who claimed to be a son of an African king, had several wives, wore large gold earrings, had two or three ritual scars cut high on each cheek, and was elaborately tattooed. "Sambo" was a name popular in Africa, and it is noteworthy that he kept it rather than becoming one of the myriad slaves named "Sam." When a Royal Navy warship came up the Potomac River to Mount Vernon in 1781, Sambo absconded along with sixteen other slaves. Details are unclear, but after Yorktown, Sambo was located in Philadelphia and returned to Washington. He remained a slave at Mount Vernon until freed by the terms of the general's will.

Sambo was a carpenter trained by William Sears, a skilled English-born craftsman who worked at Gunston Hall and Pohick Church, as well as at Mount Vernon. Sambo worked on all the Washington barns, including the famous sixteen-sided specimen that has been reconstructed. According to later recollections, Sambo shared an interesting vignette involving Washington as a builder. As Sambo was working on a corncrib, Washington came by and observed that the studding was not plumb and that Sambo must redo it. To Sambo's eye the studs seemed straight, but he remarked of his master, "His eye was a perfect plumb ball." Sambo admitted that Washington's desire to be so exact was exasperating. He described Washington as "very particular and the most correct man who ever lived." Sambo recollected that "if a rail, a clapboard, or a stone was permitted to remain out of its place," his master "complained, sometimes in language of severity." Washington asked Sambo's permission to use his small boat (something one would not expect a slave to own) and always returned that craft to the spot from which he had taken it, even if a tidal change meant the president had to drag the boat twenty yards.

Sambo may have been able to afford a boat thanks to personal industry. A skillful beekeeper, over the years he sold his master at least fifteen gallons of honey and four pounds of beeswax. Additionally, Sambo owned a gun and was an excellent hunter. In a ledger entry, Washington noted that he purchased from Sambo, for 6 shillings, 3 pence, five dozen birds—probably canvasback ducks. Sambo also bought goods from his master; the record shows him purchasing a barrel of fine flour and 162 pounds of pork.

Since few of George Washington's slaves owned firearms, Sambo may well have been involved in an interesting incident that occurred in 1787, uncharacteristic of interactions between bondsmen and whites not their owners. The year before, Washington had placed a notice in the newspaper forbidding hunting or fowling on his land without his written permission, which he was very reluctant to grant.

A letter buried in the *Washington Papers* explains what happened, at least from the author's biased perspective. He and a friend had been, with others, sailing on the Potomac when winds led them to land on the general's property. They disembarked, carrying their weapons lest the guns be stolen. Shortly afterward, three blacks, one of whom was armed (Sambo?), approached and, seeing a squirrel, suggested they shoot it, which his companion did. The blacks then led the pair to a section of woods where they said many squirrels could be found. As the white men were climbing a fence, the blacks knocked them both to the ground. The Africans seized the whites' weapons "with more barbarity than any highwayman would have done." They then ran off, declaring that they had just gained ten pounds. I interpret this passage to surmise that the letter writer and his companion were hunting illegally on Washington's land, but I was surprised to read of an attack on whites by black slaves. Apparently, they were emboldened by the fact that Washington had given "strict, and positive orders to all my people . . . if they hear a Gun fired upon my Land to go immediately in pursuit of it."

Once manumitted in 1801, Sambo supported himself by hunting wild game, which he sold to hotels and "the most respectable families" in Alexandria. This income allowed him to buy a daughter, two grandchildren, and three great-grandchildren out of bondage. Perhaps indicative of his feelings for his former master, Sambo was one of eleven blacks who voluntarily worked on the president's new tomb in 1831, the tomb that remains intact today. Following Nat Turner's rebellion in Southampton County, Virginia, in 1831, fearful authorities confiscated guns from many blacks around the state, including Sambo. Much to his delight, his weapon was eventually returned.

In old age, Uncle Sambo, as whites called him, found himself free but also impoverished. According to the recollections of a white acquaintance, Sambo considered himself better off in bondage, when he "had a good kind master to look after all my wants, but now I have no one to care for me." His statement contrasts so sharply with what Ona Judge said that one wonders to what degree Ona and Sambo were saying what they thought their interviewers wanted to hear—Ona to a northern abolitionist and Sambo to a white southerner.

Charlotte

Among Mount Vernon's enslaved workers' stories, Charlotte's is one of the most interesting and surprising. Charlotte was a household seamstress of considerable talent. Martha had a seamstress in Philadelphia, but when important garments needed repair she sent them home to Mount Vernon so Charlotte could do the work. In a letter to her niece Fanny, Mrs. Washington explained why. "She knows how work should be done."

Almost certainly a powerful and imposing figure, Charlotte chafed under the burden of bondage, seeking to make the best of a bad situation. There were often complaints about her shirking her work or feigning illness. For example, Washington's farm book for April 1797 notes that Charlotte spent eleven straight days in bed following the birth of one of her children, which seems like a longer time than normal, although slaves were regularly given time off after the birth of a child. On another occasion, Washington informed farm manager William Pearce that Charlotte had been reported sick for weeks, adding that Mrs. Washington wanted Pearce to check on her and decide whether to summon Dr. Craik. Martha griped that Charlotte feigned illness and would "lay herself up for as little as anyone will." Mrs. Washington commented that her seamstress was "so indolent that she will do nothing but what she is told." She closed, apparently without a wisp of irony, that, if allowed to be idle, a woman like Charlotte "will in a little time do nothing but work for herself." Surprise.

Charlotte figures in two fascinating and revealing incidents documented in the *Washington Papers*. In 1786, Charles MacIver, a Highlander and lecturer but not of gentry status, wrote to Washington describing a recent incident involving his wife. Two years before, evidently a white seamstress had stolen several of Mrs. MacIver's dresses. By chance, in the heart of Alexandria, Mrs. MacIver came upon Charlotte, likely intoxicated, wearing what seemed to be one of the stolen garments. Mrs. MacIver spoke to the slave about the dress and got a surprise. "My wife wanted to take a nearer view of the gown," MacIver wrote. "But Mrs. Charlotte, countenanced by another black woman, to whom she appealed as a Lady of Character and Distinction, abused my wife very grossly and threatened to beat her; nor would she demean herself so much as to be seen walking with such a Creature as my wife." In a postscript, the husband repeated, "Charlotte threatened to flog my Wife, not without abusive and contemptuous epithets." A crisis was averted only after "Mrs. Herbert politely called in my wife from such an unequal Contest."

The scene this letter paints is startling. Accepted wisdom would lead one to expect a bondswoman accused in public by a white woman of wearing a stolen garment to respond mildly, if not with slavish deference, whether or not the charge was valid, but such was not the case in this instance.

The second incident confirms that Charlotte was no shrinking violet and that while she might have been enslaved, she would stand up for herself if she felt aggrieved. During the January 1793 hog slaughter, undertaken while the Washingtons were in Philadelphia, Charlotte feuded with Washington's farm manager, Anthony Whiting. The episode began when Charlotte had Davy, a slave who was the overseer at Muddy Hole Farm, the smallest of Mount Vernon's five farms, ask Whiting on her behalf for a "spear rib as she longed for it."

Whiting did not give Davy a rib for Charlotte that Thursday. The manager later told Washington by letter that he had withheld the meat because he "thought it a piece of impudence in her which she has a great share of." Two days later, Whiting did send ribs to every woman in the slave quarters, including Charlotte. Apparently insulted by Whiting's earlier snub, she confronted him. "Affronted I suppose at my not sending it on Thursday," the manager told the general, Charlotte followed Whiting into his house, threw the proffered "spear rib" on the floor, and declared "she wanted none of my Meat & was in short very impudent." Whiting used a hickory switch as a riding crop, and he answered Charlotte's reproof with "a very good whipping," augmented by more corporal punishment over subsequent days. Charlotte continued to defy Whiting. Since then, he told his employer, she had not done any work "under a pretense of her finger receiving a blow and was swelled."

Whiting closed his report by writing that more of the same would be necessary, and that he was "determined to lower her Spirit or skin her Back." George Washington wrote back that he considered Whiting's treatment of Charlotte to be "very proper." "If She, or any other of the Servants will not do their duty by fair means, or are impertinent, correction (as the only alternative) must be administered." Outraged by her mistreatment, Charlotte stated that no one had whipped her in fourteen years and threatened to tell Mrs. Washington of her mistreatment at Whiting's hands. Apparently, Whiting had composed his account in part to get his side to the Washingtons before Charlotte presented hers.

About five months after this incident, Whiting died. The president, who was in Philadelphia at the time, initially praised the dead man, saying he would be fortunate to find a replacement of equal ability. Washington, however, soured on the late Whiting shortly after he and Martha returned to Mount Vernon. The president began writing very critically of his former farm manager, asserting that Whiting "drank freely—kept bad company at my house and . . . was a very debauched person." Was the reason for the new assessment due in part because he heard Charlotte's side of the story? While clearly speculation, it is certainly plausible. And it is worth noting that Washington didn't only say Whiting drank freely and kept bad company, but added that he was "a very debauched person." In the eighteenth-century dictionary, "debauched" is often used in a sexual context. To me, it raises questions about the relationship between Whiting and Charlotte, which of course can never be known with any certainty. Why did Charlotte expect to receive her spare rib earlier than everyone else, and why, upset with her portion, did she feel comfortable enough to follow Whiting into his house and throw it at his feet? Did she, perhaps, have reasons to expect special treatment because she had given him sexual favors? While clearly speculative, it is one explanation that makes sense out of the known facts of the story.

Caroline Branham

Charlotte's fellow enslaved seamstress, Caroline Branham (or Brannum), receives a more detailed portrait. In his records, the general lists Caroline's husband by his full name, Peter Hardiman, and each of Caroline's several children by name and age. Washington did not own Peter but rented him for twelve pounds a year from David Stuart, who had married the widow of Martha's son, Jackie Custis. Even so, Peter lived with Caroline and their children at Mount Vernon for many years as Washington was opposed to separating families. Peter's job was caring for "jacks, stud horses, mules, etc." Washington charged a stud fee of ten dollars per mule plus an extra dollar to cover Peter's work. Always worried about being taken advantage of, Washington thought Peter was finagling his travel time, supposedly to care for horses and mules at the different Mount Vernon farms, in order to pursue "other objects; either of traffic or amusement, more advancive of his own pleasures than my benefit."

Washington worried that not only Peter but also Caroline might take advantage of him. He warned his manager to not let Caroline cut out the clothing fabric because she "was never celebrated for her honesty" and would steal some of the fabric if she could. A recollection of Hannah Taylor, a resident of Alexandria, shines a light on the type of duty that Caroline performed and perhaps on her character as well. Forced to spend the night at Mount Vernon as a seven-year-old because of bad weather, Taylor later recalled her experience. "Caroline Brannum [sic], a colored maid took her to a little room at the head of the stairway. She then brought a copper-warming pan, the first Hannah had ever seen, and ran it between the sheets of the bed, and produced a nightgown of Miss Nelly's and put it on the little girl. . . . She was covered up and tucked in the feather bed, and Caroline left the candle burning until Hannah had gone to sleep."

Counted among Caroline's daily duties was lighting the fire in the Washingtons' bedchamber early in the morning during the winter months. That was what she was doing on December 14, 1799, when Washington fell desperately ill, and Martha told her to fetch help by alerting Tobias Lear. Caroline was of the four blacks with Washington when he breathed his last.

Inherited by George Washington Parke Custis, Caroline was apparently offered a chance to help win her grandson's freedom. Jared Sparks, an early (and woefully inadequate) editor of Washington's papers, was visiting Custis and eager to learn about Washington's final hours. Custis, who had been away at the time of Washington's death, indicated that if Caroline recounted a good story about Washington's death for Sparks, Custis would free her grandson, Robert Robinson. Caroline told a story and Robert was manumitted, eventually becoming a prominent Methodist clergyman in Alexandria. Probably basing his comments on what he heard from Caroline, Jared Sparks minimized the horror of Washington's death and wrote that the great man faced death with the same "patience, fortitude and submission to the divine will" he had demonstrated in life.

Christopher Sheels, William Lee, Ona Judge, Hercules Posey, Sambo Anderson, Charlotte, and Caroline Branham: each dealt uniquely with his or her place in a system forced upon them, trying as well as they could to have lives of their own. Even in these fragmentary glimpses, their humanity shines through, inspiring respect and sympathy and perhaps a clearer understanding of slavery's primal horrors. Sadly, even George Washington was not immune from "the grating chain of racism and slavery that snaked through the new republic and diminished every life it touched." It was the saddest aspect of his remarkably illustrious life—in his words, "the only unavoidable subject of regret."

7

A Sad Postscript to a Remarkable Public Career

GEORGE WASHINGTON AND THE QUASI-WAR
WITH FRANCE

ON MARCH 5, 1797, a day after his inauguration, President John Adams wrote home conveying his impression of his predecessor's reaction to that occasion. George Washington's "countenance was . . . serene and unclouded. . . . Me thought I heard him think, 'Ay! I am fairly out and you fairly in! See which of us will be happiest!'" No doubt, Washington felt relieved at being able to lay aside the heavy burdens of the presidency. As he wrote John Jay, "The trouble & perplexities . . . added to the weight of years which have passed upon me, have worn away my mind more than my body; and renders ease and retirement indispensably necessary to both, during the short time I have to remain here."

He looked forward to returning to his beloved Mount Vernon, where he fully expected to live out his remaining years in privacy. Invoking his favorite biblical reference (Washington quoted from the Bible more than is generally recognized), "Having taken my seat in the shade of my Vine & Fig tree," he concluded his thought with a line from his favorite play, Joseph Addison's *Cato.* "I shall endeavor to view things in the 'Calm lights of mild Philosophy.'" He planned to "spend the remainder of my days . . . in peaceful retirement, making political pursuits yield to the more rational amusement of cultivating the Earth." He strongly doubted he would ever again travel more than twenty miles from Mount Vernon.

Whether Washington remembered it or not, he had employed almost identical language years before, at the end of the War of Independence. "I am at length become a private citizen of America, on the

banks of the Potomac; where under my own Vine & my own Fig tree . . .
I shall view the busy world 'in the calm lights of mild philosophy.'" Of
course, subsequent events in the aftermath of the war brought Washington back to center stage in a starring role. Similar events occurred
after his presidency, but the results were less praiseworthy.

Washington's later life teetered between conflicting impulses—his
desire for autonomy and independence as the squire of Mount Vernon
versus his desire to be at the center of power and influence shaping
events. However strongly and regularly he insisted his sole wish was
to live and die an honest man on his own farm, his behavior spoke
otherwise. (See chapter 8.) As William Abbot, editor of the Retirement Series of the *George Washington Papers,* put it, Washington "was
not yet quite ready to watch the world pass him by without giving it
a nudge or two." John Adams made a similar point in an 1812 letter to
Benjamin Rush. "He soon found Solitude, more fatiguing, more dis-
gusting, and longed to return to public Bustle again."

Washington did spend most of his last thirty months on earth
managing personal affairs. Numerous things needed his attention: re-
storing Mount Vernon, which was "sadly out of repair"; attempting to
straighten out his step-grandson, George Washington Parke Custis, a
young man whom the president liked but whom he described as having
"an almost unconquerable disposition to indolence"; dealing with the
fact that he had too many enslaved workers to employ profitably but
was constrained by moral compunctions from selling them; managing
the seemingly endless stream of visitors who came to Mount Vernon
to pay homage to him (or perhaps, as he thought, "out of curiosity"), a
fact which turned Mount Vernon into a "well-resorted hotel"; bringing
order to his vast treasure trove of personal and public papers "which
might be of interest" in the future; and finally turning his vast land
holdings in the West into much-needed cash.

While all of these private concerns merit attention, my focus will
be on George Washington's active return to public life. He expressed
surprise that it had happened. As he wrote to the artist John Trumbull, "When I bid adieu last to the Theatre of public life, I thought it
was hardly possible that any event would arise, in my day, that could
induce me to tread that stage again. But this is an age of Wonders, and
I have once more consented to become an Actor in the great Drama."

It should not have been so surprising. Washington was drawn to the center stage like iron filings are drawn to a magnet.

Even as a private citizen, he subscribed to ten newspapers, although he confessed that they were contradictory enough to give him little confidence in what was actually going on. It is not insignificant that one of his earliest letters after arriving at Mount Vernon in the spring of 1797 was to his friend and former aide, and now secretary of war, James McHenry. Flattering him by saying, "You are at the source of information and can find many things to relate," Washington requested to be kept in the loop. McHenry, who idolized the former president, was happy to oblige. The situation outlined by McHenry and others like Secretary of State Timothy Pickering was grave.

The crisis centered on two closely connected issues: the prospect of war with France and the increasingly partisan political battles between Federalists and Republicans. With the exception of the decade before the Civil War, the last several years of the eighteenth century were the most politically contentious and divisive in United States history. In 1795, upon learning of the Jay Treaty and America's accommodation with Great Britain, the French immediately began seizing American ships and confiscating their cargoes. With Adams's election in 1796, Gallic belligerence intensified, with French warships seizing approximately three hundred American vessels even before Adams had taken the oath of office. France warned that its crews would treat impressed American sailors found aboard captured British ships as pirates, which meant possible execution. The Directory ruling revolutionary France refused to receive American ambassador Charles C. Pinckney and, in December 1796, expelled him, an act Washington called "unexampled."

With war increasingly likely, President Adams acted on two fronts. He called Congress into special session in May 1797, leading to a law to strengthen land forces and enlarge the army. Additionally, following his predecessor's example of sending a special envoy (John Jay) to Great Britain to avoid war, President Adams decided to send a special mission to France in an effort to find a way out of the crisis. After considerable back and forth, Pinckney, John Marshall, and Elbridge Gerry sailed for France in the spring of 1797, hoping to smooth relations between the two nations.

John Adams asserted that if he could make Washington president, he would do so, "but I never said I would hold the office & be responsible for its exercise, while he should execute it." (Courtesy of Library of Congress, Prints & Photographs Division)

The Adams administration not only faced France's hostility but also believed that France was supported by a "French party" in the United States, which seemed to be happy to do France's bidding and undermine the government of its own country. In the administration's view, these internal divisions, encouraged by foreign powers, posed the greatest threat to the nation's independence. Lacking a historical framework for legitimate principled political debate, Hamiltonian Federalists and Jeffersonian Republicans and their newspaper outlets railed at one another as if at war, poisoning the political discourse of the day. Each side viewed the other as destroying the promise of America. One cannot understand this phase of Washington's career without bearing in mind people's exaggerated fears of those who disagreed with them.

In response to events as he perceived them, George Washington, the man most often viewed as being above party, ultimately ended up as an extremely partisan Federalist, a tilt that may be disappointing but should not be surprising. His post-presidential correspondence rings with deep distrust of critics of the government. His animosity is clear even if his sentence structure is not. The Republicans, by "attempts to injure those who are supposed to stand well in the estimation of the People, and are stumbling blocks in their way (by misrepresenting their political tenets) thereby to destroy all confidence in them, is one of the means by which the Government is to be assailed, and the Constitution destroyed," he wrote to a Federalist supporter, John Nicholas, in March of 1798. "The conduct of this Party is systematized, and everything that is opposed to its execution, will be sacrificed, without hesitation, or remorse; if the end can be answered by it. . . . But as the attempts to explain away the Constitution, & weaken the Government are now become so open; and the desire of placing the Affairs of this Country under the influence & control of a foreign Nation is so apparent, & strong, it is hardly to be expected that a resort to covert means to effect these objects, will be longer regarded."

A month earlier Washington had written to Secretary of State Timothy Pickering, "But the more the views of those who are opposed to the measures of our Government are developed, the less surprised I am at the attempt, and the means—cowardly, illiberal and assassin like—which are used to subvert it." In January of 1799 he wrote his dear friend Bryan Fairfax in England that there was a "party among us which have been uniform in their opposition to all the measures of Government; in short to every act, either of Executive or Legislative authority, which seemed to be calculated to defeat French usurpations, and to lessen the influence of that Nation in our Country, hang upon, & clog its wheels as much as in them lie; and with a rancor & virulence which is scarcely to be conceived!—torturing every act, by unnatural construction, into a design to violate the Constitution, Introduce Monarchy, & to establish an Aristocracy. . . . That they have been the cause of our present disquietudes . . . I have no more doubt than that I am now in the act of writing you this letter." He essentially repeated the same opinion to Lafayette in France and to other friends in America.

Washington reached the point of no return when he realized how France had treated the three-man peace mission dispatched by Adams. That incident lives on in infamy as "the XYZ Affair," so-called because the French principals were not publicly named. Even before negotiations could begin, American envoys Marshall, Pinckney, and Gerry endured a barrage of humiliating demands, foremost among them being a huge loan to France and personal bribes to be paid to Charles-Maurice de Talleyrand-Perigord, the brilliant and wily French foreign minister and member of the Directory, before simply being granted an audience with him.

Adams announced the mission's failure in March 1798. Republicans responded by blaming Adams for making unreasonable demands. Then in April, the president made public his envoys' dispatches, and they clearly illustrated how the French had abused the trio. France's high-handedness outraged the vast majority of Americans. The slogan "Millions for defense but not one cent for tribute" well expressed the nation's mood, though Pinckney actually had said, "No, no, not a six pence!" George Washington learned the backstory of France's intransigence and hopes of conquest from one of the envoys, John Marshall, a particularly strong champion of the first president, and a man in whom Washington had complete confidence. Indeed, Washington declared that Marshall "is so capable of making accurate observations that his information may be relied on with certainty." Washington was shocked by Marshall's long and detailed letter. "What a scene of corruption and profligacy have these communications disclosed."

The impact on Washington of Marshall's letter reverberates in the journal of Polish nobleman Julian Niemcewicz, who visited Mount Vernon on June 13, 1798. In an entry made at the time, Niemcewicz said Washington read aloud to him from Marshall's communiqué, and then the former president vented. "I have never heard him speak with so much candor nor with such heat," Niemcewicz wrote, and further reported that Washington declared, "Whether we consider the wrongs and the plunder which our commerce is suffering or the affront to our national independence and dignity in the rejection of our envoys or whether we think on the oppression, ruin, and destruction of all free people through this military government, everywhere we recognize the need to arm ourselves with a strength and zeal equal to the dangers with which we are threatened. Continued patience and submission will not deliver us, any more than submission delivered Venice and others. Submission is vile. Yea, rather than allowing herself to be insulted to this degree, rather than having her freedom and independence trodden underfoot, America, every American, I, though old, will pour out the last drop of blood which is yet in my veins."

In the explosion of patriotic fever that followed the release of the envoys' report early in April 1798, several important events ensued.

The Republican party, viewed as the champions of the French cause, lost popularity—"struck dumb" in the succinct phrase of Abigail Adams, whose husband suddenly found himself immensely popular for the first and only time during his presidency. Fury at France and the specter of war spurred Congress to create the Department of the Navy, to direct the raising of an army, and to legislate against enemies foreign and domestic.

The Federalist-controlled Congress saw two major perils on the home front. One was the increasing numbers of foreign immigrants, many from France and many others from Ireland, another fount of anti-British feeling. The second was the Republican press, whose behavior Federalists regarded as scurrilous. To deal with these two issues, Congress passed the very controversial Alien and Sedition Acts in 1798.

The Alien Acts, four in all, increased the required period of residency to qualify for citizenship from five to fourteen years and allowed the president to expel all immigrants of a country with whom the United States was at war, as well as any immigrant that he considered "dangerous." The Sedition Act made it a crime punishable by fine and imprisonment to produce any "false, scandalous, and malicious" writing against the government or the president or Congress that might "stir" the people to sedition. As one supporter expressed it, there was evidence everywhere of "the necessity of purifying the country from the sources of pollution." Opponents, with good reason, viewed the Sedition Act as a direct threat to the guarantees of a free press outlined in the First Amendment. Even Alexander Hamilton warned, "Let us not establish a tyranny."

In the hysteria of the period, it is clear that George Washington supported these acts, even though they went against what he had practiced when he was president. He had suffered many unjust calumnies and unprovoked attacks from Benjamin Bache's *Aurora* and other newspapers, but he never proposed legislation to stifle the freedom of the press. Indeed, at one point he termed journalistic misrepresentations as an "evil which must be placed in opposition to the infinite benefits resulting from a free Press." Further, he had envisioned the United States to be a place of asylum for "the poor, the needy, and the oppressed of the earth" and had encouraged immigration. "The bosom of America is open to the oppressed and persecuted of all Nations and Religions."

In the tumult of the new crisis with France and the perceived threat of the Republicans, Washington now worried that certain immigrants might become a conspiratorial fifth column. "[Is it] not time and expedient to resort to protecting Laws against aliens . . . who acknowledge no allegiance to this Country, and in many instances are sent among us . . . for the express purpose of poisoning the minds of our people . . . in order to alienate their affections from the government of their choice." He clearly approved of and actively defended the Sedition Act, such as when he sent a pamphlet by Alexander Addison supporting that law to John Marshall, asking that Marshall share the broadside with Washington's nephew, Bushrod, and perhaps others. Washington's correspondence for this time period resounds with grievances of the sort Federalist sponsors intended these laws to redress. He argued that "a good deal of exertion" was necessary "for certain it is that the Agents and Partisans of France leave nothing unessayed to bring all the Acts and Actors of Government into disrepute; to promote divisions among us." If newspapers of *Aurora*'s ilk published "calumny calculated to poison the minds of the people," Washington declared that "punishment" was justified. He believed no "true American" needed to fear these laws, since the laws only targeted Jacobins and traitors.

Expanding unrest suggested Washington was not long for his vine and fig tree. The first signal that circumstance might call him back into service—to lead the new army—came from Alexander Hamilton in a letter of May 19, 1798. "You ought also to be aware, My Dear Sir, that in the event of an open rupture with France, the public voice will again call you to command the armies of your Country; and though all who are attached to you will from attachment, as well as public considerations, deplore an occasion which should once more tear you from that repose to which you have so good a right—yet it is the opinion of all those with whom I converse that you will be compelled to make the sacrifice. All your past labor may demand to give it efficacy this further, this very great sacrifice."

In retrospect, there seems to be a certain sense of inevitability about the course of events. After all, who would command the new army and save the country from France? Who else but the man who saved the country from Great Britain? President Adams recognized this from the first. "We must have your name, if you, in any case will permit us to use it. There will be more efficacy in it, than in many an army." It must have been galling to Adams, who harbored a certain jealousy toward Washington, to have to utilize his predecessor's reputation. He later wrote Benjamin Rush that he was "mortified" at the need to borrow Washington's glory to prop up his own regime.

Washington got the call and answered it—with surprising speed, by my measure. He stepped up more quickly than in either 1775 or 1789. A sign of his willingness, if not his eagerness, to serve may be seen in his decision to write President Adams in mid-June of 1798, his first letter to Adams since the latter's inauguration. The former president praised his successor's tough stance against France and invited him to Mount Vernon if Adams visited the site of the new capital, yet under construction. Washington also confessed to Secretary of War McHenry that he would find it difficult in a crisis "to remain an idle spectator under the plea of age or retirement." As always, there were the disclaimers, no doubt heartfelt, emphasizing his wish to remain at Mount Vernon enjoying "the tranquil walks of retirement." He told Hamilton that he would "go with as much reluctance from my present peaceful abode, as I should go to the tombs of my ancestors." He worried skeptics would view his taking command as "a restless act" and call his professed love of retirement "a sham." He fretted about whether "my strength and powers might be found incompetent." Was he too old? He noted that however desirous one might be, one could not simply strike forty years off one's age. He was sure others could be equally effective in the job.

Yet he also made clear to Hamilton and to the secretary of war that he would respond if the crisis reached a point where his sense of duty or a call from his country left him no choice. There would, however, be certain conditions. After all, he was once again risking his most prized possession—his reputation—and therefore needed to be in control of certain factors. Most important, he needed to be able to appoint the highest-ranking officers, especially his general staff. The former president particularly wanted to know, if his appointment became a reality, would Hamilton be willing to take "an active part" in the endeavor. Time would prove that Hamilton was more than willing on that front.

These questions had not been answered when President Adams, perhaps inferring from Washington's letters and from discussion with cabinet members that Washington would serve, acted early in July before receiving Washington's agreement. The president nominated George Washington and the Senate "unanimously confirmed" him to be "Lieutenant General and Commander in Chief of all the Armies raised or to be raised for the service of the United States." (This fifth "unanimous" call to an important post stands unparalleled as an example of Washington's stature in the eyes of his countrymen.) Secretary of War McHenry was immediately sent to Mount Vernon with the commission in hand, and with the hope and expectation that GW would accept it.

Washington's appointment would lead to three months of conflict and confusion. It would center on three very prominent Americans—Washington, Adams, and Hamilton—and none would emerge from the squabble with an enhanced reputation. The central cause of the dispute was actually quite simple. George Washington wanted Hamilton as his second in command. John Adams did not. If Washington would not serve without Hamilton as second in command, such a result seemed intolerable to Adams. Resolving the dispute proved complicated and involved more than just the three principals.

George Washington's deep admiration for Alexander Hamilton and John Adams's deep distrust of him were at the root of the clash between Washington and President Adams in 1798. (Courtesy of Library of Congress, Prints & Photographs Division)

From George Washington's perspective, it was crystal clear that he needed to have the power to control his staff. In a sharply worded letter, he emphasized that it was with that understanding that he accepted the commission to lead the army. He insisted on having Hamilton as his inspector general and second in command, which mattered greatly, because another of Washington's conditions was that he would take command of the army only if France actually invaded America. Typically, he wrote to James Marshall, "I have consented to accept the appointment to which my Country has been pleased to call me, with the reservation not to quit my private walks until the Army is in a situation to require my presence, or it becomes indispensable by the urgency of circumstances." Pending a French landing on American soil, Hamilton would lead the army in day-to-day operations.

The stage was set for trouble. Alexander Hamilton's controversial role in this crisis lies beyond the scope of this examination. Critics claim he was manipulating the crisis to establish a European-style standing army for the purpose of attacking Spain in Florida and of crushing domestic opposition, with him becoming, in Abigail Adams's words, "a second Bounoparty." Personally, I believe such charges are unfair and that his critics exaggerate his militancy, but there is no doubt that Hamilton desired military glory and that he desperately wanted to be second in command and acting general. The charge that he manipulated George Washington to win this rank is misleading, because it implies that Hamilton maneuvered the general into doing something that he would not have done otherwise. In fact, George Washington wanted Hamilton to be in this position and fought hard for him, not to please Hamilton but rather because he believed that Hamilton was the essential man for the job. As Washington explained to Secretary of State Timothy Pickering, "His Services ought to be secured at almost any price." He strongly defended his choice to President Adams. "That he is ambitious I shall readily grant, but it is of that laudable kind which prompts a man to excel in whatever he takes in hand. He is enterprising, quick in his perceptions, and his judgment intuitively great: qualities essential to a great military character, and therefore I repeat, that his loss will be irreparable."

In seeking to elevate Hamilton to the virtual command of an entire army, Washington was bypassing men of long-established military experience and reputation, such as Henry Knox and C. C. Pinckney, both of whom were major generals when Hamilton was a colonel. This posed problems on two fronts. First, it deeply offended his old and dear friend Henry Knox, a man he declared he "loved." Knox wrote a poignant and wounded letter to Washington, going so far as to call their long friendship "delusional" and insisting that he would never agree to serve under Hamilton. Washington was surprised and hurt by this response but, while reaching out to Knox, he was adamant in his choice. He told President Adams, "With respect to General Knox, I can say with truth, there is no man in the United States with whom I have been in habits of greater intimacy; no one whom I have loved more sincerely; . . . But, esteem, love & friendship, can have no influence on my mind when I conceive that the subjugation of our Government and Independence, are the objects aimed at by the enemies of our Peace; and when, possibly, our all is at stake."

The bigger problem was with President Adams. By placing conditions on his acceptance and insisting on naming his general officers, Washington undermined the president as commander in chief. It is worth noting that in the Revolutionary War Washington as commander in chief of the Continental Army had never claimed the right to nominate his subordinate officers. Now, as a private citizen, he was telling the president whom he must nominate. It was a stance I doubt he would have tolerated when he was president.

Greatly compounding the situation was Adams's deep distrust and visceral dislike of Hamilton, whom he once called that "bastard brat of a Scottish peddler." Adams saw in Hamilton a "proud, spirited, conceited, aspiring mortal always pretending to Morality, with as debauched morals as anyone I know." Hamilton, according to Adams, was "the most reckless, impatient, artful, indefatigable, and unprincipled intriguer in the United States if not in the world." Obviously, he didn't want such a man to be de facto commander of the army. If he in fact appointed Hamilton as second in command, he would "consider it as the most irresponsible action of my life, and the most difficult to justify." And, as president, Adams felt it was clearly his decision to make. In frustration, Adams asserted that if he could make Washington president, he would do so, "but I never said I would hold the office & be responsible for its exercise, while he should execute it." His order of preference was Knox, Pinckney, and Hamilton. But achieving that was problematic, especially since throughout the episode's duration Adams mystifyingly remained at his home in Quincy, Massachusetts. This made intrigue by his far-from-loyal cabinet, led by Secretary of State Pickering, easier to accomplish.

In the final analysis, the president had little choice. When Adams indicated he would rank Hamilton third behind both Knox and Pinckney, Washington wrote Pickering, "The President ought to ponder well before he consents to a change in the arrangement"—a thinly veiled threat to resign if his wishes were ignored. Washington wrote a long, tough letter to President Adams on September 25, which most historians see as decisive in forcing Adams to follow Washington's preferences for order of command. While the letter is revealing as to Washington's attitude, the evidence is that Adams had already caved on the issue, signing all three commissions on the same day, leaving the final arrangement in case of dispute up to Washington as commander in chief. As Adams later recalled, "I was no more at Liberty than a Man in a Prison, chained to the floor and bound hand and foot."

In November, Lieutenant General George Washington entered Philadelphia with full military flair, on horseback and in uniform, flanked by cavalrymen. Virtually the entire military corps was lined up on the commons to receive him. Washington never said whether the event brought back the memories of his successful role as the commander in chief of the Continental Army, but there is no question that he once again wanted to look the part of commanding general. He wrote his good friend William Fitzhugh, asking him to keep an eye out for the right mount for him to ride—a "horse of figure," preferably a "perfect white." In ordering his new uniform, the general went into exquisite detail outlining the type of uniform he wished his tailor to craft for him. (See chapter 8.)

George Washington spent six weeks in Philadelphia picking the new army's officers, a task more challenging and time consuming than one might imagine. In another example of George Washington's intense partisanship, he wanted only Federalists to make up the officer corps. He believed that while "brawlers against the government" might be silent and supportive of the government at the moment from the desire of winning commissions in the army, they could not be trusted in a crisis. He explained why in an oft-quoted letter to Secretary of War McHenry. One "could as soon scrub the blackamore [black man] white, as to change the principles of a professed Democrat." Such persons, he wrote, "will leave nothing unattempted to overturn the Government of this Country."

Interestingly, Hamilton was less doctrinaire than Washington on this issue and thought it would be expedient to commission Aaron Burr as a brigadier general. Burr was not appointed. In essence, George Washington doubted the patriotism of his political opponents. William Abbot sadly but accurately concluded, "So it had come to this: the judicious, nonpartisan, and moderate George Washington acting and talking like the most partisan of the virulently reactionary Federalists." It was certainly not George Washington's finest hour.

Washington's intense partisanship had several roots: age, political philosophy, and experience. Age certainly could have played a factor. His astute judgment and remarkable political balance might not have been as sharp as they had been in his prime, and his powers of concentration might have been diminished. Other factors, however, were more important.

George Washington was a classical republican of a conservative bent. His formula for a happy country was for "all of us [to] act the part of good citizens, contributing our best endeavors to maintain the Constitution, support the laws, and guard our independence against all assaults from whatsoever quarter they may come." That simplistic construct, coupled with an intense fear of the danger of partisanship, left little room for honest dissent. Political dissidents easily became "the foes of order and good government." Washington accepted the historical English view that once the people had elected representatives, their role was over until the next election. He could not accept that dissent and a competing vision of the common good might nourish political culture, infusing it with vitality. "The idea that there could be equally valid, but different notions of the public interest was utter nonsense to George Washington—a heresy on good republican principles. Harmony, not conflict; unity not diversity characterized his classical republican vision of society." Washington's republicanism could not accommodate the phenomenon of political parties, instead equating challenges to government policy with antipathy toward the entire constitutional system. Washington's desire for unity had the tendency to occasionally cause him to mistake candid criticism of government policy as disloyalty. If there was but one true national interest, and that national interest was synonymous with federalism, as Washington believed, then opposition was illegitimate and antirepublican. There was really no room for a loyal opposition.

Additionally, I believe the increasingly sharp partisan attacks aimed at him had a cumulative effect. Thomas Jefferson's letter to Philip Mazzei and James Monroe's fierce critique of his foreign policy (see chapter 5) clearly wounded him. Thomas Paine, author of *Common Sense,* and now bitter Washington critic, ended a personally aimed tirade against Washington, "And as to you, Sir, treacherous in private friendship . . . and a hypocrite in public life, the world will be puzzled to decide whether you are an apostate or an impostor; whether you have abandoned good principles, or whether you ever had any." Benjamin Bache's *Aurora* summarized his eight years in office. "If ever there was a period for rejoicing this is the moment—every heart, in unison with the freedom and happiness of the people ought to beat high with exaltation, and the name of WASHINGTON from this day ceases to give currency to political iniquity; and to legalize corruption" [capitalization in original]. The *Aurora* later claimed that the Washington administration was not only under British influence but also under the influence of bribery as well. It is not surprising to find Washington, always extremely sensitive to criticism, viewing his critics as men without integrity or patriotism.

Ultimately, the quasi-war with France ended more with a whimper than a bang. President Adams may have lost control of the army, but he did not lose control of the peace process. Dr. George Logan, arriving in France with an introduction to Talleyrand from Thomas Jefferson, soon reported that France was now ready to treat a new American delegation with respect. (Federalist anger at this interference led to the Logan Act, prohibiting individual citizens from conducting negotiations with foreign powers, a law still in effect.) Thus bolstered, Adams bucked the war-wing of his own party and, despite considerable criticism, sent a new set of envoys to France, which eventually led to a treaty ending the quasi-war (although it was not finalized until Adams was defeated in the election of 1800).

The gesture of sending a new peace mission deflated the national sense of urgency and with it the army-building frenzy. When neither the French invasion nor the American army materialized, Washington returned to Mount Vernon, his abortive role in the crisis over. He is subject to legitimate criticism on several fronts—his extreme partisanship, his support of the Alien and Sedition Acts, his treatment of President Adams, and his insistence on an officer corps composed entirely of Federalists—although all were errors of the head, not the heart. Perhaps his desire to be center stage once more may have magnified the French threat for him, but he surely believed it genuine. If France and its operatives in this country succeeded in making America a mere satellite of France, then all his efforts to create an American nation, proudly independent, would be in vain. Thus believing, he could see no other course than to risk all to defend his beloved country from enemies, both from within and from without.

Washington might have been thoroughly disillusioned with the ways of American politics, but he was still not willing to completely withdraw. He was soon urging Federalists like Patrick Henry and Light Horse Harry Lee to run for the Virginia state legislature, as he had earlier done with John Marshall and Bushrod Washington. Would Washington himself consider running again for president? In July of 1799 Governor Jonathan Trumbull of Connecticut, with the backing of many Federalists, urged Washington once again to stand for the presidency in 1800. Only Washington, Trumbull said, invoking the recent crisis, could unite the Federalists and save the country from "a French President." Washington saw it differently. He declared that the new political conditions made his candidacy irrelevant. In the arriving era of party politics, "personal influence" and "distinctions of character" would no longer pertain. Washington acidly observed that were the Jeffersonian Republican party to "set up a broomstick" as a candidate and label that wooden form "a true son of Liberty" or "a Democrat" or "any other epithet that will suit their purpose," the piece of lumber would "command their votes in toto."

Such an observation would seem to rule out any chance of Washington agreeing to be a candidate for president, but the issue was more complicated. He never issued a Shermanesque type of refusal. Indeed, it is worth noting that he did not rule out any kind of involvement.

With the situation with France still up in the air and the political situation unclear, Washington wrote to his nephew, Lawrence Lewis, in September of 1799 about his future plans for Mount Vernon. Interestingly, he added a proviso, "If I should not be again called into the public service of my country." No doubt, there would be increasing pressure to heed the call and prevent Jefferson from becoming the new president. Among others, Gouverneur Morris, who wrote Washington a compelling letter explaining why he must become president in 1789, wrote another one explaining why he must run again in 1800. It arrived a few days after Washington's sudden death on December 14.

Had George Washington lived would he have sought a third term as president? Certainly, there were numerous past examples of his saying he was finished with public service, only to then return to center stage. John Adams for one was convinced he would have run. "I believe he expected to be called in again . . . as he certainly would have been had he lived." I prefer to think that he would not have done so, but the possibility of his doing so cannot simply be dismissed out of hand.

If he had lived and had run, even assuming he won, I believe his ultimate reputation as "first in war, first in peace, and first in the hearts of his countrymen" would have been irreparably damaged. It was crucial for his ultimate legacy that he not die in office but rather pass power on to other, more ordinary men. Much like Abraham Lincoln, George Washington died at the optimum moment for his historical reputation. Had he lived significantly longer, he probably would not have fared as well, as the country enthusiastically embraced a type of democracy that was foreign to his political philosophy.

Ironically, the fact that most Americans think of George Washington as a man above party is at least partially due to the largely overlooked fact that Thomas Jefferson chose to embrace Washington for the Republican cause. Partly for partisan purposes—to shape his own image and that of his party as embodying the nation itself—the partisan Republican Thomas Jefferson helped transform the partisan Federalist George Washington into a symbol transcending party. It was done in a way that made Washington the single greatest symbol of American nationhood, safe for the Jeffersonian Republicanism that was becoming the American ideology. So successful was this effort that relatively few people today realize that George Washington in fact died a highly partisan Federalist.

8

What Made George
Washington Tick

IN THE SUMMER of 1783, as peace talks in Paris between Great Britain and its former American colonies were grinding on, General George Washington wrote plaintively to his brother Jack. "I wait here with much impatience, the arrival of the definitive treaty. This event will put a period not only to my military service, but also to my public life; as the remainder of my natural one shall be spent in that kind of ease and repose which a man enjoys that is free from the load of public cares, and subject to no other control than that of his own judgment, and a proper conduct for the walk of private life." The burden of public service would be lifted, and Washington could do what he really wanted to do. "The great searcher of human hearts is my witness, that I have no wish which aspires beyond the humble and happy lot of living and dying a private citizen on my farm."

No doubt, to live freely and autonomously at Mount Vernon was *one* of George Washington's central desires. He would say it was *the* central desire. The historical evidence, however, strongly suggests that George Washington was not a man to be satisfied with living and dying a private citizen on some farm, even if that farm was his beloved Mount Vernon.

The task of trying to understand what made George Washington tick is truly daunting. As a historian, I am aware of the need to be skeptical of psychohistory, and I realize I am on treacherous ground seeking to plumb the depths of George Washington's mind. Nevertheless, ideas codified by the psychoanalyst Carl Jung have helped me understand George Washington's character. Jung posits that forces in the subconscious often drive people, prompting them to erect defenses against unwanted self-knowledge. Central to understanding this mechanism are Jung's concepts of the "persona" and the "shadow self." According

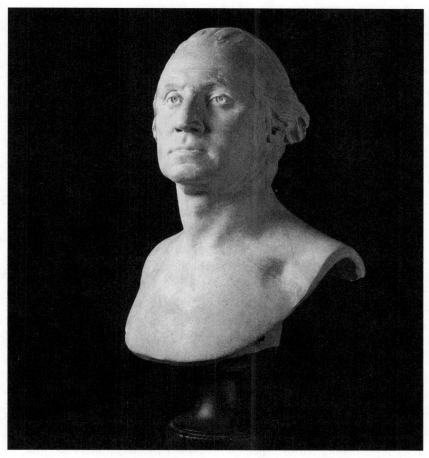

This bust of George Washington, made from life by the famed French sculptor Jean-Antoine Houdon, comes closest to conveying the force of George Washington's charismatic personality. (Courtesy of Mount Vernon Ladies' Association)

to Jung, the "persona"—Latin for "mask"—is how we present ourselves to others and how we wish the world to see us. In direct contrast, the "shadow self" resides in the subconscious. Jungian analyst Aniela Jaffe defines the "shadow self" as the "sum of all personal and collective psychic elements which, because of their incompatibility with the chosen conscious attitude, are denied expression in life." Think of your shadow self as that part of you that you hope you are not, but on some level fear you might be.

For decades, I have been examining George Washington's life and character—initially, through teaching graduate and undergraduate seminars at George Mason University, and then, upon my retirement, as an independent scholar. After these many years of study, my conclusion is that Jung's concepts are useful in deciphering what made George Washington tick. Specifically, I believe that he not only desired secular immortality—fame across the ages—but that his shadow self hungered for public acclaim while he was still on hand to revel in that acclaim.

That George Washington ardently sought fame across the ages is a commonplace claim and has been recognized by many Washington scholars. As Douglass Adair noted in his important study *Fame and the Founding Fathers,* "The love of fame encourages a man to make history, to leave the mark of his deeds and his ideals on the world . . . a being never to be forgotten." What is different in my approach is my emphasizing this powerful urge as the key to understanding George Washington.

Discovery of the Rosetta Stone in 1799 made ancient Egyptian writing comprehensible to the modern eye because on the Rosetta Stone appeared a decree on behalf of Ptolemy V inscribed both in Greek and hieroglyphs. This dual transcription allowed scholars finally to make sense of what had been indecipherable. Likewise, Washington's desire for "honest fame," especially when viewed through the overlapping lenses of his public persona and private shadow self, can serve as a Rosetta Stone for understanding core motives that drove him throughout his life. I also hypothesize that, in Jungian terms, Washington's persona and his shadow self were in conflict. At an unstated but deep level, he craved the ego-based gratification that came from public affirmation of the notion that he was special and it was his uniqueness that was needed to birth the nation.

George Washington would certainly dispute this analysis. He might admit that he desired the "good opinion of honest men, friends to freedom and well-wishers to mankind," but he would vehemently deny any suggestion that he hungered to have public adulation cascade upon him. Rather, Washington would likely prefer a term favored by his eulogists from 1799 until the present day: "selfless." I maintain that reliance on this term, with its connotations of altruism, clouds our understanding of the flesh-and-blood George Washington. No doubt, he sacrificed personal happiness on the altar of country, but he was among the least "selfless" men that ever lived. A "selfless" man does not end up possessing over fifty thousand acres of land, controlling over three hundred slaves, and qualifying as one of America's richest men. It is difficult to underestimate what has been described as Washington's "constant, wary, and often cold eye on making a profit." He was "excessively and conspicuously assiduous in the defense of his own interests."

The very vehemence with which he denied his desire for public adoration in fact lends credence to the view that George Washington's shadow self craved such acclaim. Time and again Washington went out of his way to deny having such feelings, arguing that they had no appeal for him. He responded defensively against any claim that he acted out of what he considered base motives. The fervor of his denial recalls Shakespeare's famous line in *Hamlet* to the effect that a character "doth protest too much."

Nowhere was Washington more explicit in protesting that he acted only out of love of country than in an undelivered draft of his First Inaugural Address. Written by David Humphreys and copied by Washington, this abandoned oration had sharp words for anyone who "could imagine me capable of being so smitten with the allurements of sensual gratification, the frivolities of ceremony or the baubles of ambition, as to be induced from such motives to accept a public appointment: *I shall only lament his imperfect acquaintance with my heart.*"

In another instance, he wrote a friend, "I consider it as an indubitable mark of mean-spiritedness & pitiful vanity to court applause from the pen or tongue of man." Early in his presidency, writing to ardent British admirer and historian Catharine Macaulay Graham, Washington asserted, "All see, and most admire, the glare which hovers round the external trappings of elevated Office. *To me, there is nothing in it,* beyond the luster which may be reflected from its connection with a power of promoting human felicity." He wrote his good friend David Stuart that God knew "*pride and dignity of office has no charms for me. I* can truly say I had rather be at Mount Vernon with a friend or two about me, than to be attended at the Seat of Government by the Officers of State and the Representatives of every Power in Europe." In a letter to former aide James McHenry about his journey to

Mount Vernon upon vacating the presidency, Washington declared, "The attentions we met with on our journey were very flattering, and to *some whose minds are differently formed from mine* would have been highly relished; but I avoided in every instance where I had any previous knowledge of the intention . . . all parades and escorts." (Emphasis added in all four quotations.)

Repeatedly, Washington asserted that he served the public strictly out of a sense of duty to country. To Henry Lee's prediction that Washington was bound to be elected president, he replied, "You are among the small number of those, who know my invincible attachment to domestic life, and that my sincerest wish is to continue in the enjoyment of it, solely, until my final hour. . . . Should the contingency you suggest take place, and (for argument sake alone let me say it) should my unfeigned reluctance to accept the Office be overcome by a deference for the reasons and opinions of my friends; might I not after the Declarations I have made (and Heaven knows they were made in the sincerity of my heart) in the judgment of the impartial World and of Posterity, be chargeable with levity and inconsistency; if not with rashness & ambition?"

Washington wanted observers to understand and to report that in accepting any type of public office he was not seeking adulation. Many obliged. Silas Deane, a member of the Continental Congress from Connecticut, declared, "He is no lover of parade." A French journalist, Brissot de Warville, commented, "His modesty is astonishing to a Frenchman; he speaks of the American war and his victories as of things in which he had no direction." A Dutch businessman, Gerard Vogels, noted that Washington left one concert as the chorus was about to sing a hymn in his honor set to music by Handel. "Evidently His Excellency is above hearing his praise sung and retires before the just acclaim of his people." A French nobleman commented, "He is a foe to ostentation and to vainglory. . . . Modest even to humility, he does not seem to estimate himself at his true worth. He received with perfect grace all the homages which are paid him, but he evades rather than seeks them." For example, preparing to enter New York City for his April 1789 inauguration, Washington wrote to Governor George Clinton, "I can assure you, *with the utmost sincerity,* that no reception can be so congenial to my feelings as a *quiet entry devoid of ceremony*" (emphasis added). Of course, as George Washington knew, such a request would have been impossible to honor. Indeed, if my analysis has merit, an unheralded appearance would have deeply disappointed him.

These examples demonstrate a key aspect of Washington's public persona and core identity: namely, his conviction that he always acted out of a profound sense of duty, characterized by an attitude of disinterested service pursuing only the greater good. However, an analysis of his actions, considered over his lifetime, demonstrates that Washington was not a "selfless" man or one who was simply engaging in disinterested service. Rather, a pattern emerges of a man who was deeply ambitious, massively concerned with his reputation, and in regular search of the public approbation, even as he denied such desires. Indeed, if we consider the shadow self the portion of the psyche that one fears one is but hopes one is not, we can readily interpret Washington's repeated assertions as his attempts to justify to himself and to others that he did not really seek power and influence for his own inner gratification. I believe his assertions were so strong and so frequently announced precisely because he was in denial about a significant force in his shadow self.

Where exactly Washington's incredible drive came from is impossible to pinpoint, but part of it likely emerged as a function of his basic temperament. The two most prominent traits identified by personality psychologists are extraversion and neuroticism. Extraversion is the degree to which an individual is energetic, outgoing, focused on approaching goals, and inclined toward positive emotions. Neuroticism is the degree to which an individual frets about risk, tries to avoid bad outcomes, exhibits defensiveness and pessimism, and tilts toward negative emotions. Extraversion emphasizes acquisition; neuroticism, the avoidance of loss. The arc of Washington's life—strong on energy and ambition, drive for accomplishment, and extreme risk-taking— paints a temperament very high on extraversion and relatively low on but not exempt from neuroticism. It is worth noting that, as we will see, to the extent that Washington demonstrated neurotic tendencies, those tendencies centered on the preservation of his reputation and his accompanying need to defend that reputation.

In youth, George Washington's goal was to rise to maximum prominence in Virginia society. That society was patriarchal, hierarchical, deferential, and completely dominated by members of a gentry who set themselves apart from common folk by the land they acquired, the number of slaves they held in bondage, their manner of dress, their sumptuous lifestyle, and their literacy. Young Washington faced significant obstacles in his quest. His family's admittedly second-tier status became shakier at his father's death in 1743. Besides inflicting significant financial stress, this loss also meant that young Washington, then only eleven, would be raised by a strong-willed, controlling, and emotionally demanding single mother intent on having her firstborn and favorite child focus on meeting her needs rather than achieving his independent goals. (See chapter 2.)

Of course, certain factors went George's way, such as the marriage of half-brother Lawrence, now master of Mount Vernon, into the very powerful Fairfax family. Through regular visits to the Fairfax family manor at Belvoir, which in a sense was his finishing school, George learned what it meant to be a true Virginia gentleman. Belvoir's master, William Fairfax, was cousin to Lord Thomas Fairfax and that nobleman's agent for the multimillion-acre tract known as the Northern Neck. A member of the Governor's Council and the most powerful individual in northern Virginia, William Fairfax became young Washington's mentor and patron, a crucial advantage for the youth's future. Following Fairfax's death in 1757, his protégé went to his funeral and wrote that he would cherish the "memory and friendship [for which] I shall ever retain a most grateful sense."

Given my thesis that Washington was conflicted about what drove him, it is worth noting that his hunger as a youth for worldly success and fame clashed with his widowed mother's spiritual values. More steeped in faith than her son, Mary Ball Washington held that honor, fame, and wealth paled as rewards in comparison with the eternal happiness her religion promised. Stacked against God's glory and believers' heavenly rewards, her theology saw the honors of the earth as so much "rust." Despite such an upbringing, the evidence indicates that George Washington cared more about the immortality of his legacy than he did about the immortality of his soul. In a sense, he could conquer death through fame in the manner a more traditional Christian conquered death by faith in immortality.

Always reticent about broadcasting his religious views, the mature George Washington did believe strongly in a divine power, which he believed intervened directly in human affairs, including his. Once, while enduring a grave illness during his first term as president, he remarked that he felt himself to be "in the hands of a good providence." And he believed in some type of afterlife—"the world of spirits," as he occasionally called it.

As to the nature of that afterlife, however, he was ambivalent. There is an occasional positive reference to a happy future after death. When his beloved Patsy, Martha's daughter from her first marriage, expired from epilepsy at the age of only seventeen, Washington wrote the "sweet innocent girl entered into a more happy and peaceful abode than any she has met with in the afflicted path she hitherto has trod."

More commonly, however, Washington painted the afterworld as gloomy. He normally portrayed death not as passage to a better world but as "a severe stroke," a "blow," a "test," "an afflictive trial," a "debt" all must pay. Losing friends and acquaintances left him glum: "poor Patsy," "poor Greene," "poor Laurens," "poor Mr. Custis," "poor Colo. Harrison." Not blinking at what inevitably awaited him, he wrote of "approaching decay," characterizing his death less in Christian terms than in the language of ancient classicism: going "to the shades of darkness," to "the impervious shades of death," "to sleep with my fathers," to "the shades below," to "the country from whence no Traveler returns," "to the tomb of my ancestors," to the "abyss, from whence no traveler is permitted to return," "to the dreary mansions of my fathers."

Strikingly, Washington nowhere indicates his belief in a heavenly reunion with deceased loved ones. In none of his many letters of condolence does he explicitly assure a recipient of such an eventuality, nor does he write of taking comfort himself in the concept. To the degree that he discusses death in his writings, he emphasizes separation. Upon the death of his favorite brother, Jack, in 1787, he laments that he had "just bid an *eternal* farewell to a much loved Brother who was the intimate companion of my youth and the most affectionate friend of my ripened age." In his mother's waning days, Washington visited her at Fredericksburg, writing afterward, "I took a final leave of my mother, *never* expecting to see her more." Parting at the end of Lafayette's visit to Mount Vernon in December of 1784, GW pined in a letter to his beloved Frenchman, "I often asked myself, as our carriages distended, whether that was the *last sight* I ever should have of you?

And tho' I wished to say no—my fears answered yes." (Emphasis added in all three quotations.)

Although investing little attention to his own heavenly life after death, George Washington was deeply invested in ensuring the continuation of his earthly legacy. His view on this, which never changed, appeared early in a famous 1758 letter to the bewitching Sally Fairfax. Historians, intent on explicating their relationship, have devoted much attention to this famous communiqué, but they generally overlook a revelatory sentence: "Who is there that does not rather envy, than regret a Death that gives birth to Honor & Glorious Memory." It is how one is remembered that is crucial to Washington, not the length or quality of one's life.

In a revealing letter introducing the American poet Joel Barlow to Lafayette in 1788, Washington explains one major way of achieving "glorious memory." "Mr. Barlow is considered by those who are good Judges to be a genius of the first magnitude; and to be one of those Bards who hold the keys of the gate by which Patriots, Sages and Heroes are admitted to immortality," GW wrote. "Such are your Ancient Bards *who are both the priests and door-keepers to the temple of fame.* And these, my dear Marquis, are no vulgar functions. Men of real talents in Arms have commonly approved themselves patrons of the liberal arts and friends to the poets. . . . *In some instances by acting reciprocally, heroes have made poets, and poets heroes*" (emphasis added).

The reference to heroes making poets and poets making heroes is especially pertinent in examining Washington's attitude toward becoming the subject of a biography. His public attitude was clear in denouncing any motives for personal attention: "Any memoirs of my life, distinct & unconnected with the general history of the war, would rather hurt my feelings than tickle my pride whilst I lived," he wrote. "I had rather glide gently down the stream of life, leaving it to posterity to think & say what they please of me, than by an act of mine to have vanity or ostentation imputed to me. . . . *I do not think vanity is a trait of my character*" (emphasis added).

In fact, Washington enlisted David Humphreys, his former aide, to write his biography while he was still living. "I should be pleased indeed to see you undertake this business. Your abilities as a writer," Washington wrote to Humphreys in 1785, "your discernment respecting the principles which lead to the decision by arms; your personal knowledge of many facts as they occurred in the progress of the War; your disposition to justice, candor and impartiality, and your diligence in investigating truth, combining fit you, when joined with the vigor of life, for this task."

But the general certainly knew that Humphreys would not be truly "impartial" as we use the term. In this case, I believe Washington hoped a poet would help make a hero. And Humphreys was a poet whose admiration and affection for his commander was, like Lafayette's, boundless. Consider this 1782 verse characterizing the general:

> The foe then trembled at the well-known name
> And raptur'd thousands to his standard came.
> His Martial skill our rising armies form'd;
> His patriotic zeal their gen'rous bosoms warmed;
> His voice inspired, his godlike presence led,
> The Britons saw, and from his presence fled.

Indeed, Humphreys experienced George Washington as a "godlike presence." Who better to chronicle the life of someone desiring fame across the ages? Washington offered his would-be bard total access. "I should with great pleasure, not only give you the perusal of all my papers, but any oral information of circumstances, which cannot be obtained from the former, that my memory will furnish: And I can with great truth add, that my House would not only be at your Service during the period of your preparing this work, but . . . You would be considered, & treated as one of the family."

Humphreys did reside at Mount Vernon for several years, producing an incomplete draft. Washington read over this material as Humphreys developed it, commenting on and making corrections to what is, in effect, a partial autobiography. Interestingly, Washington ordered Humphreys to destroy his notations, but Humphreys disobeyed, and the resulting record is revealing. In one comment indicative of how he wished to be remembered, Washington wrote, "whether it be necessary to mention that my time and services were given to the public without compensation, and that every direct and indirect attempt afterwards, to reward them [was refused] . . . you can best judge." Can there be any doubt that he expected Humphreys to invoke his sacrifice?

Washington similarly alerted Joseph Reed to a panegyric about him by the African American poet Phillis Wheatley. Washington praised the poem's quality but said he felt it might be seen as an act of vanity if he published it. Reed apparently took the hint and got Wheatley's verse into print.

Further evidence of Washington's desire for secular immortality appears in his extraordinary concern with preserving his papers, private and public. From youth, the record of his existence fascinated him. The late William Abbot, an early editor of the *Washington Papers,* noted that Washington "reveals perhaps most clearly, if indirectly, the sense he came to have of the importance that his life held for history, and for posterity in his attitude toward his papers, which he had gone to extraordinary lengths to gather and protect and for which he planned to erect a building to hold—in essence the first presidential library."

While leading the Continental Army amid severe fiscal constraints, the general convinced Congress to hire writers to work "under the inspection of a man of character in whom entire confidence can be placed . . . for the sole purpose of recording the voluminous papers . . . generated by the war." Washington put his recording secretary, Richard Varick, in charge of the project, which took several men more than two years to complete. Whenever the project had to be moved, His Excellency ordered, "the wagons should never be without a sentinel over them; always locked and the key in your possession." The resulting volumes, well organized and beautifully bound, pleased the general.

Concern about preserving his legacy—and his reputation—twice led Washington to edit documents he had written as a young officer during the French and Indian War. Decades later, finding the now historic materials marred by awkward constructions, faulty grammar, and misspellings, the mature hero of the Revolution painstakingly polished and repolished—albeit without changing the actual meaning of the original—his prose of more than a quarter of a century before. Signs of youthful ignorance and crudity in his early papers might lessen the value of his legacy.

Another way in which Washington courted future recognition included a dedication to the creation of likenesses of him. Offering occasional mild protests, he seemed willing to sit for virtually any artist offering to paint his portrait. In 1785, at sculptor Jean-Antoine Houdon's request, he endured the hours-long discomfort of having a life mask made. Similarly, almost anyone writing him got a reply, and any stranger who came to pay homage or simply to gawk was welcomed at Mount Vernon. Even on his deathbed, his legacy was on his mind. Tormented and gagged by epiglottitis, which made speaking very difficult, his longest speech concerned his papers and what should be done with them.

Well before that final, fatal illness, it is very likely that George Washington, out of public view, took steps to see that his tomb would be placed in the heart of the U.S. Capitol. The president put the full force of his personal authority into building a great metropolis on the banks of the Potomac. Without such a strong centripetal force at the center of the country, figuratively and literally, the president worried that the new country would dissolve into multiple—and vulnerable—confederacies.

Following Pierre L'Enfant's removal as the architect for the American capital, William Thornton was hired to design a capitol building. Almost certainly after consulting with and receiving approval from President Washington, Thornton drew up plans for a structure with two wings and a central rotunda. In that rotunda, at the Capitol's exact center, was to stand an equestrian statue of Washington, with the hero's eventual resting place immediately beneath the statue.

Upon Washington's death in 1799, Congress passed a resolution to that effect, and President John Adams moved to make it so in the form of a request to the late president's widow. Martha Washington immediately agreed, with the proviso that she should in due course be buried alongside him. Martha's surprisingly quick acceptance of Congress's offer is strong evidence that she and her husband had discussed it and decided on a course of action.

Of course, the transfer never took place, and the Washingtons lie not beneath a statue at the Capitol but at Mount Vernon. Funding for the memorial became an issue, and, with Jefferson's election, preventing the concentration of power and wealth took priority over nation building. A shrine to any man, even to Washington, and especially in the Capitol, did not fit well with the Jeffersonian Republican philosophy, and later efforts to move the body to the Capitol were rejected by the family.

George Washington's apparent decision to be entombed in the heart of the U.S. Capitol merits further examination. He had long understood his symbolic importance to American unity and the use-fulness of his own, world-famous image (and body) as a unifying force for the new country and its new capital. Yet contrast this with Washington's directive on what to do with his body following his death. "It is my *express desire* that my corpse be interred in a *private manner, without parade or funeral oration*" (emphasis added). There is a contradiction between this request and his plan to have his tomb in the center of the Capitol that highlights a tension in the forces that drove George Washington. I suspect, in Jungian terms, that his persona and his shadow self were in conflict.

Much evidence in the historical record demonstrates George Washington in fact strove to be exceptional and worked to have others see him as such from his youth until his death. Although he asserted that vanity was not part of his character, there can be little doubt that Washington took enormous pride in his appearance. He had a remarkable physicality, a natural athleticism that he diligently maintained and enhanced. He took fencing lessons not because he expected to have to run a foe through but rather to improve his existing grace and nimbleness. He became a marvelous dancer and, more significantly, the best horseman of his age, both skills that were highly admired and drew favorable notice from onlookers in Virginia society.

His horsemanship was perhaps most in evidence in his favorite sport, fox hunting. Washington apparently ridiculed the idea of it being even possible that he be unhorsed, provided the animal kept on its legs. Riding to the hounds must have gratified Washington on many levels, conscious and subconscious. Leaping ditches, streams, and fences at full gallop on a horse that he had bred and trained no doubt imbued him with the feeling of wellbeing associated with performing skillfully a challenging activity in front of others. And he got to dress to the nines to boot.

This brings us to GW's attention to apparel. In Washington's world, appearances mattered, and he wanted not only to fit in but also to be noticed. The mature Washington, always wary of excessive luxury and ostentation, may have cautioned nephew Bushrod, "Do not conceive that fine clothes make fine men, any more than fine feathers make fine birds," but GW early developed and displayed personal style. Whatever the part—junior officer on the make, fox-hunting planter, senior military commander, president—he clothed himself strategically, even theatrically, for success.

In a truly remarkable, lengthy, and detailed memorandum, the teen-aged Washington described a coat he had seen and which he wanted replicated. "Memorandum to have my Coat made by the following Directions to be made a Frock with a Lapel Breast the Lapel to Contain on each side six Button Holes and to be about 5 or 6 Inches wide all the way equal and to turn as the Breast on the Coat does to have it made very Long Waisted and in Length to come down to or below the Bent of the knee the Waist from the armpit to the Fold to be exactly as long or Longer than from thence to the Bottom not to have more than one fold in the Skirt and the top to be made just to turn in and three Button Holes the Lapel at the top to turn as the Cape of the Coat and Bottom to Come Parallel with the Button Holes the Last Button hole in the Breast to be right opposite to the Button on the Hip." That this indirect but telling self-portrait was somehow preserved testifies to what Abbot perceptively called Washington's "uncommon awareness of himself."

Examining Washington's purchases from London clothiers allows us to conjure up what Washington looked like when he dressed for one of his many fox hunts. It demonstrates not only how striking his appearance must have been but also the effort he made to achieve it. "He wore black boots and silver spurs, a pair of light-brown buckskin breeches, a scarlet waistcoat with gold lace and gilt buttons, a light-brown broadcloth riding coat with gilt buttons, buckskin gloves, and a black hunting cap covered with velvet and circled by a silk band with a silver buckle. He sat astride a hog skin hunting saddle with silver-plated stirrups; he placed a blue blanket trimmed with two white borders beneath the saddle; and he held a bridle with a silver-plated bit and a silk-covered front. He carried a hunting whip with a long silver cap engraved with his name . . ."

Washington's keen attention to his military uniforms is particularly telling, especially as it pertains to his personal sense of exceptionalism. An invoice dated October 23, 1754, on the eve of the French and Indian War, records him spending a third of his salary as adjutant for southern Virginia on a new dress uniform from England, the "rich crimson" coat glorious with gold braid and forty-eight gold-gilt buttons. Such opulent regimentals distinguished him from fellow officers lacking the wherewithal or the savvy to obtain them. The same invoice lists two handsome livery suits, emblazoned with his coat of arms, for his servants, making it clear that Colonel Washington expected to display himself in high style.

His decision to wear his new military uniform of buff and blue (the Whig colors), augmented with an expensive purchase of a gilt gorget (ornamental collar) and epaulets of gold lace with bullion fringe, to the Continental Congress in 1775 was no aberration. Interestingly, immediately after he was appointed commander in chief, he paid a Philadelphia tailor, John Galloway, twelve pounds to sew regimentals of better workmanship, materials, and trimmings than the uniform recently fabricated by Mount Vernon's indentured and less skilled tailor, Andrew Judge. Washington then soon ordered a "blue ribband" to "distinguish myself."

With the Revolution's conclusion in 1783, he did not mothball his uniform. Significantly, when he decided to attend the Constitutional Convention in the spring of 1787, he brought his uniform with him, donning it once again for a triumphant ride into Philadelphia, escorted by the city's militia to the huzzahs of the crowds. On his state-by-state nation-building circuits as president, he habitually paused outside towns to change into his vintage uniform, mount a large white stallion named Prescott, and leave onlookers with vivid memories of him in his glory.

His love of uniforms lasted all of his life. Summoned from retirement in 1798 to become commander in chief during the quasi-war with France, he focused considerable attention on what his new uniform would look like. He wrote another Philadelphia tailor, James McAlpin, to order one made of blue and buff, the "blue cloth to be of the best & softest French or Spanish; and the finest you can procure, of a deep color. And the Buff of the very best sort, fine, & not inclining to yellow or Orange, like what I have been accustomed to wear. The buttons are to be plain, flat, and of the best double gilt." The design called for extensive embroidery, prompting the general to tell McAlpin to engage whichever embroiderer he knew to be "most celebrated & esteemed the best." Nelly Custis, his beloved granddaughter, desired that Washington wear this new "splendidly embroidered uniform" on her wedding day, which was to occur on February 22, 1799, Washington's sixty-seventh birthday. Alas, the uniform was not ready, and the general died later that year without ever receiving it.

Washington's sense of style and wardrobe seems to have served him well as a means of telegraphing power and cementing loyalty. Of course, his countrymen's admiration and affection derived from much more than fabric and gilt. Americans loved him for how he conducted himself, especially in the aftermath of his appointment as commander in chief of the Continental Army in 1775, which thrust him into the spotlight. In those fraught early years, the American cause badly needed heroes, and naturally his countrymen looked first to their new military commander for heroics, as well as for a heroic presence. John Adams summed up the appeal Washington had for so many Americans then and later. "A gentleman of one of the first fortunes on the continent, leaving his delicious retirement, his family and friends, sacrificing his ease, and hazarding all in the cause of his country." That, no doubt, is how the mature George Washington wished people to see him, and indeed how the vast majority of Americans did see him.

I maintain that shortly after his appointment as commander in chief of the Continental Army, George Washington came to believe that Providence had chosen him for an epic role—to embody the noblest of Roman attributes, disinterested virtue, and to do so in a just cause that would expand republican government and human freedom. For the remainder of his life, he fashioned and wore a mask of extraordinary public virtue.

It was no easy task, and George Washington constantly wondered if he was carrying it off. His elevation offered immense possibilities but also great risks, especially for a man who, hunger though he might for fame and honor, also feared failure and its accompanying humiliation—George Washington in a thumbnail sketch. For example, he was intensely conscious of his lack of formal education and his supposed inferior mental endowments. Shortly after being nominated to lead the army, he told the great rebel Patrick Henry that with that event "I date the fall and ruin of my reputation"—a prediction he asked Henry to remember for posterity. This neuroticism persisted as a personal motif. Rather typically, he wrote on the eve of accepting the presidency, "I feel an insuperable diffidence in my own abilities. . . . I greatly apprehend that my Countrymen will expect too much from me. I fear, if the issue of public measures should not correspond with their sanguine expectations, they will turn [the] extravagant (and I may say undue) praises which they are heaping upon me at this moment, into equally extravagant (though I will fondly hope unmerited) censures."

He was a master at lowering and then exceeding expectations, declaring himself unfit for whatever his next illustrious position might be. Even in private life, he was often apologetic, whether for lacking expertise regarding art or etiquette or architecture or in the nuances of drafting a will, an undertaking he accomplished unassisted. As his perceptive and fervent admirer Eliza Powel said, "He appears to have an invincible diffidence of his own abilities."

Fear of failing and thereby wrecking his reputation fired in him an unquenchable desire for approval and hypersensitivity to anything resembling negative comment. (In his writings published to date, the word "approbation" appears over seven hundred times.) Enemy bullets never aroused in him the fear he harbored of criticism, especially from those whose approbation he courted. His public persona might declare that "the arrows of malevolence, however barbed and well pointed, never can reach the valuable part of me," but I believe that Jefferson was more accurate when he declared that Washington was "extremely affected by the attacks made & kept up on him in the public papers. He feels these things more than any man I know."

None of George Washington's actions drew more approbation than those following the end of the war. In December 1783, at Annapolis, Maryland, with victory achieved, His Excellency made the consummate republican gesture, returning his military commission to the Continental Congress in a scene rich in drama and pathos. This act, followed by his return to civilian life, termed by one historian as the "greatest moment in American history," cast him as America's Cincinnatus, a man who had interrupted his agrarian idyll to fight for and obtain his country's liberty and, mission accomplished, ceded power and returned to his beloved farm. This was the role that Washington consciously played and the role he believed Providence had given him.

Numerous theatrical references in Washington's correspondence indicate that he saw the world as a stage and life as a drama, in which each person has a role to play. It is not amiss to picture George Washington constantly "on stage" seeking to fulfill his role as the one indispensable man who was required for the successful birthing of the nation.

Yet, there was another role George Washington desired to play. His longing to live under his own "vine and fig tree" was not posturing but a key part of his essence. Mount Vernon was his hobby as well as his home, an expression of his livelihood and lineage. The house and its environs symbolized his origins, his achievements, his aspirations. Washington identified Mount Vernon with autonomy and freedom from public responsibilities, a setting in which he reigned supreme and felt secure.

Had George Washington simply desired autonomy, being Mount Vernon's master would have sufficed, but he held in his head and in his heart irreconcilable ambitions. As much as he prized autonomy, freedom from the influence of others, he prized power—that is, influence exerted through dominance—and love—influence granted through affiliation—even more.

No matter how heartfelt his desire to live quietly at Mount Vernon, George Washington time and again yielded to the call of public service and its accompanying esteem, gratification, and travail. (Courtesy of Mount Vernon Ladies' Association)

There can be little doubt that George Washington was strongly drawn to the centers of influence and power. That is why, however much he loved Mount Vernon, he often felt compelled to leave it. In the words of the hit musical *Hamilton,* GW "wanted to be in the room where it happens." He was drawn even more powerfully by a need for love—not romantic affection, but the love and admiration of right-minded men and women everywhere. To win the esteem of those he admired was his persistent goal, and he constantly strove to make himself worthy of their admiration, and he constantly fretted that he might lose it.

To be at the center of power and influence and to win and keep the affection and admiration of his compatriots demanded a great deal of time and energy, much of it expended on activities and concerns he would rather not have to do. Something had to give, and ultimately that price was his personal autonomy. No matter how heartfelt his desire to live quietly at Mount Vernon, Washington time and again yielded to the call of public service and its accompanying esteem, gratification, and travail. The price he paid was very high. Like Faust, forced to pay the price of his ambitions, George Washington discovered that a lifetime of fame and veneration could be purchased only at enormous cost.

I believe that George Washington would assert that the enormous cost of public service was worth the enormous sacrifices he made. He believed, as he wrote to Lafayette, that a nation's leader could "immortalize his name" by enhancing the "prosperity and happiness of his people." In other words, the success of the American experiment would give Washington the secular immortality he craved. George Washington's self-love and his love of country coincided. Indeed, they were inseparable.

The last words that people, especially public figures, utter before their deaths often take on special meaning. George Washington's last words were "'Tis well." Examining the actual context in which the words were uttered makes them rather mundane. Washington, genuinely fearful of being buried alive, wanted to be sure that his faithful secretary, Tobias Lear, understood that he was not to be buried until he was dead for at least two days. When Lear acknowledged that he understood, Washington responded, "'Tis well."

While mundane in one sense, in a broader sense this declaration is perfectly apt. In two syllables George Washington summed up his remarkable span on earth. To his everlasting credit, he had been able to tame whatever demons lurked in his shadow self and live a life of honor uncorrupted by what he called "left-handed attempts to acquire popularity."

Regardless of the forces of his shadow self, he was a truly remarkable man, and his sacrifices enriched his beloved country and all humankind. Among the Founding Fathers of the "great unfinished symphony" that is America, George Washington holds a place unique and immortal—first and always. He fathered no children, but in a symbolic sense the United States of America was his offspring. We might properly view the Revolution as American history's Big Bang. That uprising generated particles of energy that will last as long as the United States lasts. Without George Washington, the great experiment in republican government never would have had the chance to thrive. Simply put—no George Washington, no America.

On the occasion of his first inauguration, a New York newspaper went on at length listing honors and praises accorded him, concluding, "He deserved it all." Yes, he did. "'Tis well" that he receives it.

The Wisdom of George Washington

A SAMPLING OF QUOTATIONS

GEORGE WASHINGTON might not match Thomas Jefferson or Abraham Lincoln as a great wordsmith, but he was a much better writer than most people realize, and he was the author of many insightful quotations on a wide range of subjects. Indeed, entire books containing quotations by Washington have been published. Without any claim to being comprehensive, inclusive, or even representative, I have selected some of my favorites, a number of which were incorporated into the main text of the book. I believe they give us insight into both Washington's political philosophy and his philosophy of human nature, which of course influenced his political philosophy. I suspect people on both sides of the political spectrum will find quotes that they particularly like, as well as those they would have preferred that Washington had not written. I have also selectively included some of his advice on the best way for individuals to conduct their lives, which I believe is as relevant now as it was when he wrote it.

Philosophy of Human Nature

A small knowledge of human nature will convince us that, with far the greatest part of mankind, interest is the governing principle and that almost every man is more or less under its influence. . . . The few therefore, who act upon Principles of disinterestedness, are, comparatively speaking, no more than a drop in the Ocean.

The motives which predominate most in human affairs [are] self-love and self-interest.

Few men have the virtue to withstand the highest bidder.

What, gracious God, is man! That there should be such inconsistency and perfidiousness in his conduct?

Such is the vicissitude of human affairs, and such the frailty of human nature that no man I conceive can well answer for the resolutions he enters into.

We know little of ourselves, and still less of the ways of Providence.

In the composition of the human frame there is a great deal of inflammable matter. . . . When the torch is put to it, that which is within you must burst into a blaze.

A man who will do wrong to another in one instance, knowingly, will have no scruple in doing it in every instance where it can be done without being liable to discovery.

I well know too that small circumstances will induce and encourage great hopes, where the object of our hopes is the object of our love and strongest affection. [To the father of a sailor captured by pirates, warning how people might try to extract money on false promises of help.]

Political Philosophy

It is among the evils, and perhaps is not the smallest, of democratical governments, that the people must *feel* before they will *see* (emphasis in original).

No nation is to be trusted farther than it is bound by its interest, and no prudent statesman or politician will venture to depart from it.

But in all matters of great national moment, the only true line of conduct, in my opinion, is, dispassionately to compare the advantages and disadvantages of the measure proposed, and decide from the balance.

If any power on earth could, or the great power above would, erect the standard of infallibility in political opinions, there is no being that

inhabits this terrestrial globe that would resort to it with more eagerness than myself, so long as I remain a servant of the public. But as I
have found no better guide hitherto than upright intentions, and close
investigation, I shall adhere to these maxims while I keep the watch;
leaving it to those who will come after me to explore new ways, if they
like; or think them better.

Men in responsible situations cannot, like those in private life, be governed solely by the dictates of their own inclinations, or by such motives as can only affect themselves.

It is our duty to make the best of our misfortunes and not to suffer
passion to interfere with our interest and the public good.

We must make . . . the best use of mankind as they are, since we cannot have them as we wish.

To anticipate and prevent disastrous contingencies would be the part
of wisdom and patriotism.

If we cannot convince the people that their fears are ill-founded, we
should (at least in a degree) yield to them and not suffer that which
was intended for the best of purposes to produce a bad one which will
be the consequence of divisions.

It is to be lamented that Gentlemen of talents and character should disagree in their sentiments for promoting the public weal, but unfortunately, this ever has been, and more than probable, ever will be the case.

How unfortunate, and how much is it to be regretted then, that whilst
we are encompassed on all sides with avowed enemies and insidious
friends, that internal dissensions should be harrowing and tearing
at our vitals. [Unless corrected] in my opinion the fairest prospect
of happiness and prosperity that ever was presented to man will be
lost—perhaps forever!

My earnest wish, and my fondest hope therefore is, that instead of
wounding suspicions, and irritable charges, there may be liberal

allowances, mutual forbearances, and temporizing yieldings on all sides. Under the exercise of these, matters will go on smoothly, and, if possible, more prosperously. Without them everything must rub; the Wheels of Government will clog; our enemies will triumph, and by throwing their weight into the disaffected Scale, may accomplish the ruin of the goodly fabric we have been erecting.

In a word if the Government and the Officers of it are to be the constant theme for Newspaper abuse, and this too without condescending to investigate the motives or the facts, it will be impossible, I conceive, for any man living to manage the helm, or to keep the machine together.

And let me conjure you, in the name of our common Country, as you value your own sacred honor, as you respect the rights of humanity, and as you regard the Military and National character of America, to express your utmost horror and detestation of the Man who wishes, under any specious pretenses, to overturn the liberties of our Country, and who wickedly attempts to open the flood Gates of Civil discord, and deluge our rising Empire in Blood.

It is not difficult by concealment of some facts, and the exaggeration of others, [where there is an influence] to bias a well-meaning mind, at least for a time; truth will ultimately prevail where pains is [sic] taken to bring it to light.

I am sure the mass of Citizens in the United States mean well; and I firmly believe they will always act well whenever they can obtain a right understanding of matters; but in some parts of the Union, where the sentiments of their delegates and leaders are adverse to the government, and great pains are taken to inculcate a belief that their rights are assailed, and their liberties endangered, it is not easy to accomplish this.

The bosom of America is open to receive not only the Opulent and respectable stranger, but the oppressed and persecuted of all Nations and Religions; whom we shall welcome to a participation of all our rights and privileges, if by decency and propriety of conduct they appear to merit the enjoyment.

All possess alike liberty of conscience and immunities of citizenship. It is now no more that toleration is spoken of, as if it was by the indulgence of one class of people, that another enjoyed the exercise of their inherent natural rights. For happily the Government of the United States, which gives to bigotry no sanction, to persecution no assistance, requires only that they who live under its protection should demean themselves as good citizens.

If men are to be precluded from offering their sentiments on a matter which may involve the most serious and alarming consequences . . . Freedom of speech may be taken away and, dumb and silent, we may be led, like sheep, to the slaughter.

If there were good grounds to suspect that the proscribed and banished characters were engaged in a conspiracy against the Constitution of the People's choice, to seize them even in an irregular manner, might be justified upon the ground of expediency, or self-preservation; but after they were secured and amenable to the Laws to condemn them without a hearing, and consign them to punishment more rigorous perhaps than death is the summit of despotism.

Of all the animosities which have existed among mankind, those which are caused by a difference of sentiments in religion appear to be the most inveterate and distressing, and ought most to be deprecated.

No punishment in my opinion is too great for the man who can build his greatness upon his country's ruin.

The tumultuous populace of large cities are ever to be dreaded. Their indiscriminate violence prostrates for the time all public authority, and its consequences are sometimes extensive and terrible.

I want an American character. . . . We must never forget that we are Americans, the remembrance of which will convince us we act for ourselves and not for others.

I see so many instances of the rascality of Mankind that I am convinced the only way to make men honest, is to prevent their being otherwise.

Is the consideration of a little dirty pelf, to individuals, to be placed in competition with the essential rights & liberties of the present generation, & of millions yet unborn? Shall a few designing men for their own aggrandizement, and to gratify their own avarice, overset the goodly fabric we have been rearing at the expense of so much time, blood, & treasure?

It is a melancholy thing to see such a decay of public virtue, and the fairest prospects overcast & clouded by a host of infamous harpies, who to acquire a little pelf [money] would involve this great Continent in inextricable ruin.

Experience has taught us, that men will not adopt and carry into execution measures the best calculated for their own good, without the intervention of a coercive power.

I do not conceive that we are more inspired—have more wisdom—or possess more virtue that those who will come after us. The power under the Constitution will always be with the people.

Advice for Living a More Purposeful and Meaningful Life

The good opinion of honest men, friends to freedom and well-wishers to mankind . . . is the only kind of reputation a wise man would ever desire.

It is assuredly better to go laughing than crying thro' the rough journey of life.

Happiness depends more on the internal frame of a person's own mind than on the externals of the world . . . the riches of the Indies cannot purchase it.

Live and let live is, in my opinion, a maxim founded in true policy, and is one I am disposed to pursue.

Being no bigot myself to any mode of worship I am disposed to indulge the professors of Christianity in the church, that road to heaven which to them shall seem the most direct.

Shall I arrogantly pronounce that whosoever differs from me, must discern the subject through a distorting medium, or be influenced by some nefarious design? The mind is so formed in different persons as to contemplate the same object in different points of view.

Liberality and charity instead of clamor and misrepresentation (which latter only serve to foment the passions, without enlightening the understanding) ought to govern in all disputes about matters of importance.

Among individuals, the most certain way to make a man your enemy is to tell him you esteem him as such. . . . I never say anything of a man that I have the smallest scruple of saying to him.

I have accustomed myself to judge of human actions very differently, and to appreciate them, by the manner in which they are conducted, more than by the Events; which, it is not in the power of human fore- sight or prudence to command.

To inveigh against things that are past and irremediable is unpleasing, but to steer clear of the shelves and rocks we have struck upon is the part of wisdom.

I can bear to hear of imputed or real errors. The man, who wishes to stand well in the opinion of others, must do this; because he is thereby enabled to correct his faults, or remove prejudices which are imbibed against him.

I hope I shall always possess a sufficient degree of fortitude to bear without murmuring any stroke which may happen.

I have no hesitation in declaring that I shall never relinquish the right of judging, in my own concerns (though I may be pleased always to hear opinions) to any Man living while I have health & strength to look into my own business.

I trust we are not too old, or too proud to profit by the experience of others.

Experience will convince you that there is no truth more certain than that all our enjoyments fall short of our expectations, and to none does it apply with more force than the gratifications of the passions.

To be under little or no control may be pleasing to a mind that does not reflect, but this pleasure cannot be of long duration.

Consider how little a drunken man differs from a beast; the latter is not endowed with reason, the former deprives himself of it; and when that is the case acts like a brute, annoying and disturbing everyone around him.

Do not then in your contemplation of the marriage state look for perfect felicity before you consent to wed. . . . Love is a mighty pretty thing; but like all other delicious things, it is cloying; and when the first transports of the passion begins [*sic*] to subside, which it assuredly will do, and yield—oftentimes too late—to more sober reflections, it serves to evince, that love is too dainty a food to live upon *alone,* and ought not to be considered farther, than as a necessary ingredient for that matrimonial happiness which results from a combination of causes (emphasis in original).

In my estimation, more permanent and genuine happiness is to be found in the sequestered walks of connubial life than in the giddy rounds of promiscuous pleasure.

We must consult our means rather than our wishes; and not endeavor to better our affairs by attempting things, which for want of success may make them worse.

In every transaction of your life, let honor and probity be your polar star.

Be honest and just ourselves, and . . . exact it from others.

Be courteous to all, but intimate with few, and let those few be well tried before you give them your confidence; true friendship is a plant of slow growth, and must undergo and withstand the shocks of adversity before it is entitled to the appellation.

For it is a fixed principle with me, that whatever is done should be well done.

The debt of nature however sooner or later must be paid by us all, and although the separation from our nearest relatives is a heart rending circumstance, reason, religion and philosophy, teach us to bear it with resignation, while time alone can ameliorate, and soften the pangs we experience at parting.

ACKNOWLEDGMENTS

It may not take a village to produce a book, but getting this one into print took a number of knowledgeable, dedicated, and helpful people.

The two most important contributors were my wife, Marlene, and my friend and personal editor, Michael Dolan. Without Marlene's constant—if genial—prodding and her steadfast belief that I could in fact produce another worthwhile contribution to the study of George Washington, I would have succumbed to the various distractions and obstacles that inevitably intervene between having an idea and producing a finished product. The second essential factor resulted from a dinner at the conclusion of the March 2016 session of the Annual Conference on the American Revolution, which placed me opposite Michael Dolan, editor of *American History Magazine.* Our encounter led to my writing several articles for that magazine, and learning firsthand how skilled an editor Mike is. Happily, he has an interest in George Washington and agreed to edit my manuscript. The final result is much stronger as a result of our partnership, and I am much in his debt.

Two other family members gave of their time and expertise. My brilliant son, Gregg, a professor of psychology at James Madison University, sharpened my understanding of George Washington and led me to utilize Carl Jung's theory of the shadow self as a way to better understand George Washington. Gregg is also the author of the wise words that I paraphrased in my dedication to my grandchildren. My sister, Judy Pierce, "mistress of the comma," closely read the entire manuscript, much of it more than once, and saved me from many grammatical errors as well as catching numerous typographical mistakes.

I was both pleased and gratified by numerous busy scholars' willingness to share their knowledge and insights. Professors Stuart Leibiger and Rob McDonald both gave the manuscript a careful reading and, while admiring it, suggested improvements, which I hope they will see in the final product. Despite his busy schedule and renown, Joseph Ellis found time for several long phone conversations rich in both encouragement and suggestions. Bill Ferraro, despite heavy responsibilities as senior associate editor with the *Washington Papers* at the University of Virginia, always found time to respond promptly to various queries, help me locate certain quotations, and recommend how to improve passages of my writing. Martha Saxton shared her manuscript on Mary Ball Washington (now in print as *The Widow Washington*) with me and deepened my understanding of the woman who played so critical a role in my subject's early life and development.

The folks at Mount Vernon were universally helpful. President Doug Bradburn and his staff arranged for me to stay in the scholars' residence at the beautiful Fred W. Smith National Library, where the library's director, Kevin Butler, made me feel welcome. Samantha Snyder was particularly helpful in tracking down books and endnotes. Susan Schoelwer gave a sharp and constructive reading of my chapter on Washington's enslaved workers. Few if any people have more factual knowledge about George Washington than Mount Vernon's research historian, Mary Thompson, and none is more generous about sharing that knowledge. I want to give a special thank-you to Dawn Bonner, manager of Visual Resources, who suggested a number of illustrations used in the book. She is as pleasant to work with as she is capable at her job.

The list of other helpful people is long. Laura Galke of the George Washington Foundation at Ferry Farm generously shared the results of new discoveries at George Washington's birthplace, which enrich our knowledge about Washington's formative years. Ray Soller was particularly helpful in obtaining documents used in the chapter on myths about George Washington. Dan Preston of the James Monroe Papers helped me track down a key letter by Monroe. Many other people encouraged the project by reading parts of the manuscript, arranging talks, tracking down citations, or sharing useful information—Trish Balderson, Velma Berkey, Rick Brookhiser, Gretchen Bulova, Sarah Combs, Gordon Garney, Larry and Diana Henriques, Marvin Hicks, Ron Hurst, Lynn McIntosh, Nat Philbrook, Philip Smucker, and Liz Williams.

I feel fortunate that the book is being published by the University of Virginia Press. For a long time, Mark Saunders, director of the University Press, and the Press's history editor, Dick Holway, both strong advocates of my first book, *Realistic Visionary,* had encouraged me to write another volume. When, after many years, I informed them that I was actually going to undertake the project, the two of them arranged a luncheon meeting in Charlottesville to explore the idea in more depth. Tragically, the very night before our meeting, Mark was stricken with a massive and fatal heart attack. After the initial shock passed, Dick Holway renewed the project, and this book is the end result. It is my hope—and belief—that Mark would be proud of the final result.

The people at the University of Virginia Press have been universally encouraging and supportive of the project and of getting it published in a timely manner. I want to thank Ellen Satrom, Managing Editor and Editorial, Design, and Production Manager; Emily Grandstaff, publicity and social media director; Jason Coleman, marketing and sales director; Helen Chandler in acquisitions; art director Cecilia Sorochin; and particularly project editor Niccole Coggins. Special thanks to Marilyn Campbell, who did such a fine job copyediting the manuscript and is just the type of person that I enjoy working with, and to Kate Mertes for preparing an excellent index. Last, but certainly not least, I want to express my gratitude to Nadine Zimmerli, who took over the project when Dick Holway retired. What a joy to work with. She became my "most fervent advocate" during the entire process, and I am much in her debt.

For the first time, I employed an agent in one of my writing projects, and I don't think I could have found a better one than Jane Dystel, who not only obtained a better contract than I would have, but was also a fount of good advice as well.

BIBLIOGRAPHICAL ESSAY

In the appendix, I cited a variety of quotations from George Washington that I personally found interesting, but I made clear that the selection was not to be viewed as a comprehensive or inclusive or even a representative selection. Similarly, in this essay, I highlight works on George Washington that I found helpful and believe have particular value for readers who wish to explore the life and character of George Washington in more depth. There are many fine works that I have not cited.

The most encouraging aspect in the historiography of George Washington over approximately the past twenty years is the emphasis that is now regularly placed on what a strong and powerful personality George Washington possessed. He was no one's puppet or front man. The three best books demonstrating that point are Ron Chernow's *Washington: A Life,* Joseph J. Ellis's *His Excellency,* and John Rhodehamel's *George Washington: The Wonder of the Age.* All three scholars know their subject well and all are excellent wordsmiths, something in short supply among historians. Chernow's work is a massive 900-page "womb to tomb" biography, while the other two are significantly shorter.

There are other full-scale treatments of Washington's life that are worth mentioning. Douglas Southall Freeman and James Flexner both produced multivolume biographies, although they are now over fifty years old. (Flexner summarized his findings in a popular work, *Washington: The Indispensable Man.*) Freeman's work is more authoritative; Flexner's is more readable. John Ferling's *First of Men* is a scholarly but rather unsympathetic treatment of its subject. Personally, I like a book that is rarely mentioned in the Washington historiography. That is Noemie Emery's *Washington.* While occasionally inaccurate, it is very readable and contains a perceptive analysis of Washington with numerous psychological insights that are helpful in coming to grips with its subject.

The following specific aspects of Washington's career have received excellent treatment. Paul Longmore's *Invention of George Washington* is one of the very best books on Washington, but it follows him only until 1775. Edward Lengel's *General George Washington: A Military Life* and Robert O'Connell's *Revolutionary* both focus on the Revolutionary War. Another good book on the subject of GW and arms is Stephen Brumwell's *George Washington: Gentleman Warrior.* Nathaniel Philbrick's *In the Hurricane's Eye: The Genius of George Washington* focuses on the Battle of Yorktown. Edward Larson's *The Return of George Washington* focuses on the years between 1783 and 1789. Richard Norton Smith's volume, *Patriarch,* examines GW's years as president. T. H. Breen in *George Washington's Journey* looks at Washington's tour of both the northern and southern states. Stuart Leibiger's *Founding Friendship* centers on the key relationship between Washington and James Madison. Glenn Phelps's *George Washington and American Constitutionalism* helps the reader understand Washington's conservative republican position. Edmund Morgan examines Washington's understanding of power in *The Genius of George Washington.* Martha Saxton's book, *The Widow Washington,* sheds necessary light on Washington's mother. Mary Thompson's two books, *"In the Hands of a Good Providence"* and *"The Only Unavoidable Subject of Regret,"* are exhaustive examinations of Washington's religious views and his connection with slavery. Four newer works that were not consulted for this book but hold promise for increasing our understanding of Washington are Jonathan Horn's *Washington's End: The Final Years and Forgotten Struggle,* Peter Stark's *Young Washington,* Kevin Hayes's *George Washington: A Life in Books,* and Colin Calloway's *The Indian World of George Washington.*

For people who wish to find various specific tidbits relating to GW, there is a very valuable resource in Frank Grizzard's *George Washington: A Biographical Companion.* There is a wonderful collection of articles on various aspects of George Washington's life collected by the late Don Higginbotham in his volume *George Washington Reconsidered.* In addition to articles by Higginbotham, one of the leading Washington scholars until his death, the book contains contributions from such famous scholars as Gordon Wood ("The Greatness of George Washington") and Edmund Morgan ("The Aloof American"). Don's outstanding student, Robert McDonald, edited a similarly fine set of articles, *Sons of the Father.* A more uneven set of essays is edited by Edward

Lengel, *A Companion to George Washington.* My own volume, *Realistic Visionary,* attempts to zoom in on various interesting topics that cannot be adequately covered in a regular biography.

Three older volumes that are not easy to categorize but are worth reading are Marcus Cunliffe, *George Washington, Man and Monument,* Charles Wall, *Citizen-Soldier,* and Garry Wills, *Cincinnatus: George Washington and the Enlightenment.*

For readers who wish to learn about Washington through historical novels, I recommend *Citizen Washington* by William Martin.

NOTES

Abbreviations

FOL	Founders Online
GWPCL	*Colonial Series, George Washington Papers*
GWPRV	*Revolutionary War Series, George Washington Papers*
GWPCF	*Confederation Series, George Washington Papers*
GWPP	*Presidential Series, George Washington Papers*
GWPRT	*Retirement Series, George Washington Papers*
MVLA	Mount Vernon Ladies' Association Library

Note to Users

Happily, the large majority of the writings of the Founding Fathers (and Mothers) is easily accessible through the website Founders Online—https://founders.archives.gov/.

I have found the best way to use this wonderful site is to cut and paste a section of the quote you are looking for in quotation marks next to the author of the words, and the site will take you to the entire letter. The quote must be exact.

If a letter is cited that I did not find on Founders Online, even if it might be on the site, I give the more traditional citation.

The second remarkably helpful site is Google Advance Search—https://www.google.com/advanced_search. Cutting and pasting the quote you are looking for in the box "this exact word or phrase" will usually take you directly to the book (or books) where it appears. It will often take you to the Founders Online site. When looking for a quote from a book, I suggest doing the same thing with Google Advanced Book Search—https://books.google.com/advanced_book_search.

Author's Note

xi   *In both of those dramatic achievements:* Joseph J. Ellis, *His Excellency: George Washington* (New York, 2004), 271.

xi   *More clearly than any other Founding Father:* Don Higginbotham, *George Washington: Uniting a Nation* (Lanham, MD, 2002), 2.

xii   *"have been so great had not many of the members":* The delegate was Pierce Butler from Maryland. Quoted in James Flexner, *George Washington and the New Nation* (Boston, 1969), 134.

xii   *"achievement must be recovered before":* Ellis, *His Excellency,* 188.

xiii   *The presidency is the powerful entity:* Gordon Wood, "The Greatness of George Washington," in *George Washington Reconsidered,* edited by Don Higginbotham (Charlottesville, VA, 2001), 322.

xiii   *"I fancy the skill":* GW to Jonathan Boucher, 21 May 1772, *GWPCL* 9:49.

xiv   *As more and more of his papers:* More information is constantly being made available through the publication of the *Papers of George Washington,* a project wonderfully carried on by the Washington Papers staff at the University of Virginia in conjunction with the Mount Vernon Ladies' Association.

1. Matchless

1   *"Never did nature and fortune":* Thomas Jefferson to Dr. Walter Jones, 2 January 1814, FOL.

1   *Although asserting that GW:* Robert O'Connell, *Revolutionary: George Washington at War* (New York, 2019), xxv.

1   *"when the greatest lawgivers":* John Adams to John Penn, 27 March 1776, FOL.

1   *Of course, like his fellow founders:* Joseph Ellis, *American Creation: Triumphs and Tragedies at the Founding of the Republic* (New York, 2007), 15.

3   *It consisted of nearly 8,000 acres:* Ron Chernow, *Washington: A Life* (New York, 2010), 98.

4   *"a deportment so firm":* Quoted in David McCullough, *1776* (New York, 2005), 247.

4   *"There was in his whole appearance":* Quoted in Albert Bushnell Hart, ed., *Tributes to Washington, Pamphlet No. 3* (Washington, DC: George Washington Bicentennial Commission, 1931), 7. Copy accessed online.

4   *His "public & private Virtues":* Mercy Otis Warren to Catharine Sawbridge Macaulay, 24 August 1775, in *Mercy Otis Warren: Selected Letters,* edited by Jeffrey H. Richards and Sharon M. Harris (Athens, GA, 2005), 59.

4   *"You may laugh":* Quoted in T. H. Breen, *George Washington's Journey: The President Forges a New Nation* (New York, 2016), 128.

4   *Washington "has the soul, the look":* Quoted in Chernow, *Washington,* 567.

4 "I sat down beside him": Quoted in the *Century Illustrated Magazine* 63 (1901–2), 515. Copy accessed online.

4 "I have sometimes thought him": Quoted in Washington Irving, *Life of Washington*, 6 vols. (New York, 1855), 5:138. Copy accessed online.

5 "polite with dignity": Abigail Adams to Mary Smith Cranch, 5 January 1790, FOL.

5 "No man could approach him": Gouverneur Morris, "An Oration on the Death of George Washington," New York, 31 December 1799. Copy at MVLA.

5 "awestruck": Henry Knox to Lucy Knox, 22 July 1776. Quoted in Nathaniel Philbrick, *Valiant Ambition: George Washington, Benedict Arnold, and the Fate of the American Revolution* (New York, 2016), 30.

5 French officer after French officer: Gilbert Chinard, *George Washington as the French Knew Him* (Princeton, NJ, 1940), passim.

5 "martial dignity": Lyman Butterfield, ed., *The Letters of Benjamin Rush*, 2 vols. (Princeton, NJ, 1951), 1:92.

5 "He was ambitious": Edmund Morris, *Dutch: A Memoir of Ronald Reagan* (New York, 1999), 386.

5 "If it be a sin": William Shakespeare, *Henry V*, act 4, scene 3.

5 "What toils do I undergo": Quoted in *The Works of Oliver Goldsmith* (New York, 1885), 3:454. Accessed online.

5 "Throughout his life": Paul Longmore, *The Invention of George Washington* (Berkeley, CA, 1988), 1.

6 "feeds and thrives on misfortune . . . patience in suffering": Robert Morris to GW, 27 February 1777, FOL.

6 "I am bereft": GW to Lund Washington, 30 September 1776, FOL.

6 "You can form no Idea": GW to Samuel Washington, 18 December 1776, FOL.

6 "Such is my situation": GW to Lund Washington, 30 September 1776, FOL.

6 "Those who have seen him strongly moved": Morris, "An Oration on the Death of George Washington."

6 "totally different . . . savage tribes": Quoted in Isaac Weld, *Travels through the States of North America*, 2nd ed. (London, 1799), 1:105–6. Copy at MVLA.

7 "was naturally irritable": Thomas Jefferson to Walter Jones, 2 January 1814, FOL.

7 "empire over yourself": Elizabeth Willing Powel to GW, 17 November 1792, FOL.

7 Visibly controlling: Richard Brookhiser, *Founding Father: Rediscovering George Washington* (New York, 1996), 107.

7 only remarkable powers of self-control: Ellis, *His Excellency*, 38.

7 *"Like Socrates"*: Quoted in James C. Rees, *George Washington's Leadership Lessons* (Hoboken, NJ, 2007), 97.

7 *"votary of love"*: GW to Sally Cary Fairfax, 12 September 1758, FOL.

7 *"the dead—the dying—the groans"*: Rosemary Zagarri, ed., *David Humphreys' "Life of Washington" with George Washington's "Remarks"* (Athens, GA, 1991), xlii.

7 *"The supplicating tears"*: GW to Robert Dinwiddie, 22 April 1756, *GWPCL* 3:33–34.

8 *"I flatter myself"*: GW to Robert Dinwiddie, 29 May 1754, *GWPCL* 1:107–8.

8 *knocking soldiers' rifles up*: Zagarri, ed., *David Humphreys' "Life of Washington,"* xliii. Sadly, men were killed in the incident.

8 *Washington "seemed incapable of fear"*: Thomas Jefferson to Walter Jones, 2 January 1814, FOL.

8 *"The firm, composed and majestic countenance"*: Quoted in Chernow, *Washington*, 279.

8 *"His personal bravery"*: Samuel Shaw, *The Journals of Major Samuel Shaw* (Boston, 1847), 29–30. Accessed online.

8 *"His appearance alone gave confidence"*: Quoted in Rick Atkinson, *The British Are Coming: The War for America, Lexington to Princeton, 1775–1777* (New York, 2019), 117.

8 *"the General had "as commanding a physical presence"*: Philbrick, *Valiant Ambition*, 68.

8 *"there is something charming"*: GW to John Augustine Washington, 31 May 1754, *GWPCL* 1:118.

9 *steely will*: John Rhodehamel, *George Washington: The Wonder of the Age* (New Haven, CT, 2017), 22.

9 *"a hard master"*: Joshua Brooks, "A Dinner at Mount Vernon: From the Unpublished Journal of Joshua Brookes (1773–1859)," edited by R.W.G. Vail, *New-York Historical Society Quarterly* 31, no. 2 (April 1947), 82. Copy at MVLA.

9 *"I have a Constitution hardy enough"*: GW to Robert Dinwiddie, 29 May 1754, FOL.

9 *"With the spring of a deer"*: The story is summarized in David Hackett Fischer, *Washington's Crossing* (New York, 2004), 25.

10 *"It is the General's express orders"*: General Orders, 23 August 1776, FOL.

10 *"found within the Enemies lines"*: Quoted in Harry M. Ward, *George Washington's Enforcers: Policing the Continental Army* (Carbondale, IL, 2006), 195.

10 *"the most effectual way"*: GW to Colonel Joseph Kirkbride, 20 April 1778, FOL.

10   *"To this day"*: Seneca Chiefs to GW, 1 December 1790, FOL. Washington's role in the destruction of Native towns is examined in Susan Sleeper-Smith, *Indigenous Prosperity and Indian Women* (Charlottesville, VA, 2018).

10   *"gave me such a slap"*: Quoted in Mary Thompson, *"The Only Unavoidable Subject of Regret": George Washington, Slavery, and the Enslaved Community at Mount Vernon* (Charlottesville, VA, 2019), 253.

10   *great fondness for money*: Robert and Lee Dalzell, *George Washington's Mount Vernon* (Oxford and New York, 1998), 27.

10   *"As you are now receiving my money"*: GW to Valentine Crawford, 30 March 1774, FOL.

10   *"If then a man receives [pay]"*: GW to Thomas Green, 31 March 1789, FOL.

11   *"What brave fellows"*: Quoted in Rhodehamel, *Wonder of the Age*, 129.

11   *"the hardest of war's hard truths"*: Atkinson, *The British Are Coming*, 553.

11   *"rock-ribbed realist"*: Joseph J. Ellis, *Founding Brothers: The Revolutionary Generation* (New York, 2000), 151.

11   *he never would have agreed that it should be "by the people"*: This point is well developed by Glenn A. Phelps, *George Washington and American Constitutionalism* (Lawrence, KS, 1993), chapter 2, "The Republican General."

12   *"an inestimable gift"*: Gouverneur Morris to GW, 24 January 1790, FOL.

12   *"It happens somewhat unfortunately"*: Quoted in Breen, *George Washington's Journey*, 7.

12   *"What, gracious God, is man!"*: GW to David Humphreys, 26 December 1786, FOL.

12   *"I have seen so many instances of the rascality"*: GW to Lund Washington, 17 December 1778, *GWPRV* 18:439.

12   *"We must take the passions of men"*: GW to John Banister, 21 April 1778, FOL.

12   *"A small knowledge of human nature"*: GW to a Continental Congress Camp Committee, 29 January 1778, FOL.

12   *"The motives which predominate most in human affairs"*: GW to James Madison, 3 December 1784, FOL.

12   *"It is vain to exclaim against the depravity of human nature"*: GW to a Continental Congress Camp Committee, 29 January 1778, FOL.

12   *"the only cement that will bind"*: GW to James Warren, 7 October 1785, FOL.

12   *"We must make the best of mankind as they are"*: GW to Major General Philip Schuyler, 24 December 1775, FOL.

12   *"awash in talents"*: I am indebted to Richard Norton Smith for this phrase.

13   *he "never became"*: Marcus Cunliffe, *George Washington: Man and Monument* (Mount Vernon, VA, 1958, 1982), 23.

13   *"lacking . . . slow of mind"*: Alexander DeConde, *Entangling Alliance: Politics and Diplomacy under George Washington* (Durham, NC, 1958), 510.

13   *"an intellect no better than average"*: Andrew Burstein and Nancy Isenberg, *Madison and Jefferson* (New York, 2010), 284.

13   *"Washington's writings"*: William M. Ferraro, "George Washington's Mind," in *A Companion to George Washington,* edited by Edward G. Lengel (West Sussex, UK, 2012), 548, 553.

13   *visiting Polish nobleman:* Richard Norton Smith, *Patriarch: George Washington and the New American Nation* (Boston, 1993), 322.

13   *Washington's "executive talents are superior"*: Thomas Jefferson to Francis Hopkinson, 13 March 1789, FOL.

13   *"much abler heads"*: GW to Bryan Fairfax, 24 August 1774, *GWPCL* 10:155.

14   *"the two great requisites"*: Quoted in Smith, *Patriarch,* 132.

14   *Washington "possessed the gift of silence"*: John Adams to Benjamin Rush, 11 November 1807, FOL.

14   *"the politics of self-presentation"*: I am indebted to Philip Smucker for this phrase.

14   *"He spoke like a man"*: Quoted in Smith, *Patriarch,* 305.

14   *"He was habituated to view things on every side"*: Quoted in William S. Baker, ed., *Early Sketches of George Washington* (Philadelphia, 1893), 132. Accessed online.

14   *"To grow upon familiarity"*: GW to William Pearce, 18 December 1793, FOL.

14   *that remoteness complicates the task:* Edmund Morgan, *The Genius of George Washington* (New York, 1980), 6–7.

15   *"a dignity that forbids familiarity"*: Quoted in Chernow, *Washington,* 199.

15   *"art of making himself beloved"*: Quoted in ibid., 377.

15   *"The man who wishes to stand well"*: GW to Lieutenant Colonel Joseph Reed, 14 January 1776, FOL.

15   *"Act well your part"*: Alexander Pope, "An Essay on Man," Epistle IV. Accessed online.

15   *At Monmouth in 1778:* "General Washington seemed to arrest fate with a single glance," Lafayette wrote. "His nobility, grace, and presence of mind were never displayed to better advantage." Quoted in Edward G. Lengel, *General George Washington: A Military Life* (New York, 2005), 303.

15   *near mutiny at Newburgh:* A detailed account of the Newburgh Conspiracy may be found in William M. Fowler Jr., *American Crisis: George Washington and the Dangerous Two Years after Yorktown, 1781–1783* (New York, 2011).

15   *"Unutterable sensations"*: GW to the Mayor, Corporation, and Citizens of Alexandria, 16 April 1789, FOL.

15 *He awed members:* Washington, a witness said, announced the document's uncontrolled presence, then bowed, picked up his hat, and left the room "with a dignity so severe that every person seemed alarmed." James Madison, The Report of 1800, 7 January 1800, FOL.

16 *He was not only a consummate actor:* Philip G. Smucker, *Riding with George: Sportsmanship and Chivalry in the Making of America's President* (Chicago, 2017), xvii.

16 *a concern for appearance and a love of theater:* Breen, *George Washington's Journey,* 50.

16 *"The Unifier":* Don Higginbotham, ed., *George Washington Reconsidered* (Charlottesville, VA, 2001), 141.

16 *During the Constitutional Convention:* Stuart Leibiger, *Founding Friendship: George Washington, James Madison, and the Creation of the American Republic* (Charlottesville, VA, 1999), 79.

16 *"I have undergone more than most men":* GW to Richard Henry Lee, 16 October 1777, FOL.

16 *"A great Mind knows how to make personal Sacrifices":* GW to François-Joseph-Paul, comte de Grasse-Tilly, 27 September 1781, FOL.

16 *"Let it suffice for me to add":* GW to Joseph Jones, 7 June 1781, FOL.

17 *"Surely every post ought to be deemed honorable":* GW to Brigadier General John Thomas, 23 July 1775, FOL.

17 *"How strange it is that Men":* GW to Brigadier General James Mitchell Varnum, 4 November 1777, FOL.

17 *"How unfortunate":* GW to Thomas Jefferson, 23 August 1792, FOL.

17 *"passion to interfere with our interest":* GW to Major General William Heath, 28 August 1778, FOL.

17 *"Courage is rightly esteemed":* "Winston Churchill Quotes." Accessed online. https://www.brainyquote.com/quotes/winston_churchill_130619.

17 *"I hope I shall always possess":* GW to Lund Washington, 29 May 1779, FOL.

17 *"No man is free who is not master of himself":* "Epictetus Quotes." Accessed online. https://www.brainyquote.com/quotes/epictetus_121419.

17 *drunkards:* A good example is "Consider how little a drunken man differs from a beast; the latter is not endowed with reason, the former deprives himself of it; and when that is the case acts like a brute, annoying and disturbing everyone around him." GW to John Christian Ehlers, 23 December 1793, FOL.

18 *"I do not recollect that in the course of my life":* GW to William Triplett, 25 September 1786, FOL.

18 *"His justice [was] the most inflexible I have ever known":* Thomas Jefferson to Walter Jones, 2 January, 1814. FOL.

18   *"It is difficulties that show what men are."* "Epictetus Quotes." Accessed on-line. https://www.azquotes.com/quote/520057.

18   *"study to be what you wish to seem"*: Quoted in Peter R. Henriques, "George Washington: America's Atlas," *American History,* December 2016, 41.

18   *"a very dangerous" man:* Quoted in Phyllis Lee Levin, *Abigail Adams: A Biography* (New York, 1987), 261.

2. "Complicated, Very Complicated"

19   *"Termagant [Mother]":* James Flexner, *George Washington: The Forge of Experience, 1732–1775* (Boston and Toronto, 1965), 18.

19   *"George Washington defined himself as the* antithesis *of his mother":* Chernow, *Washington,* 11.

20   *His estate's inventory makes clear the Balls were very prosperous:* Martha Saxton, *The Widow Washington: The Life of Mary Washington* (New York, 2019), 14–15. I wish to acknowledge a particular debt to Ms. Saxton for sharing with me her then unpublished manuscript on Mary Washington, which was very helpful to me in writing this chapter.

20   *Mary had not turned three when Colonel Ball died:* Ibid., 26–27.

21   *Mary's mother described Eskridge:* Ibid., 51–52.

21   *Bequests to young Mary:* Ibid.

22   *"young dapple-gray riding horse":* Ibid., 63.

22   *"That the young man should register his birth":* Rhodehamel, *Wonder of the Age,* 13.

23   *for Mary "this was an irreplaceable intimacy":* Saxton, *Widow Washington,* 127.

23   *Additionally, he stipulated:* Ibid., 133.

24   *"She was an imperious woman":* Henry Cabot Lodge, *Life of George Washington,* 2 vols. (New York and Boston, 1920), 1:40.

24   *"In her dealings with her servants":* Douglas Southall Freeman, *George Washington: A Biography,* 7 vols. (New York, 1948), 1:193.

24   *One vignette describes Mary's farm manager:* George Washington Parke Custis, *Recollections and Private Memoirs of George Washington* (New York, 1860), 140.

24   *"The matron held in reserve an authority":* Ibid., 130.

24   *"Of the mother I was ten times more afraid . . . it is impossible to describe":* Ibid., 131.

25   *George signed it, too:* Kevin J. Hayes, *George Washington: A Life in Books* (New York, 2017), 13.

25   *"Labor to get thy peace with God"*: Matthew Hale, *Contemplations Moral and Divine* (London, 1676), 347.

25   *"abstracted from the world and worldly things"*: Custis, *Recollections*, 141.

25   It *"was upon this spot"*: Quoted in Freeman, *George Washington*, 6:231.

26   recommended her soul *"into the hands of my Creator"*: Quoted in Saxton, *Widow Washington*, 287.

26   *"Powerful Virginia elders"*: Freeman, *George Washington*, 2:384.

26   she *"taught him the duties of obedience"*: Custis, *Recollections*, 130.

26   *"I hope you will make use of your natural resolution"*: GW to Ann Fairfax Washington, September–November 1749, *GWPCL* 1:38.

26   *"The careful analysis of small finds"*: Laura J. Galke, "The Mother of the Father of Our Country: Mary Ball Washington's Genteel Domestic Habits," *Northeast Historical Archaeology* 38 (2009): 29–48.

27   *"The long-ago inventory of textiles"*: Saxton, *Widow Washington*, 171.

27   *"7 Shirts"*: *GWPCL* 1:39.

27   typical of *"fond and unthinking mothers"*: Freeman, *George Washington*, 1:195.

28   *"cut and staple him"*: Quoted in ibid., 1:198–99.

28   *"Mistress of much or of little"*: Ibid., 1:193.

28   *When Lawrence died in 1752:* A copy of the will is in the Fred W. Smith library of the Mount Vernon Ladies' Association.

29   *"alarmed at the report of my intentions"*: GW to Robert Orme, 2 April 1755, *GWPCL* 1:246.

30   butter *"cannot be had here"*: GW to Mary Ball Washington, 7 June 1755, *GWPCL* 1:304.

30   *"There was no end to my troubles"*: Quoted in Saxton, *Widow Washington*, 201.

30   *Washington absorbed all the myriad expenses incurred in this move:* They are carefully summarized in the appendix of Volume 3 of Douglas Southall Freeman's massive and still very valuable biography of Washington.

31   *there was a move in the Virginia legislature:* Benjamin Harrison to GW, 25 February 1781, FOL.

31   *"Confident I am"*: GW to Benjamin Harrison Sr., 21 March 1781, FOL.

31   *"I learn from very good authority"*: GW to John Augustine Washington, 16 January 1783, FOL.

32   *"Fredericksburg is where General Washington's mother lives"*: Quoted in Chernow, *Washington*, 423.

32   *"This fighting and killing is a sad thing!"*: Mason Weems, *The Life of George Washington: With Curious Anecdotes* (Philadelphia, 1833), 29.

32   *the citizens of Fredericksburg . . . heaped praise upon her*: From the Citizens
    of Fredericksburg, c. 14 February 1784, *GWPCF* 1:121.

32   *"For whilst I have a shilling left"*: GW to Mary Ball Washington, 15 Febru-
    ary 1787, FOL.

32   *"My house is at your service"*: Ibid.

33   *By following "the mode I have pointed out"*: Ibid.

33   *"She has had a great deal of money from me at times"*: GW to Betty Wash-
    ington Lewis, 13 September 1789, FOL.

34   *"His Excellency! What nonsense!"*: Quoted in Chernow, *Washington*, 423.

34   *"wishes to hear from you"*: Betty Lewis to GW, 24 July 1789, *GWPP* 3:301.

35   *"I give to my son"*: Quoted in Saxton, *Widow Washington*, 288.

35   *"the strangest mystery of Washington's life"*: Freeman, *George Washington*,
    5:491.

35   *not only out of duty but by* "inclination": GW to Charles Thomson, 22 Jan-
    uary 1784, FOL.

35   *"My Mother will receive the compliments"*: GW to Adrienne, Marquise de
    Lafayette, 10 May 1786, FOL.

36   *"as I was prepared to expect"*: GW to Robert Morris, 5 May 1787, FOL. It is
    very unlikely that the story of his mother giving her blessing for Washing-
    ton to accept the presidency is accurate.

36   *"In this point of view"*: GW to Betty Washington Lewis, 13 September 1789,
    FOL.

36   *"It affords us great joy"*: From the Citizens of Fredericksburg, c. 14 Febru-
    ary 1784, *GWPCF* 1:121.

36   *"the honorable mention"*: GW to the Citizens of Fredericksburg, 14 Febru-
    ary 1784, FOL.

38   *"Whoever has seen that awe-inspiring air and manner"*: Custis, *Recollec-
    tions*, 131.

3. "I Cannot Tell a Lie"

39   *"The most successful statesman"*: Rhodehamel, *Wonder of the Age*, 9.

39   *"When George was about six years old"*: Peter Onuf, *The Life of Washing-
    ton, Mason Locke Weems, A New Edition* (New York and London, 1996),
    9–10.

40   *Lawrence Washington weeping with joy*: Ibid., 18.

41   *"Swift on angels' wings"*: Ibid., 134–35.

42   *"The story must have had some circulation"*: Peter Lillback, *George Wash-
    ington's Sacred Fire* (Bryn Mawr, PA, 2006), 95–97.

42   *photograph of the tankard:* R. T. Halsey, *Pictures of Early New York on Dark Blue Staffordshire Pottery* (1889; rpt. New York, 1974). The Fred W. Smith Library of the MVLA has a copy of the book.

43   *Washington purchased teeth from his own slaves:* Thompson, "*The Only Unavoidable Subject of Regret*," 200.

43   *"the most sublime picture in American History":* Quoted in Lillback, *Sacred Fire,* 397.

43   *"a kind of American Gethsemane":* Ellis, *American Creation,* 60.

44   *Washington's character, habits, and gentlemanly reticence:* Samuel Eliot Morison, "The Young Man Washington," in *George Washington: A Profile,* edited by James Morton Smith (New York, 1969).

44   *"would have soiled his uniform":* Rhodehamel, *Wonder of the Age,* 159.

44   *"in none of these":* Bob Drury and Tom Clavin, *Valley Forge* (New York, 2018), 241. Accessed online.

44   *"If George Washington be not a man of God":* Onuf, *Weems,* 147.

44   *Potts was in Pottsgrove:* Lorett Treese, *Valley Forge: Making and Remaking a National Symbol* (State College, PA, 1995), 12.

45   *"Are these the men with whom I am to defend America?" . . . "Good God! Have I got such troops as these?":* Both quoted in Chernow, *Washington,* 254.

45   *"swore that day till the leaves shook on the trees":* Quoted in ibid., 342.

46   *"Washington was careful of his words":* Quoted in Michael Newton, *Alexander Hamilton: The Formative Years* (Phoenix, AZ, 2015), 428.

46   *"No sir! no sir!":* Quoted in ibid.

46   *"the wanton practice of swearing":* General Orders, 21 October 1778, FOL.

46   *"The foolish and wicked practice of profane cursing":* General Orders, 3 August 1776, FOL.

46   *Washington's body language . . . was stronger "than the expressions themselves":* Dominick Mazzagetti, *Charles Lee: Self Before Country* (New Brunswick, NJ, 2015), 248.

47   *"During the meeting of the Constitutional Convention . . . Morris retreated abashed into the crowd":* Morgan, *Genius of George Washington,* 5–6.

47   *be "not too familiar":* GW to Colonel William Woodford, 10 November 1775, FOL.

47   *"The first record we have of this story":* Garry Wills, *Cincinnatus: George Washington and the Enlightenment* (New York, 1984), xxii–xxiii.

48   *"He is a complete gentleman":* Quoted in Peter R. Henriques, *Realistic Visionary: A Portrait of George Washington* (Charlottesville, VA, 2006), 38.

48   *"those who believed George Washington was always proper":* James Thomas Flexner, *Washington: The Indispensable Man* (Boston, 1969), 255.

48   *"the story so often repeated of his never laughing"*: Quoted in Leibiger, *Founding Friendship*, 6.

48   *"it is assuredly better to go laughing than crying"*: GW to Theodorick Bland, 15 August 1786, FOL.

49   *"the Cyprian mystery"*: Gouverneur Morris was very frank in his letters to GW, of whom he said, "It is the pride of my life to consider that man as my friend." *GWPP* 12:143.

49   *"I promised you some Chinese pigs"*: Gouverneur Morris to GW, 12 November 1788, *GWPP* 1:104.

49   *"I am glad to hear that my old acquaintance Colo. Ward"*: GW to William Gordon, 20 December 1784, FOL.

50   *"General Washington throws off the hero"*: Quoted in Flexner, *Indispensable Man*, 134.

50   *"You apply to me, My dear Madam"*: GW to Annis Boudinot Stockton, 2 September 1783, FOL.

51   *"Tell her . . . that I have a heart susceptible"*: GW to Major General Lafayette, 30 September 1779, FOL.

51   *he could "but regret"*: GW to Elizabeth Powel, 30 July 1787, FOL.

51   *All have been shown to be slanders*: These alleged scandals are examined in John C. Fitzpatrick, *The George Washington Scandals* (Alexandria, VA, 1929).

51   *"After that fateful night"*: Linda Allen Bryant, *I Cannot Tell a Lie: The True Story of George Washington's African-American Descendants* (San Jose, CA, 2001), 16.

52   *it is "possible—if not probable"*: Marie Jenkins Schwartz, *Ties That Bound: Founding First Ladies and Slaves* (Chicago, 2017), 108.

52   *"The possibility remains"*: Henry Wiencek, *An Imperfect God: George Washington, His Slaves, and the Creation of America* (New York, 2003), 308–9.

53   *The child probably was born in 1784*: Thompson, *"The Only Unavoidable Subject of Regret,"* 150–51.

53   *If that visiting maid was Venus*: Wiencek, *An Imperfect God*, 304.

53   *"lad West"*: Thompson, *"The Only Unavoidable Subject of Regret,"* 150.

54   *"the shock was too great for her infirm frame to bear"*: John Augustine Washington to GW, 4 April 1784, *GWPCF* 1:261.

54   *the wonderful journal*: John Rogers Williams, ed., *Philip Vickers Fithian: Journal and Letters, 1767–1774* (New York, 1900).

56   *Washington selflessly refusing the offer of a crown*: Robert F. Haggard, "The Nicola Affair: Lewis Nicola, George Washington, and American Military Discontent during the Revolutionary War," *Proceedings of the American Philosophical Society* 146, no. 2 (June 2002), 139. Accessed online.

56   *"never yield to any dishonorable or disloyal plans"*: Continental Congress Remarks on the Revenue and the Situation of the Army, 20 February 1783, FOL.

56   *"You could not have found a person to whom your schemes are more disagreeable"*: GW to Lewis Nicola, 22 May 1782, FOL.

57   *"As you value your sacred honor"*: GW to Officers of the Army, 15 March 1783, FOL.

57   Washington *"saw himself as a mere steward"*: Ellis, *His Excellency*, 143.

57   *"I am not less sure that General Washington"*: James Madison to Henry Colman, 25 August 1826, FOL.

57   *"Probably the most startling example of a living oral tradition"*: Lillback, *Sacred Fire*, 418–19.

58   *the evidence is overwhelming*: Much of this section is drawn from Amicus Brief (https://docs.justia.com/cases/federal/district-courts/district-of -columbia/dcdce/1:2008cv02248/134560/44) filed in conjunction with the December 31, 2008, Newdow v. Roberts lawsuit.

58   *Moustier transcribed the oath as in the Constitution*: Charlene Bickford and Ken Bowling, eds., *Documentary History of the First Federal Congress of the United States of America, March 4, 1789–March 3, 1791: Correspondence: First Session, March–May 1789* (Baltimore, 2004), 15:404–5.

58   *"Chancellor Livingston read the oath"*: E. S. Quincy, ed., *Memoir of the Life of Eliza S. M. Quincy* (Boston, 1861), 52.

59   *Early arrivals to the House of Representatives*: Annals of Congress, House of Representatives, 1st Congress, 1st Session, 101.

59   *passed a new oath act*: Annals of Congress, House of Representatives, 1st Congress, 1st Session, 215.

59   *The Senate, after adding unrelated amendments*: Annals of Congress, Senate, 1st Congress, 1st Session, 31.

60   *"There is not a shadow of right"*: General Defense of the Constitution, 12 June 1788, FOL.

60   *"a dim-witted tool"*: Quoted in Peter R. Henriques, "Don't Print the Legend," *American History Magazine*, December 2018, 41.

60   *That conclusion was equally unacceptable to Jefferson*: Joanne Freeman, *Affairs of Honor: National Politics in the New Republic* (New Haven, CT, 2001), 76.

61   *at his core lived a steely will*: Rhodehamel, *Wonder of the Age*, 22.

61   *"I can see no propriety"*: GW to Lafayette, 28 April–1 May 1788, FOL.

62   *"Simple truth is his best eulogy"*: Abigail Adams to Mary Smith Cranch, 28 January 1800, FOL.

4. "Unfortunate"

63   *"Dangerland"*: O'Connell, *Revolutionary*, chapter 6.

63   *In the aftermath of Washington's victories*: This paragraph draws heavily from an article by Allan L. Damon, "A Melancholy Case," *American Heritage* 21, no. 2 (February 1970). Copy accessed online.

64   *Two years later*: Katherine Mayo, *General Washington's Dilemma* (New York, 1938), 80–81. Although written in the 1930s, this work is well written, well researched, and an excellent resource.

64   *Joshua "Jack" Huddy was a controversial figure*: Matthew H. Ward, "Joshua Huddy: The Scourge of New Jersey Loyalists," *Journal of the American Revolution*, October 8, 2018. Copy accessed online.

65   *a troop of Loyalists took Huddy from prison at Sandy Hook*: Mayo, *General Washington's Dilemma*, 82–83.

65   *they would "open to view a scene"*: Ibid., 94.

65   *"Tho' my Indignation"*: GW to Major General Adam Stephen, 20 April 1777, FOL.

66   *"Justice and policy will require recourse"*: GW to John Hancock, 15 July 1776, FOL.

66   *"I know how apt men are"*: Alexander Hamilton to Major General Henry Knox, 7 June 1782, FOL.

66   *"in the morally ambiguous territory of irregular warfare"*: O'Connell, *Revolutionary*, 288.

66   *"the most wanton, unprecedented and inhuman Murder"*: GW to Sir Henry Clinton, 21 April 1782, FOL.

66   *All favored retaliation*: GW to John Brooks, 19 April 1782, FOL. In this interesting and little-used report, Washington summarizes the views of all of the officers he polled.

67   *"In Failure of it"*: GW to Sir Henry Clinton, 21 April 1782, FOL.

67   *"I cannot conceal my surprise"*: Sir Henry Clinton to GW, 22 April 1782, FOL.

67   *"Deeply impressed"*: Quoted in Damon, "A Melancholy Case."

67   *"under the disagreeable necessity"*: GW to Moses Hazen, 3 May 1782, FOL.

67   *"to save the innocent"*: GW to Sir Henry Clinton, 21 April 1782, FOL.

67   *"I am therefore under the disagreeable necessity"*: GW to Moses Hazen, 18 May 1782, FOL.

68   *a macabre lottery*: Mayo, *General Washington's Dilemma*, 124–31.

69   *"Washington had determined to revenge"*: Quoted in Daniel Epstein, *Loyal Son: The War in Ben Franklin's House* (New York, 2017), 345. Accessed online.

70   *"A sacrifice of this sort"*: Alexander Hamilton to Major General Henry Knox, 7 June 1782, FOL.

70   *the incident "has distressed me exceedingly"*: GW to Benjamin Lincoln, 7 October 1782, FOL.

70   *"Having formed my opinion"*: GW to Henry Knox, 20 April 1782, FOL.

70   *"The Enemy ought to have learnt"*: GW to Elias Dayton, 11 June 1782, FOL.

70   *"My resolutions having been taken up"*: GW to John Dickinson, 19 June 1782, FOL.

71   *the tribunal said, "was not the effect of malice or ill will"*: Quoted in Mayo, *General Washington's Dilemma*, 191.

71   *wartime service:* Ward, "Joshua Huddy."

71   *"I fear an act of retaliation . . . an individual ought not to decide"*: GW to John Hanson, 19 August 1782, FOL.

71   *"chalk a line for me"*: GW to James Duane, 30 September 1782, FOL.

71   *It "interested every feeling mind"*: Quoted in Mayo, *General Washington's Dilemma*, 218–19.

72   *Jay wrote General Washington:* Ibid., 212–13.

72   *"sensibly affected"*: Moses Hazen to GW, 27 May 1782, FOL.

72   *"My son, my only son, . . . this act of clemency"*: Quoted in Mayo, *General Washington's Dilemma*, 229–30.

73   *France had reasons besides a mother's grief:* Ibid., 200–203.

73   *"Was I to give my private opinion"*: GW to Benjamin Lincoln, 7 October 1782, FOL.

73   *"The goodness of their majesties' hearts"*: Quoted in Mayo, *General Washington's Dilemma*, 231.

73   *Benjamin Franklin:* Epstein, *Loyal Son*, 349–50.

74   *"We got clear of shedding innocent blood"*: Quoted in Mayo, *General Washington's Dilemma*, 233.

74   *"Captain Asgill would certainly have paid the forfeit"*: Quoted in ibid., 248.

74   *"It would have been a horrid damp"*: Quoted in ibid., 249.

74   *Tilghman reported that among other insults:* Ibid., 272–73.

74   *Asgill later wrote:* Anne Ammundsen, "Saving Captain Asgill," *History Today* 61, no. 12 (December 2011). Copy accessed online.

75   *"the continual indulgencies & procrastinations"*: GW to James Tilghman, 5 June 1786, FOL.

75   *"I was not without suspicions"*: Ibid.

75   *"I am informed that Capt. Asgill is at Chatham"*: GW to Elias Dayton, 11 June 1782, FOL.

76   *"My judgement told me"*: Quoted in Ammundsen, "Saving Captain Asgill."

76   *Serving in Ireland during the Rebellion of 1798*: Ibid.

5. FRACTURED FRIENDSHIPS

77   *"George Washington, more than any member of the Revolutionary genera-tion"*: Higginbotham, *Uniting a Nation*, 2.

78   *"The disinclination of the individual states"*: GW to Benjamin Harrison, 18 January 1784, FOL.

78   *"Thus believing"*: GW to Edmund Randolph, 8 January 1788, FOL.

78   *"our natural enemies"*: Thomas Jefferson to William Carmichael, 15 December 1787, FOL.

78   *"The cause of France is the cause of man"*: Quoted in Gordon S. Wood, *Empire of Liberty: A History of the Early Republic, 1789–1815* (New York, 2009), 183.

79   *"rock-ribbed realist"*: Ellis, *Founding Brothers*, 151.

79   *President Washington sought to take the crisis out of the hands of Congress*: A detailed look at the events surrounding the Jay Treaty may be found in Stanley Elkins and Eric McKitrick, *The Age of Federalism: The Early American Republic, 1788–1800* (New York, 1993), chapter 9. See also, Todd Estes, *The Jay Treaty Debate, Public Opinion, and the Evolution of Early American Culture* (University of Massachusetts Press, 2006).

79   *"If people are convinced of my integrity"*: GW to Joseph Reed, 23 June 1777, FOL.

80   *"Shall I set up my judgment as the standard of perfection?"*: Undelivered First Inaugural Address: Fragments, 30 April 1789, FOL.

80   *"My friendship is not in the least lessened"*: GW to Benjamin Harrison, 9 March 1789, FOL.

80   *"The hints you have communicated from time to time"*: GW to Lieutenant Colonel Joseph Reed, 14 January 1776, FOL.

80   *The "favorable manner"*: GW to Joseph Reed, 11 June 1777, FOL.

81   *"I do it on the presumption"*: GW to Gouverneur Morris, 28 January 1792, FOL.

81   *Born in 1725, Mason alone*: I examined the relationship between Washington and Mason in "Uneven Friendship," *Virginia Magazine of History and Biography* 97, no. 2 (April 1989), 185–204.

81   *"Much abler heads than my own"*: GW to Bryan Fairfax, 24 August 1774, *GWPCL* 10:155.

82   *"I could think of no person"*: GW to George Mason, 10 May 1776, FOL.

82   *"a zealous and able supporter"*: GW to George Mason, 27 March 1799, in John C. Fitzpatrick, ed., *The Writings of George Washington* (Washington, DC, 1938), 14:298n.

83   *the friendship was showing strains:* These and other incidents are expanded upon in my article "Uneven Friendship."

83   *Most academics:* Scholars referring to the November dinner include Robert Rutland, Helen Hill Miller, Julian Boyd, Kate Mason Rowland, and Elswyth Thane.

84   *"Colo. Mason is certainly a man of superior abilities"*: Tobias Lear's letters to Governor John Langdon of New Hampshire are cited in my article "Uneven Friendship," 198–200. Archived at the Langdon-Elwyn Papers, New Hampshire Historical Society, Concord, these letters have been made available since the publication of my article.

84   *"Mr. Mason & Mr. [Patrick] Henry still continue their opposition"*: Ibid.

85   *"quandom friend"*: GW to Alexander Hamilton, 29 July 1792, FOL.

85   *"I always expected"*: GW to James Craik, 8 September 1789, FOL.

85   *"I will also unite my regret to yours"*: GW to James Mercer, 1 November 1792, FOL.

85   *"In this important trust"*: George Mason to John Mason, 13 March 1789, in Robert Rutland, ed., *The Papers of George Mason, 1725–1792*, 3 vols. (Chapel Hill, NC, 1970), 3:1172.

86   *"I feel happy at my emancipation:* Edmund Randolph to James Madison, 1 November 1795, FOL.

87   *"the poorest chameleon I ever saw"*: Quoted in Mary K. Bonsteel Tachua, "George Washington and the Reputation of Edmund Randolph," *Journal of American History* 73 (June 1980), 16.

89   *"Your confidence in me"*: Edmund Randolph to GW, 19 August 1795, FOL. The accompanying text note summarizes Randolph's account of the meeting.

89   *The entire episode:* One account concludes, "The result was a shameful episode, possibly the worst incident to mar an almost unblemished life." David S. Heidler and Jeanne T. Heidler, *Washington's Circle: The Creation of the Presidency* (New York, 2015), 367.

89   *Washington appeared unable to forgive:* Ibid., 371.

89   *Randolph composed and published a 100-page apologia:* Edmund Randolph, *A Vindication of Mr. Randolph's Resignation* (Philadelphia, 1795).

90   *"full liberty to publish"*: GW to Edmund Randolph, 21 October 1795, FOL.

90   *"Randolph sets his defense within the context of a diatribe against Washington"*: Tachua, "George Washington and the Reputation of Edmund Randolph," 32. Tachua's is the best summary of the impact of the incident on both men.

90   *"Under the influence of Wolcott and Pickering"*: Randolph, *A Vindication*, 49.

90   *"The silence that the president had maintained publicly"*: Tachua, "George Washington and the Reputation of Edmund Randolph," 34.

90   *Randolph's "greatest enemies"*: James Madison to James Monroe, 26 January 1796, FOL.

91   *"dull and stupid"*: Burr's longer quote was "Naturally dull and stupid; extremely illiterate; indecisive to a degree that would be incredible to one who did not know him." Quoted in John Sedgwick, *War of Two: Alexander Hamilton, Aaron Burr, and the Duel That Stunned the Nation* (New York, 2015), 259.

92   *"a deportment so firm"*: Quoted in McCullough, *1776*, 247.

92   *"The esteem I have for him"*: GW to Archibald Cary, c. 22 May 1779, FOL.

92   *"I have a boundless confidence in him"*: James Monroe to Thomas Jefferson, 12 July 1788, FOL.

92   *"candor and liberality"*: Quoted in William M. Ferraro, "George Washington and James Monroe," in *Sons of the Father: George Washington and His Protégés*, edited by Robert McDonald (Charlottesville, VA, 2013), 106.

92   *The Washington/Monroe split*: The most complete biography remains Harry Ammon, *James Monroe: The Quest for National Identity* (Charlottesville, VA, 1990).

93   *Thus, for America to slip back into the orbit of France's mortal enemy, Britain*: Elkins and McKitrick, *Age of Federalism*, 512.

93   *"I alone am responsible"*: This letter is quoted in an "Introductory Note: To George Washington," 14 April 1794, in the correspondence of Alexander Hamilton, FOL.

93   *Monroe was a partisan Republican*: Elkins and McKitrick, *Age of Federalism*, 498.

94   *"If it is ratified"*: James Monroe to James Madison, 23 October 1795, FOL.

94   *"If you supposed that I would submit in silence"*: James Monroe to Timothy Pickering, quoted in Ammon, *James Monroe*, 161.

95   *"Such a collection of vain, superficial, blunderers"*: James Monroe to James Madison, 1 January 1797, FOL.

95   *"Our navigation is destroyed"*: Quoted in Ammon, *James Monroe*, 166. Ammon's entire book is available online.

95   *"Too long have they been the dupes"*: Daniel Preston, ed., *The Papers of James Monroe*, Vol. 4, *Selected Correspondence and Papers, 1796–1802* (Santa Barbara, CA, 2012), 301–4.

95 *he took up his pen to jot down in the margins:* All of the marginalia are found in the editorial note in the *George Washington Papers*: "Comments on Monroe's A View of the Conduct of the Executive of the United States," March 1798, FOL.

96 *"remarks on Monroe and his book":* Ibid.

96 *Washington, Lear wrote later, appeared "much affected":* Tobias Lear's Narrative Accounts of the Death of George Washington, Diary Account, *GWPRT* 4:547.

96 *Washington came to view Jefferson as a deceitful man:* I examine their relationship in more detail in *Realistic Visionary*, "Reluctant Enemies: The Increasingly Strained Relationship between George Washington and Thomas Jefferson." Most of this segment is drawn from that chapter.

97 *"fullest latitude of a friend":* GW to Thomas Jefferson, 8 April 1784, FOL.

97 *"a man of whom I early imbibed the highest opinion":* GW to Lafayette, 10 May 1786, FOL.

97 *the president admired his character:* Andrew Burstein, *The Inner Jefferson: Portrait of a Grieving Optimist* (Charlottesville, VA, 1995), 221.

97 *"you are to marshal us as may be best for the public good":* Thomas Jefferson to GW, 15 December 1789, FOL.

98 *"attracting Freneau to Philadelphia":* Noble Cunningham, *In Pursuit of Reason: The Life of Thomas Jefferson* (Baton Rouge, LA, 1987), 171.

99 *"My Dear Friend":* Thomas Jefferson to Philip Mazzei, 24 April 1796, FOL.

100 *President Washington had been turned:* Brian Steele, "George Washington Did Not Harbor One Principle of Federalism," in *Sons of the Father*, edited by Robert McDonald (Charlottesville, VA, 2013), 90–92.

100 *"one of the most detestable of mankind":* Quoted in the *Life, Journals and Correspondence of the Rev. Manasseh Cutler*, 2 vols. (Cincinnati, 1888), 2:56ff. The quote is included with a collection of quotes about Martha Washington at MVLA.

101 *Madison "is uncorrupted and incorruptible":* Alexander Hamilton, Conversation with George Beckwith, October 1789, FOL.

101 *"the noblest work of God: an honest man":* Abigail Smith Adams to Elizabeth Smith Shaw Peabody, 10 February 1814, FOL.

101 *"the most virtuous, calm, and amiable of men":* Quoted in Leibiger, *Founding Friendship*, 7. Leibiger's book is excellent on the relationship between these two men, and I have used it extensively in this brief summary.

102 *"I am very troublesome, I know":* GW to James Madison, 23 September 1789, FOL.

102 *these brief phrases reveal a great deal:* Stuart Leibiger, "Founding Friendship: George Washington, James Madison, and the Creation of the American Republic," *History Today* 51 (July 2001), 23.

102   *His ego would not get in the way:* David O. Stewart, *Madison's Gift: Five Partnerships That Built America* (New York, 2015), 80.

102   *"Moderate exercise, and books occasionally":* GW to James Madison, 23 June 1788, FOL.

103   *Ultimately, after much debate and maneuvering:* It was apparently a moving speech by Fisher Ames that brought some delegates to tears and carried the day. Elkins and McKitrick, *Age of Federalism,* 448.

104   *President Washington was less popular in Virginia than in any of the other states:* Quoted in Chernow, *Washington,* 676.

104   *Washington confided in him:* Ibid.

104   *the least Virginian of all the great Virginia leaders:* W. W. Abbot, "The Young George Washington and His Papers," 11 February 1999, in *Washington Papers.* Copy accessed online.

6. Lives of Their Own

105   *Over the next fifty-six years:* Thompson, *"The Only Unavoidable Subject of Regret,"* 15.

105   *At the time of his death:* The most complete treatment of the subject is Thompson, *"The Only Unavoidable Subject of Regret."*

105   *"ecstasy of sanctimony":* Philip Roth, *The Human Stain* (New York, 2001), 2.

107   *Washington bade Christopher sit:* In contrast to Brookhiser, *Founding Father,* 199, Tobias Lear in his account of Washington's death makes clear that Christopher did sit down.

107   *"For besides the call of Humanity":* GW to William Stoy, 14 October 1797, FOL.

108   *"the servant got them about his head":* Quoted in Thompson, *"The Only Unavoidable Subject of Regret,"* 253.

108   *"salary" of four dollars a month:* GWPP 5:223.

109   *"always at his [GW's] side":* Quoted in Thompson, *"The Only Unavoidable Subject of Regret,"* 53.

110   *"Will, the huntsman[,] . . . rode a horse called Chinkling":* Custis, *Recollections,* 387.

110   *"His Excellency, with his usual dignity":* James Thacher, *Military Journal, 1779,* AmericanRevolution.org. Accessed online.

110   *If Will had been a white man:* Fritz Hirschfeld, *George Washington and Slavery: A Documentary Portrayal* (Columbia, MO, 1997), 111.

111   *Smith . . . learned about Lafayette's discomfort "from one of General Washington's domestics":* I wish to acknowledge William Ferraro of the Washington Papers for this information. William M. Ferraro, "A Glimpse of

William 'Billy' Lee: George Washington's Enslaved Manservant," *Washington's Quill* blog post, 4 October 2019, *GW Papers*. Accessed online.

111 *"as he could neither Walk, stand, or ride"*: GW Diary Entry, 22 April 1785, FOL.

111 *"(if it can be complied with on reasonable terms)"*: GW to Clement Biddle, 28 July 1784, FOL.

111 *"If he is still anxious to come on here"*: Quoted in Chernow, *Washington*, 563.

112 *"Ah, colonel, I am a poor cripple"*: Quoted in Custis, *Recollections*, 451.

112 *"Paid Dr. Dangerfield"*: Eugene E. Prussing, *The Estate of George Washington, Deceased* (Boston, 1927), 159.

112 *In recent years, Ona Judge:* Ona is the subject of a recent and I think not always accurate new book: Erica Armstrong Dunbar, *Never Caught: The Washingtons' Relentless Pursuit of Their Runaway Slave, Ona Judge* (New York, 2017). Dunbar believes that Ona should be held on a par with the likes of Frederick Douglass and Harriet Tubman. Her dramatic rendering of Ona's confrontation with GW's nephew, Burwell Bassett (which may well have never happened), reads like a historical novel (165–67).

113 *"being Perfect a Mistress of her needle"*: GW to Oliver Wolcott Jr., 1 September 1796, FOL.

113 *"without the least provocation"*: GW to Joseph Whipple, 28 November 1796, FOL.

113 *more "like a child than a servant"*: GW to Oliver Wolcott Jr., 1 September 1796, FOL.

113 *monthly "salary" of four dollars:* GWPP 5:223.

113 *"Although well enough used as to work and living"*: Quoted in Thompson, "The Only Unavoidable Subject of Regret," 289.

114 *insisting that a Frenchman had seduced her:* GW to Joseph Whipple, 28 November 1796, FOL.

114 *"to seize, and put her on board a vessel"*: GW to Oliver Wolcott Jr., 1 September 1796, FOL.

114 *"a thirst for complete freedom"*: Quoted in Wiencek, *An Imperfect God*, 326.

115 *"Ten Dollars Reward"*: *Claypoole's American Daily Advertiser*, May 25, 1796, 3, *America's Historical Newspapers*. Accessed online.

115 *"discontent her fellow servants"*: GW to Joseph Whipple, 28 November 1796, FOL.

115 *violated the Fugitive Slave Act:* Wiencek, *An Imperfect God*, 324.

116 *"She never received the least mental or moral instruction of any kind"*: Rev. Benjamin Chase, "Interview with Ona Judge Staines," *The Liberator*, January 1, 1847. Accessed online on website of The President's House in Philadelphia.

116   *"No, I am free"*: *The Granite Freeman*, Concord, NH, May 22, 1845. Accessed online on website of The President's House in Philadelphia.

117   *three bottles of rum*: Thompson, *"The Only Unavoidable Subject of Regret,"* 283.

117   *"dirty figures"*: GW to Tobias Lear, 9 September 1790, FOL.

117   *"his linen was of exceptionable whiteness and quality"*: Custis, *Recollections*, 423. Custis wrote "unexceptional whiteness" although he clearly meant exceptional whiteness.

118   *"This advice may be known to none but yourself and Mrs. Washington"*: GW to Tobias Lear, 12 April 1791, FOL.

118   *"mortified to the last degree"*: Tobias Lear to GW, 5 June 1791, *GWPP* 8:232.

118   *Hercules did not run away in Philadelphia*: Thompson, *"The Only Unavoidable Subject of Regret,"* 284.

118   *Hercules . . . was relegated to hard labor at Mount Vernon*: Ibid.

119   *"for if Hercules was to get the least hint of the design"*: GW to Frederick Kitt, 10 January 1798, FOL.

119   *"It's a fantasized image of what people want"*: Quoted in Craig LeBan, "George Washington's Enslaved Chef, Who Cooked in Philadelphia, Disappears from Painting, but May Have Reappeared in New York," *Philadelphia Inquirer*, Updated, 1 March 2019. Accessed online.

119   *Researchers have recently discovered a New York City death*: Ibid.

120   *she was "very glad, because he is free now"*: Quoted in Thompson, *"The Only Unavoidable Subject of Regret,"* 285.

120   *"His eye was a perfect plumb ball"*: Quoted in Susan P. Schoelwer, ed., *Lives Bound Together: Slavery at George Washington's Mount Vernon* (Mount Vernon, VA, n.d.), 31.

120   *"very particular"*: Ibid.

120   *"if a rail, a clapboard, or a stone"*: Quoted in Thompson, *"The Only Unavoidable Subject of Regret,"* 36.

120   *Washington asked Sambo's permission*: Ibid., 49.

121   *A skillful beekeeper*: Schoelwer, ed., *Lives Bound Together*, 32.

121   *A letter buried in the* Washington Papers: Joseph Lewis Jr. to GW, 12 November 1787, *GWPCF* 5:431–32.

121   *"strict, and positive orders to all my people"*: Quoted in Thompson, *"The Only Unavoidable Subject of Regret,"* 198.

121   *"the most respectable families"*: Ibid.

122   *he "had a good kind master"*: Quoted in ibid., 323.

122   *Charlotte feigned illness and would "lay herself up for as little as anyone will"*: Martha Washington to Fanny Bassett Washington, 29 August 1791,

in Joseph E. Fields, ed., *Worthy Partner: The Papers of Martha Washington* (Westport, CT, 1994), 233.

123 *"My wife wanted to take a nearer view of the gown"*: Charles MacIver to GW, 17 June 1786, *GWPCF* 4:113–15.

124 "Affronted I suppose at my not sending it on Thursday": Anthony Whiting to GW, 16 January 1793, *GWPP* 12:11–12.

124 *"If She, or any other of the Servants"*: GW to Anthony Whiting, 20 January 1793, FOL.

124 *Whiting "drank freely"*: GW to William Pearce, 18 December 1793, FOL.

125 *"other objects; either of traffic or amusement"*: GW to Anthony Whiting, 30 December 1792, FOL.

125 *she "was never celebrated for her honesty"*: GW to Anthony Whiting, 17 February 1793, *GWPP* 12:165.

125 *"Caroline Brannum . . . , a colored maid"*: Quoted in Schoelwer, ed., *Lives Bound Together*, 10.

126 *Jared Sparks minimized the horror of Washington's death*: Mary G. Powell, *The History of Old Alexandria, Virginia* (Richmond, VA, 1928), 244.

126 *"the grating chain of racism and slavery"*: Roger Wilkins, *Jefferson's Pillow: The Founding Fathers and the Dilemma of Black Patriotism* (Boston, 2001), 122.

126 *"the only unavoidable subject of regret"*: Zagarri, ed., *David Humphreys' "Life of Washington,"* 78.

7. A Sad Postscript to a Remarkable Public Career

127 *Washington's "countenance was . . . serene and unclouded"*: John Adams to Abigail Adams, 5 March 1797, FOL.

127 *"The trouble & perplexities"*: GW to John Jay, 8 May 1796, FOL.

127 *"Having taken my seat in the shade of my Vine & Fig tree"*: GW to David Humphreys, 26 June 1797, FOL. The ending lines, in Addison, *Cato,* Act 1, scene 1, are: "Thy steady temper, Portius,/Can look on guilt, rebellion, fraud, and Caesar,/In the calm lights of mild Philosophy."

127 *"the remainder of my days"*: GW to James Anderson (of Scotland), 7 April 1797, FOL.

127 *"I am at length become a private citizen of America"*: GW to Chastellux, 1 February 1784, FOL.

128 *Washington "was not yet quite ready"*: W. W. Abbot, "George Washington in Retirement," Lowell Lecture Series, 5 December 1999. Accessed online.

128 *"He soon found Solitude, more fatiguing"*: John Adams to Benjamin Rush, 12 June 1812, FOL.

128 *"an almost unconquerable disposition to indolence"*: GW to Samuel Stanhope Smith, 24 May 1797, FOL.

128 *"When I bid adieu"*: GW to John Trumbull, 25 July 1798, FOL.

129 *"You are at the source of information"*: GW to James McHenry, 29 May 1797, FOL.

129 *politically contentious and divisive*: Wood, *Empire of Liberty*, 209.

129 *"unexampled"*: GW to Timothy Pickering, 10 April 1797, FOL.

130 *"attempts to injure those . . . will be longer regarded"*: GW to John Nicholas, 8 March 1798, FOL.

131 *"But the more the views of those"*: GW to Timothy Pickering, 6 February 1798, FOL.

131 *there was a "party among us . . . in the act of writing you this letter"*: GW to Bryan Fairfax, 20 January 1799, FOL.

132 *"No, no, not a six pence!"*: Wood, *Empire of Liberty*, 243.

132 *Marshall "is so capable of making accurate observations"*: GW to James Lloyd, 27 June 1798, FOL.

132 *"What a scene of corruption and profligacy"*: GW to James Lloyd, 15 April 1798, FOL. See John Marshall to GW, 8–10 March 1798, *GWPRT* 2:123.

132 *"I have never heard him speak with so much candor nor with such heat"*: Quoted in *GWPRT* 2:127.

133 *"struck dumb"*: Abigail Smith Adams to Cotton Tufts, 25 May 1798, FOL.

133 *As one supporter expressed it*: These events are well summarized in Wood, *Empire of Liberty*, chapter 7.

133 *an "evil which must be placed in opposition"*: GW to Gouverneur Morris, 20 October 1792, *GWPP* 11:245.

133 *"the poor, the needy, and the oppressed of the earth"*: GW to the Members of the Volunteer Association and other Inhabitants of the Kingdom of Ireland, 2 December 1783, in Fitzpatrick, ed., *Writings of Washington*, 27:254.

134 *"Is it not time and expedient"*: GW to Alexander Spotswood Jr., 22 November 1798, FOL.

134 *asking that Marshall share the broadside*: GW to John Marshall, 30 December 1798, *GWPRT* 3:297.

134 *Washington's correspondence for this time period*: For a thorough examination, see Marshall Smelser, "George Washington and the Alien and Sedition Acts," *American Historical Review* 59, no. 2 (January 1954), 322–34.

134 *"a good deal of exertion"*: GW to William Heth, 5 August 1798, FOL.

134 *"calumny calculated to poison the minds of the people"*: GW to Charles Cotesworth Pinckney, 10 August 1799, FOL.

134 *"You ought also to be aware"*: Alexander Hamilton to GW, 19 May 1798, FOL.

134 *"We must have your name"*: John Adams to GW, 22 June 1798, *GWPRT* 2:352.

135 *praised his successor's tough stance*: GW to John Adams, 17 June 1798, FOL.

135 *"to remain an idle spectator"*: GW to James McHenry, 4 July 1798, FOL.

135 *he would "go with as much reluctance"*: GW to Alexander Hamilton, 27 May 1798, *GWPRT* 2:298.

135 *"my strength and powers might be found incompetent"*: GW to James Mc-Henry, 4 July 1798, FOL.

135 *"an active part"*: GW to Alexander Hamilton, 27 May 1798, *GWPRT* 2:298.

136 *The central cause of the dispute*: Chernow, *Washington*, 785.

137 *In a sharply worded letter*: GW to James McHenry, 16 September 1798, *GWPRT* 3:4.

137 *"I have consented to accept the appointment"*: GW to James Markham Marshall, 16 July 1798, *GWPRT* 2:426.

137 *"His Services ought to be secured at almost any price"*: GW to Timothy Pickering, 11 July 1798, *GWPRT* 2:397.

137 *"That he is ambitious I shall readily grant"*: GW to John Adams, 25 September 1798, *GWPRT* 3:42. This is a long angry letter that takes up seven pages in *GWPRT*.

138 *"delusional"*: Henry Knox to GW, 29 July 1798, *GWPRT* 2:469.

138 *"With respect to General Knox"*: GW to John Adams, 25 September 1798, *GWPRT* 3:42.

138 *"proud, spirited, conceited, aspiring mortal"*: John Adams to Abigail Adams, 9 January 1797, FOL.

138 *"the most reckless"*: John Adams to James Lloyd, 17 February 1815, FOL.

138 *"consider it as the most irresponsible action of my life"*: Quoted in Sedgwick, *War of Two*, 277.

138 *"but I never said I would hold the office"*: John Adams to James McHenry, 29 August 1798, FOL.

139 *"The President ought to ponder well"*: GW to Timothy Pickering, 9 September 1798, *GWPRT* 2:597.

139 *"I was no more at Liberty than a Man in a Prison"*: John Adams to Benjamin Rush, 11 November 1807, FOL.

139 *"horse of figure"*: GW to William Fitzhugh, 5 August 1798, FOL.

139 *"brawlers against the government"*: GW to James McHenry, 30 September 1798, FOL.

140 One *"could as soon scrub . . . to overturn the Government of this Country"*: Ibid.

140 *"So it had come to this"*: Abbot, "George Washington in Retirement."

140 *"all of us act the part of good citizens"*: GW to the Citizens of Alexandria, March 1797, *GWPRT* 1:41.

140 *"the foes of order and good government"*: GW to Alexander Hamilton, 29 July 1795, FOL.

140 *"The idea that there could be equally valid"*: Phelps, *George Washington*, 81.

141 *"And as to you, Sir"*: Quoted in Chernow, *Washington*, 745.

141 *"If ever there was a period for rejoicing"*: Quoted in James D. Tagg, "Benjamin Franklin Bache's Attack on George Washington," *Pennsylvania Magazine of History and Biography* 100, no. 2 (April 1976), 219.

142 *He was soon urging Federalists:* See for example GW to Patrick Henry, 15 January 1799, *GWPRT* 3:317–20.

142 *"set up a broomstick"*: GW to Jonathan Trumbull Jr., 21 July 1799, FOL.

143 *"If I should not be again called"*: GW to Lawrence Lewis, 28 September 1799, *GWPRT* 4:325.

143 *"I believe he expected to be called in again"*: John Adams to Benjamin Rush, 12 June 1812, FOL.

143 *So successful was this effort:* Steele, "George Washington," 90–92.

8. WHAT MADE GEORGE WASHINGTON TICK

144 *"I wait here with much impatience"*: GW to John Augustine Washington, 15 June 1783, FOL.

144 *"The great searcher of human hearts"*: GW to Charles Pettit, 16 August 1788, FOL.

144 *The task of trying to understand what made George Washington tick:* I would like to acknowledge a particular debt to my son, Professor Gregg Henriques, without whose insights this chapter would not have been possible.

145 *"shadow self"*: Aniela Jaffe was a coworker of Jung's and a prolific author. The quoted definition may be readily accessed online.

146 *"The love of fame"*: Douglass Adair, *Fame and the Founding Fathers* (Indianapolis, 1974), 14–16.

146 *the "good opinion of honest men"*: GW to Edward Pemberton, 20 June 1788, *GWPCF* 6:170.

147 *"constant, wary, and often cold eye"*: Edmund S. Morgan, "The Aloof American," in *George Washington Reconsidered*, ed. Higginbotham, 289.

147 *"excessively and conspicuously assiduous"*: Ellis, *His Excellency*, 46.

147 *Shakespeare's famous line:* William Shakespeare, *Hamlet*, Act 3, scene 2. The line is spoken by Queen Gertrude, commenting on a character in her son's play within a play. "The lady protests too much, methinks."

147 *anyone who "could imagine me capable of being so smitten"*: Undelivered First Inaugural Address: Fragments, 30 April 1789, FOL.

147 *"I consider it as an indubitable mark"*: GW to Chastellux, 18 August 1786, *GWPCF*, 4:219.

147 *"All see, and most admire"*: GW to Catharine Sawbridge Macaulay Graham, 9 January 1790, FOL.

147 *"pride and dignity of office has no charms for me"*: GW to David Stuart, 15 June 1790, FOL.

148 *"The attentions we met with on our journey"*: GW to James McHenry, 3 April 1797, FOL.

148 *"You are among the small number"*: GW to Henry Lee Jr., 22 September 1788, *GWPCF* 6:530.

148 *"He is no lover of parade"*: Silas Deane to Mrs. Elizabeth Deane, 18 June 1775, in *Collections of the New-York Historical Society for the Year 1886: The Deane Papers, Vol. 1, 1774–1777* (New York, 1887). Accessed online.

148 *"His modesty is astonishing"*: Quoted in Chernow, *Washington*, 469.

148 *"Evidently His Excellency"*: Quoted in ibid., 453.

148 *"He is a foe to ostentation"*: Quoted in Brad Meltzer, *The First Conspiracy: The Secret Plot to Kill George Washington* (New York, 2018), 20.

148 *"I can assure you"*: GW to George Clinton, 25 March 1789, *GWPP* 1:444.

149 *Where exactly Washington's incredible drive came from*: I want to acknowledge my debt to Gregg Henriques for the bulk of this paragraph.

150 *cherish the "memory and friendship"*: GW to Robert Dinwiddie, 17 September 1757, *GWPCL* 4:408.

150 *he could conquer death*: Adair, *Fame and the Founding Fathers*, 16.

151 *"in the hands of a good providence"*: Quoted in Mary Thompson, *"In the Hands of a Good Providence": Religion in the Life of George Washington* (Charlottesville, VA, 2008), 114.

151 *"the world of spirits"*: GW to Robert Morris, 5 May 1787, FOL.

151 *"sweet innocent girl"*: GW to Burwell Bassett, 20 June 1773, FOL.

151 *Washington painted the afterworld as gloomy*: Peter R. Henriques, "The Final Struggle between George Washington and the Grim King: Washington's Attitude toward Death and an Afterlife," in *George Washington Reconsidered*, ed. Higginbotham, 250–71. The essay includes all citations.

151 *"just bid an eternal farewell"*: GW to Henry Knox, 27 April 1787, *GWPCF* 5:157.

151 *"I took a final leave of my mother"*: GW to Betty Washington Lewis, 13 September 1789, *GWPP* 4:32.

151 *"I often asked myself"*: GW to Lafayette, 8 December 1784, *GWPCF* 2:175.

152 *"Who is there that does not rather envy"*: GW to Sally Cary Fairfax, 12 September 1758, FOL.

152   *"Mr. Barlow is considered"*: GW to Lafayette, 28 May 1788, *GWPCF* 6:297–98.

152   *"Any memoirs of my life"*: GW to James Craik, 25 March 1784, *GWPCF* 1:235.

152   *"I should be pleased"*: GW to David Humphreys, 25 July 1785, FOL.

153   *"The foe then trembled at the well-known name"*: Poem is located in *GW-PCF* 3:133.

153   *"I should with great pleasure"*: GW to David Humphreys, 25 July 1785, FOL.

153   *"whether it be necessary to mention"*: Quoted in Zagarri, ed., *David Humphreys' "Life of Washington,"* xl.

154   *panegyric*: See Phillis Wheatley to GW, 26 October 1775, *GWPRV* 2:242–3. The poem is included.

154   *Washington praised*: GW to Joseph Reed, 10 February 1776, FOL.

154   *"reveals perhaps most clearly"*: W. W. Abbot, "An Uncommon Awareness of Self: The Papers of George Washington," *Washington Papers*. Accessed online.

154   *"under the inspection of a man of character"*: Quoted in ibid.

154   *"the wagons should never be without a sentinel over them"*: Quoted in Chernow, *Washington*, 471. The papers are only now being completely published by the University of Virginia Press in conjunction with the Mount Vernon Ladies' Association. The Revolutionary War series of *The Papers of George Washington* will fill approximately forty-two volumes of more than seven hundred pages each. The entire edition (all series) will run approximately ninety volumes.

154   *the mature hero of the Revolution painstakingly polished and repolished*: Abbot, "An Uncommon Awareness of Self."

155   *his longest speech concerned his papers*: For a detailed discussion of George Washington's death, see Henriques, *Realistic Visionary*, chapter 9.

155   *his tomb would be placed in the heart of the U.S. Capitol*: C. M. Harris, "Washington's Gamble, L'Enfant's Dream: Politics, Design, and the Founding of the National Capital," *William and Mary Quarterly*, 3rd ser., 56, no. 3 (July 1999), 527–64. Much of my discussion of this issue is based on this article.

155   *Thornton drew up plans*: Ibid., 553.

155   *Martha Washington immediately agreed*: Martha Washington to John Adams, 31 December 1799, in Fields, ed., *Worthy Partner*, 332.

155   *Funding for the memorial became an issue*: Harris, "Washington's Gamble," 553.

156   *"It is my express desire"*: GW's "Final and Will Testament," *GWPRT* 4:491.

156   *his favorite sport, fox hunting*: Alexander Mackay-Smith, *The American Foxhound, 1747–1967* (Millwood, VA, 1968). For example, according to GW's diaries, in January and February of 1768 he "went a fox hunting" fourteen or fifteen times.

156   *"Do not conceive"*: GW to Bushrod Washington, 15 January 1783, in Fitz-patrick, ed., *Writings of Washington*, 26:39–40.

157   *"Memorandum to have my Coat made . . . to the Button on the Hip"*: Memorandum, *GWPCL* 1:43–44.

157   *"He wore black boots and silver spurs"*: Quoted in Guthrie Sayen, "'A compleat gentleman': The Making of George Washington, 1732–1775" (PhD diss., University of Connecticut, 1998). Copy in possession of author. It is a shame this very fine dissertation was never published.

157   *"rich crimson" coat*: Invoice, 23 October 1754, *GWPCL* 1:217.

158   *he paid a Philadelphia tailor*: Carol Cadou, "Silver Swords to Silk Waistcoats: The Personal Style of George Washington," in *The George Washington Collection: Fine and Decorative Arts at Mount Vernon* (Mount Vernon, VA, 2006), 213.

158   *he habitually paused outside towns to change*: Breen, *George Washington's Journey*, 72–73.

158   *"blue cloth to be of the best"*: GW to James McAlpin, 27 January 1799, *GWPRT* 3:341.

158   *"splendidly embroidered uniform"*: Ibid., 3:342.

159   *"A gentleman of one of the first fortunes"*: John Adams to Elbridge Gerry, 18 June 1775, FOL.

159   *"I date the fall and ruin of my reputation"*: Quoted in James Flexner, *George Washington in the American Revolution* (Boston, 1967), 9.

159   *"I feel an insuperable diffidence in my own abilities"*: GW to Edward Rutledge, 5 May 1789, FOL.

160   *"He appears to have an invincible diffidence"*: Eliza Powel to Martha Washington, 7 December 1796, in Fields, ed., *Worthy Partner*, 294.

160   *"the arrows of malevolence"*: GW to Henry Lee, 21 July 1793, *GWPP* 13:261.

160   *"extremely affected by the attacks made"*: Thomas Jefferson to James Madison, 9 June 1793, FOL.

162   *Like Faust, forced to pay the price of his ambitions*: The analogy is from Smith, *Patriarch*, 250.

162   *"immortalize his name"*: GW to Lafayette, 18 June 1788, *GWPCF* 6:337.

162   *George Washington's self-love and his love of country coincided*: Rhodehamel, *Wonder of the Age*, 112.

162   *"'Tis well"*: Lear, Journal Account, *GWPRT* 4:551.

163   *"left-handed attempts"*: GW to Bryan Fairfax, 20 January 1799, *GWPRT* 3:325.

163   *the "great unfinished symphony" that is America*: "Great unfinished symphony" comes from the Broadway musical *Hamilton*.

163   *Simply put—no George Washington, no America*: I wish to credit George F. Will for this phrase.

Appendix

165 *entire books:* They include Stephen E. Lucas, ed., *The Quotable George Washington: The Wisdom of an American Patriot* (Madison, WI, 1999), and John Frederick Schroder, ed., *Maxims of George Washington: Political, Military, Social, Moral and Religious* (Mount Vernon, VA, 1989).

165 *"A small knowledge of human nature":* GW to a Continental Congress Camp Committee, 29 January 1778, FOL.

165 *"The motives which predominate":* GW to James Madison, 3 December 1784, FOL.

165 *"Few men":* GW to Major General Robert Howe, 17 August 1779, FOL.

166 *"What, gracious God, is man":* GW to David Humphreys, 26 December 1786, FOL.

166 *"Such is the vicissitude of human affairs":* GW to David Humphreys, 26 December 1786, FOL.

166 *"We know little of ourselves":* GW to Bryan Fairfax, 20 January 1799, *GW-PRT* 3:323.

166 *"In the composition of the human frame":* GW to Eleanor Parke Custis, 16 January 1795, *GWPP* 19:575.

166 *"A man who will do wrong":* GW to Anthony Whiting, 3 February 1793, *GWPP* 12:126.

166 *"I well know too that small circumstances":* GW to Matthew Whiting, 18 November 1789, *GWPP* 4:225.

166 *"It is among the evils":* GW to Henry Knox, 8 March 1787, *GWPCF* 5:74.

166 *"No nation is to be trusted farther":* GW to Henry Laurens, 14 November 1778, *GWPRV* 18:151.

166 *"But in all matters of great national moment":* GW to Henry Lee, 31 October 1786, *GWPCF* 4:319–20.

166 *"If any power on earth":* GW to Henry Knox, 20 September 1795, FOL.

167 *"Men in responsible situations":* GW to François Alexandre Frederic, Duc de La Rochefoucauld-Liancourt, 8 August 1796, in Fitzpatrick, ed., *Writings of Washington*, 35:167.

167 *"It is our duty":* GW to Major General William Heath, 28 August 1778, *GWPRV* 16:401.

167 *"We must make . . . the best use of mankind":* GW to Major General Philip Schuyler, 24 December 1775, FOL.

167 *"To anticipate and prevent disastrous contingencies":* GW to John Jay, 15 August 1786, *GWPCF* 4:213.

167 *"If we cannot convince the people":* GW to Jonathan Trumbull Jr., 4 April 1784, FOL.

167 *"It is to be lamented"*: GW to Alexander Hamilton, 18 October 1787, FOL.

167 *"How unfortunate"*: GW to Thomas Jefferson, 23 August 1792, FOL.

167 *"My earnest wish"*: Ibid.

168 *"In a word"*: GW to Edmund Randolph, 26 August 1792, *GWPP* 11:45–46.

168 *"And let me conjure you"*: GW to Officers of the Army, 15 March 1783, FOL.

168 *"It is not difficult"*: GW to Charles Mynn Thruston, 10 August 1794, FOL.

168 *"I am sure the mass of Citizens"*: GW to John Jay, 8 May 1796, FOL.

168 *"The bosom of America"*: GW to the Members of the Volunteer Association and other Inhabitants of the Kingdom of Ireland, 2 December 1783, in Fitzpatrick, ed., *Writings of Washington*, 27:254.

169 *"All possess alike"*: GW to the Hebrew Congregation in Newport, RI, 18 August 1790, FOL.

169 *"If men are to be precluded"*: GW to Officers of the Army, 15 March 1783, FOL.

169 *"If there were good grounds"*: GW to John Marshall, 4 December 1797, *GWPRT* 1:501.

169 *"Of all the animosities"*: GW to Edward Newenham, 20 October 1792, FOL.

169 *"No punishment"*: GW to Joseph Reed, 12 December 1778, FOL.

169 *"The tumultuous populace"*: GW to Lafayette, 28 July 1791, *GWPP* 8:378.

169 *"I want an American character"*: GW to Patrick Henry, 9 October 1795, *GWPP* 19:37.

169 *"I see so many instances"*: GW to Lund Washington, 17 December 1778, *GWPRV* 18:439.

170 *"Is the consideration of a little dirty pelf"*: GW to James Warren, 31 March 1779, *GWPRV* 19:673–75.

170 *"It is a melancholy thing"*: GW to William Fitzhugh, 10 April 1779, FOL.

170 *"Experience has taught us"*: GW to John Jay, 15 August 1786, FOL.

170 *"I do not conceive"*: GW to Bushrod Washington, 9 November 1787, FOL.

170 *"The good opinion of honest men"*: GW to Edward Pemberton, 20 June 1788, *GWPCF* 6:170.

170 *"It is assuredly better to go laughing than crying"*: GW to Theodorick Bland, 15 August 1786, *GWPCF* 4:210.

170 *"Happiness depends"*: GW to Mary Ball Washington, 15 February 1787, FOL.

170 *"Live and let live"*: GW to James Anderson, 10 September 1799, FOL.

170 *"Being no bigot myself"*: GW to Lafayette, 15 August 1787, FOL.

171 *"Shall I arrogantly pronounce"*: Undelivered First Inaugural Address: Fragments, 30 April 1789, FOL.

171 *"Liberality and charity"*: GW to Benjamin Harrison, 9 March 1789, FOL.

171 *"Among individuals"*: GW to Robert Morris, 16 June 1782, FOL.

171   *"I have accustomed myself"*: GW to Benjamin Tallmadge, 10 December 1782, FOL.

171   *"To inveigh against things that are past"*: GW to Major General John Armstrong, 26 March 1781, in Fitzpatrick, ed., *Writings of Washington,* 21:378.

171   *"I can bear to hear of imputed or real errors"*: GW to Joseph Reed, 14 January 1776, *GWPRV* 3:87.

171   *"I hope I shall always possess"*: GW to Lund Washington, 29 May 1779, FOL.

171   *"I have no hesitation"*: GW to James Anderson, 22 May 1798, *GWPRT* 2:288.

171   *"I trust we are not too old"*: GW to John Jay, 18 July 1788, *GWPCF* 6:386.

172   *"Experience will convince you"*: GW to Elizabeth Parke Custis, 14 September 1794, FOL.

172   *"To be under little or no control"*: GW to Harriot Washington, 30 October 1791, *GWPP* 9:130–31.

172   *"Consider how little a drunken man"*: GW to John Christian Ehlers, 23 December 1793, FOL.

172   *"Do not then in your contemplation of the marriage state"*: GW to Elizabeth Parke Custis, 14 September 1794, FOL.

172   *"In my estimation"*: GW to Armand [marquis de la Rouërie], 10 August 1786, FOL.

172   *"We must consult our means"*: GW to Lafayette, 30 October 1780, FOL.

172   *"In every transaction of your life"*: GW to Bushrod Washington, 23 February 1794, *GWPP* 15:266–67.

172   *"Be honest and just"*: GW to Dr. James Anderson, 24 December 1795, *GWPP* 19:291.

172   *"Be courteous to all"*: GW to Bushrod Washington, 15 January 1783, FOL.

173   *"For it is a fixed principle with me"*: GW to William Pearce, 22 March 1795, *GWPP* 17:679.

173   *"The debt of nature"*: GW to George Lewis, 9 April 1797, *GWPRT* 1:90.

INDEX

Page numbers in *italics* indicate illustrations. Page numbers with an "n" appended indicate a page number in the notes section. Women are generally listed under the final married name provided in the text.

Lee, Charles, 45–46
Lee, Frank (enslaved worker), 107, 109
Lee, Henry, 100, 148
Lee, John, 109
Lee, Light Horse Harry, 142
Lee, Margaret Thomas (Peggy), 111
Lee, Mary Smith Ball, 109
Lee, William "Billy" (enslaved worker), 107, 108–12, *109*, 113, 126
Leibiger, Stuart, 101, 102, 201n
L'Enfant, Pierre, 155
letters of marque, 64
Lewis, Elizabeth Washington (Betty; sister), 22, 23, 24, 27, 30–31, 33, 34, 35
Lewis, Fielding (brother-in-law), 30–31
Lewis, Howell (nephew), 4–5
Lewis, Lawrence (nephew), 25, 107–8, 142
life mask of GW, 155
life philosophy of GW, 170–73
Lillback, Peter, *George Washington's Sacred Fire,* 42, 57–58
Lincoln, Abraham, xii, 11, 143, 165
Lincoln, Benjamin, 70, 73
Lippencott, Richard, 65, 67, 71
Livingston, Edward, 94
Livingston, Robert, 74
Lodge, Henry Cabot, 24
Logan, George, and Logan Act, 141
Longmore, Paul, 5
Lossing, Benson, 112
Louis XVI (king of France), 73, 93
love and marriage, views of GW on, 171. *See also* marriage; sexuality
Loyalists. *See* Tories
Lucy (enslaved worker), 107

MacIver, Charles, and wife, 123
Madison, Dolley Payne Todd, 103
Madison, James: on amiability of GW, 48; career advanced by GW, 14; on commitment of GW to republicanism, 57; French ambassadorship

declined by, 94; Freneau and, 98; friendship with GW severed, 100–104; Hamilton and, 101; Jay Treaty, opposition to, 103; Jefferson and, 98, 100; marriage of, involvement of GW and Martha in, 103; on Mason's *Objections to the Constitution,* 84; on "modest dignity" of GW, 15; Monroe nominated for governor of Virginia by, 96, 104; portrait of, *101;* presidential oath and, 59; Edmund Randolph and, 86, 90; secretary of state position declined by, 102–3; on separation of church and state, 60; Virginia, ratification of Constitution by, 60, 78, 102
Marie Antoinette (queen of France), 73, 76
marriages: courtship and marriage of Martha by GW, 3, 50; of Nelly Custis, 158; of Eliza Custis and Thomas Law, 113; of Mary Bennett Johnson Ball Hughes, 20, 21; Madison and Dolley Payne Todd, 103; views of GW on, 171; of Mary Ball and Augustine Washington (parents of GW), 20–23; of Lawrence Washington and Anne Fairfax, 2, 150; of Betty Washington and Fielding Lewis, 113
Marshall, John, 129, 131, 132, 134, 142
Mason, George, 81–85, *82; Objections to the Constitution,* 84–85
Mason, George, Jr., 83
Mayo, Katherine, 196n
Mazzei, Philip, 99–100, 141
McAlpin, James, 157
McHenry, James, 129, 136, 140, 147
memory of GW, 13
Mercer, James, 85
Minerva (periodical), 99
modesty of GW, 4–5, 15, 48, 92, 148
Monmouth, Battle of, 8, 15, 45–46, 110
Monroe, James: as anti-Federalist, 92; France, appointment and recall as

political philosophy of GW, 166–70
political skill of politician, 14–15, 90
Pope, Alexander, 15, 101
Posey, Hercules (enslaved worker), 112, 117–20, 126
Posey, John, 83, 117
Posey, Richmond (enslaved worker), 117, 118
Potts, Isaac, 44
Powel, Eliza, 7, 51, 160
power: GW's understanding of, 14; peaceful transfer of, 61–62
Prescott (horse), 158
presidency: contributions of GW to development of, xi–xiii; figurehead under control of Hamilton, GW viewed as, 60–61; First Inaugural Address, undelivered draft of, 147; kingship, myth of GW's consideration of, 56–57; myths about GW associated with, 55–62; oath, presidential, 57–60; power, peaceful transfer of, 61–62; state-by-state circuits during, 158; third term after quasi-war with France, GW considering, 142–43; two-term tradition, 61–62
press, GW on freedom of, 133–34, 168
Princeton, Battle of, 8, 63
private life and public service, tension between: quasi-war with France and, 127–29, 135, 143; reputation, GW's concern for, 144, 147–49, 156, 160–62; two-term presidential tradition and, 61–62
prudence of GW, 13–14, 18, 65, 140
public acclaim. See reputation, GW's concern for

Quakers, 64
quasi-war with France, x, 127–43; Alien and Sedition Acts, 133–34, 142; army, raising of, 129, 133, 134–42; initial hostilities and attempted mission

to France, 129–32; Navy, creation of Department of, 133; partisanship and political parties in, 129–30, 139–43; peace process, 141–42; private life and public service, GW's conflict over, 127–29, 135, 143; third term, GW's consideration of, 142–43; uniform worn by GW in, 158; XYZ Affair, 131–32
Quincy, Eliza (Susan) Morton, 58

rabies, treatment of, 107
Ramsey, David, 14
Randolph, Edmund: on allegiance of GW in division between North and South, 104; commendation of Monroe as ambassador to France, 94; Fauchet papers and, 87–89, 199n; friendship with GW severed, 86–90; Jay Treaty and, 87, 88; portrait of, 86; Vindication, 89–90; Whiskey Rebellion and, 87–88
Randolph, John, 86
Randolph, Peyton, 86
Reagan, Ronald, 5, 43
realism of GW, 11–12
Reed, Joseph, 15, 80, 154
Reign of Terror, 93
religion/religious belief: afterlife, GW's view of, 150–52; freedom of religion, GW on, 169, 170–71; of mother of GW, 24–26, 150; presidential oath, addition by GW of "So help me God" to, 57–60; separation of church and state, 60; Valley Forge, myth of GW praying on his knees at, 43–45; of GW, 43–44, 116, 150–52
republican/revolutionary virtue, GW as embodiment of, x, 16, 18, 38, 56
Republicans: constitutional disagreements with Federalists, 78–79, 87, 93, 103; Jefferson's embrace of GW for, 143; quasi-war with France and,